Ray Grasse is an astute observer of human culture, past and present. His eyes firmly fixed on the symbolic content of events, he uses a combination of astrosymbolism, the principle of synchronicity, and mythology to examine a wide range of cultural expressions. *Signs of the Times* is an attempt, firmly anchored in the age-old tradition of spiritual symbology, to make sense of what often strikes us as utterly chaotic, arbitrary, and senseless. Grasse makes fascinating and sometimes surprising links that reveal the deeper structure of our lives. Both this and his previous book furnish us with important clues for shaping our individual and collective life more consciously and wisely.

—**Georg Feuerstein, Ph.D., author of *Structures of Consciousness, Lucid Waking, The Shambhala Encyclopedia of Yoga*, etc., and founder-president of Yoga Research and Education Center**

In times of information overload and media glut, Ray Grasse provides a key for seeing beneath the confusing surface of events to the underlying patterns and meaning. Grasse illuminates the soulful dynamics that are emerging in our cultural forms and provides a compass for navigating the currents.

—**Eric Klein, co-author of *Awakening Corporate Soul: Four Paths to Unleash the Power of People at Work***

Ray Grasse has written a book that serves as a powerful guide for those seeking to understand the symbolism and deeper meaning of current events in the world. This book is a masterpiece carefully crafted gathering data over decades. Reading it I said again and again "aha" and "of course," as I was led through history to contemporary events in a brilliant view of what the Aquarian Age really is about. This book is profound, prolific, and prophetic.

—**Laurence Hillman, co-author of *Alignments: How to Live in Harmony with the Universe***

Our accepted view of history, perhaps any view of history, is little more than factual information selected, tailored, skewed and arranged to fit individual historians' culturally determined preconceptions. Astrology is never, ever, taken into account. But without astrology as a determining or at least corresponding factor, history is effectively incomprehensible and/or meaningless.

Signs of the Times is a unique and extremely interesting examination of both history and the unfolding present as seen through the prism of astrological significance; in other words, history viewed as a civilization-wide response to the precession of the equinoxes. This will not please skeptics, but then, nothing that does not correspond to what skeptics already believe (or disbelieve as the case may be) will. The new science of archeoastronomy proves the almost obsessive attention directed at astronomy (really, astrology!) by the ancients.

Without necessarily agreeing with all Grasse's conclusions, I think he is re-inventing a very old but very valid perspective. No more than a basic acquaintance with the signs of the Zodiac and their meanings is needed to understand Grasse's book and at the very least provoke a spirited inner dialogue.

—**John Anthony West, author of *Serpent in the Sky: The High Wisdom of Ancient Egypt* and *The Traveler's Key to Ancient Egypt: A Guide to the Sacred Places of Ancient Egypt***

To penetrate through the surface of scattered historical facts and then discern the underlying archetypal patterns of history requires an exceptional visionary consciousness. Ray Grasse, in *Signs of the Times*, has managed to describe the dynamic shift of archetypal patterns emerging in our contemporary life.

Fifty years ago, Carl Jung's *Aion* showed a similar form of symbolic insight as it traced the development of the Piscean Age from Christ to the Twentieth Century. Grasse's courageous and holoscopic picture of the vast changes ahead for our planet deserves the same consideration as Jung's classic.

Anton Lysy, Ph.D., dean of studies, The Olcott Institute

Signs of the Times

For Renata,
I hope you enjoy my
book! Be well!
Warmly,
Ray Grasse
Aug. 11, 2011

Also by Ray Grasse

The Waking Dream:
Unlocking the Symbolic Language of Our Lives

Signs
of the
Times

Unlocking the
Symbolic Language
of World Events

RAY GRASSE

HAMPTON ROADS
PUBLISHING COMPANY, INC.

Cover design by Steve Amarillo
Cover art © 2002 by Digital Imagery PhotoDisc, Inc.
Digital Vision Ltd., Rubberball, NASA
Interior illustrations by Anne L. Dunn

Hampton Roads Publishing Company, Inc.
1125 Stoney Ridge Road
Charlottesville, VA 22902

434-296-2772
fax: 434-296-5096
e-mail: hrpc@hrpub.com
www. hrpub.com

If you are unable to order this book from your local
bookseller, you may order directly from the publisher.
Call 1-800-766-8009, toll-free.
Library of Congress Catalog Card Number: 2001095581
ISBN 1-57174-309-X
10 9 8 7 6 5 4 3 2 1
Printed on acid-free paper in the United States

For my mother, Catherine,
and the memory of my father, Raymond
with great love.

Acknowledgments

I would like to extend a heartfelt thanks to all those who provided feed-back, insight, or support of one kind or another during the writing of this book: Diana Amato, Richard Andresen, David Blair, Thea Bloom, Stan Brakhage, Vija Bremanis, Maureen Cleary, Dan Doolin, Normandi Ellis, Rand and Rose Flem-Ath, Georg and Trisha Feuerstein, George Gawor, Linda Gawor, Nathan Greer, Lacey Grillos, Dave and Donna Gunning, Kirsten Hansen, Willis Harman, Laurence Hillman, Bill Hogan, Alice O. Howell, Bill Hunt, James Hurtak, Clarke Johnston, Barbara Keller, Goswami Kriyananda, John Kranich, Mark Lerner, John Daido Loori, Tony Lysy, Mike McDonald, Paul Mahalek, Maggie Piero, William W. Ross, Boris Said, Kate Sholly, Rick Tarnas, Tem Tarriktar, Russell Taylor, Shelly Trimmer, Bonnie Myotai Treace, Anna van Gelder, John Anthony West, and Donna Wimberly.

I would also like to extend a special thanks to Richard Leviton, whose editorial skills helped shape this book in many valuable ways, and to the entire staff at Hampton Roads for their diligent work on this project. Finally, a special thanks to Judith Wiker, who not only provided endless support throughout the years but conducted the original interview back in 1989 (for the Chicago-based publication *The Monthly Aspectarian*) in which I introduced the general themes of this research for the first time, and which served as the basis for this present volume.

Table of Contents

Introduction

This book is an attempt to understand the complex developments of our times, based on a worldview some have called symbolist. "Every history," the American poet and essayist Ralph Waldo Emerson once remarked, "should be written in a wisdom which divined the range of our affinities, and *looked at facts as symbols.*" For thousands of years, mystics of all traditions have affirmed that our world is the reflection of a deeper spiritual intelligence made visible, rich in meaning and interconnectedness. They have said that beyond surface phenomena lies a hidden network of subtle correspondences and archetypal meanings; coming trends announce themselves ahead of time through an intricate language of omens and predictable cycles.

To the symbolist, all events are part of a vast symphony of meaning that extends to every aspect of our world. Weather patterns, the movements of animals and humans, the paths of the stars and planets, and the rise and fall of civilizations—all these are intricately coordinated within an orderly whole, with no occurrence accidental, no pattern superfluous. Like dream symbolism, a historical event can connect with a larger matrix of meaning in time and space far beyond itself. A simple example from recent history may help to illustrate this point.

In 1992, Windsor Castle in England was heavily damaged by fire and many of its priceless contents destroyed. For most observers, this event was simply an accident with no greater significance; but for the esotericist, the historical significance of this building suggested a larger pattern might be at work. Dating back to the time of William the Conqueror, this structure had been a fixture of both English society and the royal family for many centuries. And when we see the other developments taking place during this same time, we find a provocative link with the broader turbulence taking place in English culture that year (which Queen Elizabeth II famously referred to as the *annus horribilis*, or "horrible year"). Among these dramatic events were: Princess Anne's divorce, the publication of a controversial book by Andrew Morton on Princess Diana, the separation of Prince Andrew and Princess Sarah, and the announcement of a separation between Prince Charles and Princess Diana. In this context, the burning of the royal palace became a vivid metaphor for the broader problems besetting the royal family and English society, perhaps even for the declining state of royalty in modern times.

The symbolist approach toward history takes this same holistic perspective and applies it to many kinds of world developments, including natural disasters, scientific breakthroughs, political shifts, religious changes, cultural events, and celestial phenomena. With an eye for symbolism and metaphor, we can discern the shapes buried deep within history and uncover important clues about the trends taking shape before our eyes on the global stage. We live in astonishing times—but not completely incomprehensible ones!

As aids in this process of investigation, I will be employing three primary tools: astrology, synchronicity, and mythology.

Astrology: Just as astrology can shed light on the lives of ordinary individuals, so have astrologers long believed that this discipline can offer important insights into the hidden patterns underlying history. Traditionally, this has been approached from one of two different perspectives. The method preferred by most astrologers today has been to study the horoscopes (birth charts) created for key moments in time, like the founding of nations or the signing of important treaties. Others examine the great planetary cycles that weave through history, such as the interaction of slower-moving planets like Saturn and Jupiter, or Uranus and Pluto. Through this, astrologers can uncover important clues into the hidden archetypal dynamics at work in culture over many years, or even centuries.

This general perspective has much to offer, and I will draw on it myself from time to time throughout this book. However, it has one notable disadvantage; namely, it provides an essentially piecemeal approach to history. Focusing on isolated planetary cycles or horoscopes is in some ways like reading selected lines from a play: It doesn't provide a true understanding of the larger historical *context* involved that informs those smaller cycles.

For this, we need to turn our attention to a broader astrological concept—the notion of the Great Ages.

According to this ancient doctrine, world history is governed by a succession of vast stages lasting roughly 2100 years each. With each new Great Age arrives a new framework of archetypal possibilities that reflects itself in such wide-ranging areas as religion, art, politics, and science. As even many nonastrologers now realize, we find ourselves moving out of the Piscean Age and about to enter the Aquarian Age. But what does this *mean*, beyond the simplistic concepts we hear about it from popular culture? This book will provide some answers to this question, and demonstrate how the doctrine of the Great Ages helps explain many of the changes taking place in our world now, and ones likely to occur in the millennia to come.

Synchronicity: We have all experienced them at some point or another—startling coincidences that appear to be more than just "chance." You receive a phone call from an old friend just moments after stumbling upon a postcard sent twenty years ago, or an obscure name keeps recurring over the course of a day, in surprisingly similar contexts. Carl Jung called such events "synchronicities": coincidences which exhibit a quality of "meaning" beyond their obvious appearances. At times, they may seem like subtle messages from the world around us sent to reinforce some insight or truth we need to grasp at the moment.

In my last book, *The Waking Dream: Unlocking the Symbolic Language of Our Lives*, I suggested that such synchronistic events, rather than being an isolated phenomenon, may actually be occurring *all the time*—indeed, the entire world could be described as "synchronistic," in that everything coincides. Viewed in this way, world history reveals many synchronistic patterns in its diverse forms, from politics and religion to the arts. Throughout this book, I will consider a wide range of synchronicities which help us understand the subtler dynamics of our time. These range from the curious parallels that underlie the lives (and deaths) of John F. Kennedy and Abraham Lincoln to the more metaphoric synchronicities that constellated around such historic events as the *Challenger* disaster and the death of Princess Diana.

Mythology: Carl Jung once remarked that as dreams are to the individual, so myths are to society. The stories we tell ourselves as a culture reveal many insights into the deeper workings of our psyches with its myriad desires, fears, and values. By studying a society's mythologies, one can gain valuable glimpses into the archetypal dynamics that underlie history in its course from one era to the next.

But where shall we look for those mythic "clues" when the primary source of our stories—religion—has been displaced by a more secular and scientific society? Rather than study scriptural sources, one option is to turn our attention to more popular forms like cinema, television, and modern literature—what Joseph Campbell collectively termed modern culture's creative mythology. Not only do these sources offer us a glimpse into the values and attitudes of our own time, but hint at those which promise to shape civilization in our future. Ezra Pound once remarked that artists are the antennae of a society. By studying those recurring themes already surfacing throughout popular culture, we can discern the broad outline of trends which are forming deep in the collective unconscious, and which will continue to take shape in the millennia to come. Make no mistake: Our stories are already beginning to change. By studying these shifting details, we can better grasp the great transformation that is currently sweeping our world, affecting all of us.

Sometimes even ancient sources of myth can provide useful clues into our times. How? Specifically, each astrologically-defined Great Age is associated with a particular group of stars. For example, the Age of Aries is linked with the constellation of the ram, while the Age of Pisces is linked to the constellation of the fishes, and so forth. In each case, these star patterns were traditionally associated with one or more great tales. For the Greeks, the ram constellation was tied directly to the story of Jason and the Golden Fleece, while the constellation of the fish was linked with a story of Aphrodite and her son Eros. These sets of associations continue on throughout the zodiac, thus forming a great round of celestial tales. In their own way, these symbolic associations remain subliminal forces within the collective unconscious whether or not we are aware of them.

By carefully studying these mythic associations, we can thereby uncover further synchronistic clues into the subtle patterns that shape society through the ages. For instance, the above-mentioned tale of Aphrodite and her son, linked by the Greeks to Pisces, involved a story of their efforts to flee a great monster pursuing them, the mighty Typhon. In that light, it is interesting to note how the Piscean Age itself centered so powerfully on themes of persecution, both received and given. In this style, we will look closely at some of the key stories related in ancient times to the constellation of Aquarius—in particular, the Greek tale of Ganymede. As we will see, society may already be acting out the great drama of this immortal youth who was abducted into the sky to serve as cupbearer to the gods.

And what is it we will learn specifically about the coming age? For one, each era possesses certain unique qualities that distinguish it in broad ways, and the Aquarian Age will be characterized by its intensely *mental* quality. We are entering a time when information will become the driving force of society, and the primary challenges and opportunities facing us will be those of the mind. Constructively, this could mean we will experience huge advances in our collective intellectual development—or it may simply mean we'll become a society that devotes its energies to cerebral pastimes like TV or virtual reality games.

Another key quality associated with the coming age is *decentralization.* Just as democracy decentralizes power from a single ruling monarch to multiple voters, society will find itself decentralizing in a wide range of ways. A modern-day example of this would be a technology like the Internet, which has no central hub, but multiple "centers" spread out across the Earth. In the arts, we'll see how this decentralizing trend is already visible in the stylistic innovations of modern cinema, as filmmakers reinvent the traditional storyline by giving us multiple narratives and interweaving plot lines, as exemplified by directors like Robert Altman *(Nashville)* and Steven Soderbergh *(Traffic).*

A third quality associated with the coming age might be described as *electrification.* Society will no doubt continue its heavy reliance on electricity in practical ways; but in a more metaphorical sense, global culture will likely become even more kinetic and fast-paced in its lifestyle and ways of thinking. A current example of this quality would be rock music. At its best, it conveys an electrified dynamism and passion that is exhilarating and life-affirming, while at its worst it reflects a manic, aggressive energy that can be pedestrian in tone and emotionally scattering. These same extremes may well foreshadow those of the Aquarian Age itself.

To help bring the varied qualities of Aquarius into sharper focus, we will also draw on a variety of root metaphors from contemporary society that point the way to emerging trends. Among them:

- *jazz,* that distinctly American art form which balances part and whole, person and group, and mirrors developments as diverse as democracy and modern religion;

- *solar power,* a modern technology that draws down higher energies into practical application, and reflects a process occurring on many fronts in society, intellectually, spiritually, and politically;

- *the spectrum,* the splintering of unity into multiplicity which serves as a metaphor for the broader trend toward diversification taking place in contemporary culture;

- the concept of the *network,* the linkage of different information relay systems across space in a way which aptly parallels how individuals, nations, ideas, and even worlds will become interlocked in the emerging age.

In simple terms, the message of this book might be summarized like this: the Aquarian Age cannot be thought of in terms of the simplistic clichés familiar to many of us through popular sources. Familiar notions of a utopian brotherhood or an oppressive Orwellian society will have to be set aside if we hope to create a more nuanced portrait that takes into account the many ambiguities and paradoxes that will characterize the coming era. In some ways, the Aquarian Age might prove to be the age of paradoxes if current trends are any indication.

For instance, will the Aquarian Age be a time when the individual reigns supreme, or when the larger collective becomes the dominant factor? We'll look at the possibility that it could be *both* and consider examples that suggest a growing trend toward personal empowerment side-by-side with a trend toward greater globalization and collectivism. Think of the paradoxical way our communication technologies are allowing us to become more connected to the world while simultaneously causing us to become more isolated from one another in flesh-and-blood ways. Thanks to a gridwork of wires, antennae, and fiber-optic cables, we are becoming closer to our fellow Earthlings at the same time we are moving farther apart.

Another paradox of the Aquarian Age will probably center around our growing obsession with freedom, whether in connection with political reforms or the numerous technological gadgets designed to grant us more leisure time and mobility in the world. The freedoms afforded by these developments could eventually lead to a form of imprisonment. For example, think of the problems that arise when a society fails to distinguish between *liberty* and *license,* resulting in moral chaos; or when men and women become overly dependent on their everyday conveniences and discover the potential of these things to enslave (a fact that hit home for many by the Y2K scare of 1999).

Anyone hoping to grasp the meaning of the Aquarian Age must grapple with complexities like these. There are archetypal roots underlying the changes happening in our world; yet as with all archetypal concepts, there are nuances involved that can only be understood from a multileveled and multiperspectival standpoint. Over the course of these pages we will attempt to sort out many of these subtleties with help from such diverse fields as psychology, the Hindu philosophy of the chakras, contemporary cinema, political theory, quantum physics, and esoteric philosophy.

While this book draws partly on astrological ideas, I've attempted to make my arguments understandable to both astrologers and non-astrologers alike. Where astrological terms do appear throughout the text, I either explain them as they arise, or present them in such a way that their context makes them reasonably self-explanatory. For those who are new to this discipline, I recommend taking these passages slowly and carefully, digesting each one a point at a time. For those who wish to explore these arguments in greater depth, a more extensive study of astrology will enhance your understanding of the points raised in this book.

As the ancient Chinese historians knew, the events of history are neither random nor disconnected, but elements of an integral whole, no more separate from their era than are single waves from the entire ocean. Weaving together insights from these sources and approaches, we can begin to discern the overarching trends and "constellating archetypes" of the emerging global *Zeitgeist*. We are all participants in an archetypal drama spanning thousands of years and influencing our world in ways far beyond normal comprehension, but which we can begin to glimpse through the timeless language of symbolism.

In *The Magic Mountain,* German novelist Thomas Mann wrote that a "man lives not only his personal life, as an individual, but also, consciously or unconsciously, the life of his epoch and his contemporaries." Whether we realize it or not, our inner life is inextricably bound up with the spirit of our age—our values, tastes, religions, even our fears and desires are all, to a certain extent, products of our culture. The question is, how is that greater drama affecting us? How do the trends and currents of modern times shape our own values or perceptions? To this extent, understanding the drama of our times is the struggle to understand each of our own stories. The tale of the emerging Aquarian Age is therefore the story of *every* man and *every* woman in the millennia ahead. With that said, let us begin our journey into the maze of future history.

The Wheel of History: Tracking the Spirit of the Age

He who cannot see himself within the context of at least a 2,000-year expanse of history is all his life shackled to days and weeks.
—Rainer Maria Rilke

Imagine the world as it might appear from the perspective of an ant wandering onstage briefly during a performance of Shakespeare's *A Midsummer Night's Dream*. All around you there unfolds a great and colorful drama, replete with exotic colors, sounds, and dynamic actions; characters step onto and off of the stage, and mysterious transformations unfold before your eyes. Yet for all of that wondrous spectacle, the great meaning of it all escapes you; due to your limited perspective, you cannot comprehend the multilayered significance of what lies before you, nor see how these diverse elements fit into a greater unfolding narrative. Perhaps if you could see the larger story being played out over the course of several acts, you might begin to recognize how these transitory developments actually comprise integral facets of a larger pattern of meaning.

In a way, our predicament is like that. We find ourselves meandering across a great "stage"—history. To the casual eye, the events transpiring around us may seem at times like little more than a chaotic jumble of random occurrences: a rocket explodes in midair; a world leader finds himself embroiled in a scandal with a young woman; a new computer technology suddenly takes the world by storm. At first glance, there is little to suggest that such things might harbor some deeper meaning or possess subtle interconnectedness. Yet as with the ant, our problem may be one of proximity—we are *too close* to the action to grasp what is going on. If our perspective were broad enough, perhaps we would see that these isolated events are part of a larger unfolding narrative.

For the esotericist, understanding that larger story resides in a concept known as the Great Ages. At the present moment, humanity finds itself "between acts," as it were—slowly leaving the Piscean Age and about to enter the Aquarian Age. Like vast tectonic plates shifting deep within the collective unconscious, this epochal transition has already begun manifesting as a series of historic changes in our world, as the symbols of an older order make way for those of a radically new one, and our attention is transfixed by a different set of issues and values.

In the pages that follow, I will explore how this great age-shift has already begun and is affecting our world. By grasping the larger story underlying our time, we stand to gain a better sense of orientation regarding where we are and where we may be heading in the millennia before us. What can we expect during the next Great Age? As we will see, the early clues are already right before our eyes, only in "seed" form. Just as the distinguishing features of the adult are already present in childhood, so the archetypal themes of the next Great Age may already be taking shape across our world for those who have eyes to see. But before we begin our exploration of this subject, let's first take a moment to consider the workings of these Great Ages.

Understanding How the Great Ages Work

The concept of the Great Ages is based on a phenomenon astronomers call the precession of the equinoxes. On the first day of spring each year, referred to by astronomers as the vernal equinox, day and night are equally balanced. For astrologers, this yearly occurrence has long held great importance as a time of balance and of new beginnings, when the proverbial "crack between worlds" has opened and humanity is more receptive to the inflow of cosmic energies from the universe (see figure 1-1).

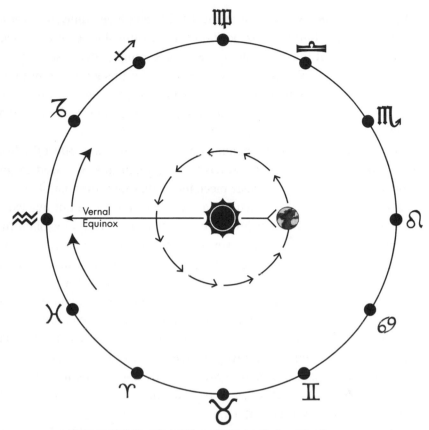

Figures 1-1. The Precession of the Equinoxes

The doctrine of the Great Ages arises from the astronomical phenomenon known as Precession. Each year on the first day of spring (the vernal equinox), the sun rises against a particular constellation located along the sun's yearly path. Due to small variations in the Earth's axis, however, this vernal point shifts slightly over time, moving *backward* through all twelve ecliptical constellations over the course of roughly 26,000 years. It is currently moving out of the constellation of Pisces and into Aquarius, giving rise to what is commonly known as "the Age of Aquarius."

Each time this occurs, the sun is superimposed against a particular constellation within the band of stars located along its path through the year, what astronomers call the ecliptic. While the brightness of the sun makes it impossible to see what specific constellation lies behind this point, it is easy for astronomers to determine this. To the astrologically minded, this point of the sky is regarded as an important marker that holds key clues into the values, dreams, and motives of humanity.

Because of the slow wobble of the Earth's axis over time, this vernal point is gradually shifting in its position through the sky, moving through the constellations at the slow rate of one degree roughly every seventy-two years. On average, it takes a little over 2100 years for this vernal point to traverse a single constellation, a period that comprises a single Great Age.[1] Over the course of nearly 26,000 years, it completes a full circuit of the sky, giving rise to what is called a Great Year (see figure 1-2).

How can an astronomical phenomenon like this possibly affect the lives of men and women down here on Earth? To explain this, we need to first understand something of the basic mechanism that underlies astrology.

At its core, astrology is based upon a way of thinking about our world that is both symbolic and synchronistic in nature. One way to explain this dual nature is through an analogy. For thousands of years, indigenous tribes across the Americas paid great attention to the seemingly "chance" events in the environment surrounding the birth of a child. If a deer was seen running by the moment a child came into the world, that child might be named "Running Deer" in the belief that this occurrence represented an important significator for that child's destiny and character. Its power as an image lay not within hidden energies or "rays" emanating from the deer to the child, but in the appropriateness of its symbolism to that moment in time, as indicative of a thread in the larger web of meaning encompassing the child and its environment at that time.

Astrology rests upon a similar presumption. For example, when calculating a horoscope, an astrologer incorporates several kinds of data, including the positions of the planets in the signs at the moment of birth, the geometric relationship between these bodies (what astrologers call "aspects"), and the exact areas of the sky these bodies inhabit at that moment (the "houses"). Like a seed-blueprint for that individual's destiny, the horoscope provides the astrologer with insight into the potentials of that person's life and character. In turn, by examining the way these birth configurations are affected by the ongoing movements of the planets through the sky throughout that person's life, the astrologer can also predict general trends about that person's inner and outer experiences in many areas.

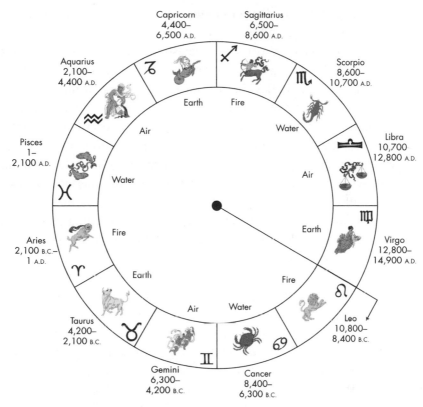

**Figure 1-2. The Round of the Great Ages
from 10,800 B.C. to 14,900 A.D.**

There is considerable dispute over the exact starting and ending times for the different Great Ages; the dates shown here are approximate. Each Age has its own qualities and symbolic correspondences, which are in turn reflected in the historical manifestations of its period.

None of this happens because of some energy or force that emanates down to Earth from the stars (which isn't to deny that there may be energies involved on some level). Rather, astrology works because of the inherent *symbolism* of these celestial patterns. Exactly as the deer's appearance at the child's birth was a sign reflecting that child's destiny, so the configurations at one's moment of birth offer a mirror into the individual's destiny, but written in the language of symbols.

"As above, so below," an ancient axiom declares. We are a reflection of the cosmos at the moment we are born, and in that sense are synchronous with the greater world around us. A person born with Jupiter in a harmonious relationship with Venus may feel lucky in love or when dealing with money;

yet that planetary signature doesn't produce this archetypal quality in their life so much as symbolize and mirror it.

In an even broader way, astrology suggests that this sense of interlocking harmony includes all phenomena; the stars and planets are but threads in a universal web of affinities that embraces everything within the outer and inner worlds. As the Neoplatonic philosopher Plotinus argued, the stars are meaningful in our lives just as everything in our world is meaningful, such as birds sailing through the sky, sounds emanating around us, even the people we unexpectedly encounter in our comings and goings. Ours is a fundamentally synchronistic universe, in which everything interlocks in tight accord. Like an elaborately written play, all events dovetail to form an intricate web of significance, each element linking to the other in a precise and complementary fashion. For the individual with an eye for symbolism, these patterns can be discerned and subtle connections duly interpreted.

The "mechanism" of the Great Ages can be understood in the same manner. The shifting of the vernal point into a new constellation doesn't cause changes on Earth so much as it mirrors them. The "effect" or "mechanism" involved is therefore one of synchronicity, or meaningful coincidence. These are the terms Carl Jung used to define seemingly separate phenomenon that appear to arise hand-in-hand, as though parts of a larger framework of meaning. As noted astrologer Robert Hand states:

> The constellation of Pisces does not signify events because of "radiation" from the fixed stars that constitute it. Instead, the constellation of Pisces takes on the form that it has because consciousness is ready to project upon it a particular drama. The drama occurs within the psyche of each person alive at the time of its occurrence. The effect of this in every person operates cumulatively to produce a cultural effect. . . . No causation is involved, yet the form of the physical universe evolves in a way that is parallel to the form of the psychic universe within us. We create our universe, which in turn recreates us in its image of our image (Hand 1982).

For the esotericist, each of the twelve Great Ages represents a universal, archetypal principle of consciousness, each with its own unique qualities and sets of correspondences. With the emergence of a new Great Age, different impulses surface within the collective psyche, and a host of related themes and symbols synchronistically constellate themselves throughout the culture.

During the Age of Aries, for example, we saw the rise of a more assertive and ego-oriented impulse in our world, and with this came the rise of many great empires and military leaders, as well as an emphasis on ram symbolism (this being the animal associated with Aries). During the Age of Pisces, a more emotional approach to the world occurred, one result of which was the emergence of a world-religion with significant fish symbolism. In both cases this occurred because of an interlocking harmony between Heaven and Earth. As astrologer Robert Hand wrote, "the form of the physical universe evolves in a way that is parallel to the form of the psychic universe within us." The archetypes that arise during each Age are elements within a mutually arising matrix of meaning that encompasses the universe and ourselves as we progress through various stages of consciousness.

But precisely because human consciousness is part of this equation, the Great Ages are not eternally fixed in their meanings or manifestations from one round to the next. The Ages are cosmic triggers that activate the latent potentials of humanity at whatever level we are, and these potentials can radically change over time. To use a simple analogy, how a season like autumn will be experienced by a freshly planted apple seed will differ radically from how it will be experienced by a twenty-five-year-old apple tree! Though the seasonal cycle is in both cases essentially the same, the response differs depending on the maturity of the life form experiencing it, especially in terms of whether fruit will result or not.

In this way, the Aquarian Age has a range of archetypal meanings which dispose us to think or act in certain ways, but it's useful to recall that there have been at least two hundred Aquarian Ages over the last five million years. It would be foolish to think that the Aquarian Age experienced by Neanderthals is exactly the same as it will be for us now. An Age bears whatever "fruit" is appropriate to the level of consciousness rising to meet it. The point here is that the Ages do not cause us act in particular ways, but only serve to synchronize with the unfoldment of our latent potentials.

Our goal then is to understand these broad patterns during the millennia ahead, and their range of possible expressions in our future. In this book, I suggest there are three skeleton keys that offer insight into the archetypal dynamics of the Aquarian Age, and which will serve as leitmotifs throughout our study. These are:

• The elemental symbolism of the zodiacal signs
• The Leo/Aquarius polarity
• The sign of Aquarius in the esoteric system of the chakras

To begin with, let us turn our attention to the four "elements" and their relationship to the unfolding Great Ages.

The Elemental Symbolism of the Zodiacal Signs

Astrological philosophy holds that the twelve signs of the zodiac break down to four primary elements, or seed qualities—earth, water, air, and fire. As symbols, these relate to the four primary states of consciousness that underlie human experience (see figure 1-3). For example, the element of earth (including the signs Taurus, Virgo, and Capricorn) relates to the quality of groundedness in daily life in terms of a person's capacity for practical thought and action. When we say someone is earthy or down-to-earth, we are acknowledging their attunement to manifest realities. Were we to choose a profession

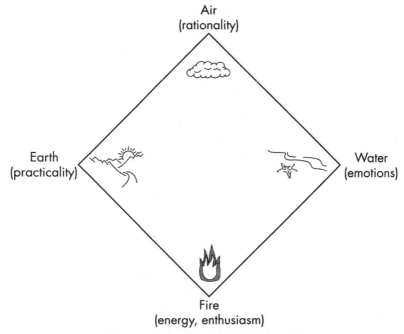

Figure 1-3. The Four Elements

Astrologers hold that the twelve zodiacal signs represent variations on four fundamental principles referred to as elements—earth, water, fire, and air. These principles can be thought of as symbolizing archetypal states of consciousness: earth relates to a sense of practicality and groundedness, water to emotionality and feeling, fire to impulsive action and consciousness in its most fundamental sense, and air to thinking and rationality.

that best symbolizes this principle, it would be a farmer or a sculptor, both of whom reflect a talent for working with tangible materials and resources.

In contrast with the more reserved, conservative qualities of earth, the element of fire (the signs Aries, Leo, and Sagittarius) relates to a sense of dynamic enthusiasm and assertiveness. Like a young child charging out into the world saying, "Here I am!" fire reflects the emergence of a primal self-awareness that thrives on the rush of pure, impulsive action. When we say someone has a fiery temperament, we are picking up on this elemental quality in their personality. A profession that symbolizes this principle would be an athlete or a show-business performer, since these express similar qualities of dynamic action along with a capacity for self-confident assertion within the world.

The element of water (the signs Cancer, Scorpio, and Pisces) relates to emotions and a person's capacity to experience emotion in their dealings with others. How are you feeling right now? How well do you empathize with those around you? Your ability to notice such factors depends on your attunement to the water element. When a highly sentimental movie hits the theaters, we talk about how people "water up" at key scenes. Here an appropriate figure to symbolize this elemental energy might be a mother cooking for a large family; this expresses the nurturing qualities associated with water. A musician absorbed in his music also symbolizes the quality of pure feeling expressed by this element.

Fourth is the mental element of air (the signs Gemini, Libra, and Aquarius). This is the astrological energy relating to rationality, our ability to communicate with others. When someone is caught up in their thoughts or ideals, we say they have "their head in the clouds" or that they have become an "airhead." An appropriate symbol for this energy is a news reporter or a writer, because of this element's great concern with information and communication.

Astrologers have long believed there is a close correspondence between the symbolism of the Great Ages and the historical developments associated with them. To illustrate this, let us briefly review the last several ages and some possible illustrations of this correspondence using the elemental meaning of the zodiacal signs as a starting point.

The Age of Taurus: The Earth Element (4200 to 2100 B.C.)

As a period governed by the element of earth, this was an unparalleled time of monumental earthworks and constructions, as perhaps best exemplified by the pyramids of Egypt. In Egyptian history, this is a period commonly called the Old Kingdom (2686 to 2181 B.C.), considered by many to represent the height of Egyptian culture in both beauty and refinement. During the Age of Taurus, artisans achieved a mastery of matter that still astonishes in terms of their ability to work with some of the hardest stone available. It is difficult to look at achievements like this and not be struck by what these ancient sculptors were able to accomplish supposedly using only crude implements. Just as impressive, though, is the sense of timeless calm conveyed by many of these artifacts and monuments, a quality that reflects the aesthetic side of the sign Taurus.

In astrological terminology, Taurus is the sign most associated with qualities of durability and consistency, so it is also fitting how many of the creations from this period have remained intact up to the present time. For example, the only one remaining of the original Seven Wonders of the World is the Great Pyramid of Egypt which stems from this period. This sense of durability is also reflected in the Egyptians' obsession with mummification during this era, a medical art that sought to preserve the body for eternity.

Symbolically, Taurus is associated with the bull, and this period saw a proliferation of bull imagery in many cultures. For instance, the cult of the bull became widespread in areas like India, Crete, and Mesopotamia. In Egypt, this was especially evident in the influential Hathor cult of the Old Kingdom, in images that depicted Hathor, the horned goddess, as a celestial cow; these date back as early as 4,100 B.C. Within the Hebrew culture, some Biblical scholars believe that the earliest god for this group was a bull deity.[2]

The earth element is regarded as the symbol of foundations, *par excellence*. Appropriately, the period of 4200 to 2100 B.C. is seen by many as marking the beginning of modern civilization, with the rise of large-scale, stable, urban societies concerned with amassing wealth and resources. Large-scale agriculture and farming played an important role during this period. Astrologer Alice O. Howell adds an interesting observation about this period when she points out how our modern terms for money and wealth have linguistic roots in the economic customs of this particular era. When we speak of capitalism, for instance, we are unconsciously referring, in an etymological way, to earlier notions of heads (Latin: *caput*) of cattle and livestock. Notice how we also speak of "stock markets," or say that the market is "bullish" (Howell 1990).

The Age of Aries: The Fire Element (2100 B.C. to 1 A.D.)

With the shift from Taurus to Aries, we see a shift from the element of earth to that of fire which is the principle of energetic, assertive ego-consciousness. During the Aries Age, we find a pervasive emphasis on military conquests and war-imagery in classic texts like the Indian Bhagavad-Gita, the Greek *Iliad,* and the Hebrew Torah. This period saw the founding of great empires in Egypt, Greece, and Rome, and the rise of historic warriors like Alexander the Great and Ramses II. In China, great empires arose like those of Shih Huang Ti who unified the warring provinces throughout China in 221 B.C.

Just as the previous Taurean age saw a filtering of spiritual sensibilities through the earth-principle, so the Age of Aries gave rise to a trend in religious imagery based on fire. For example, while Judaic custom forbade personalized depictions of God, we are told that Moses encountered the Lord in the form of a burning bush. During this age, Zoroastrianism emphasized the importance of fire rituals, while in Egypt, Ahkenaton founded a new order based on the adoration of the sun called Aton.

While the Taurean age saw a proliferation of bull images, so the Age of Aries saw a marked emphasis on the symbolism of rams. For instance, exactly on the eve of the Middle Kingdom in Egypt (roughly 2000 to 1786 B.C.), there occurred a sudden shift in emphasis from the bull-god Montu to the ram-god Amon. Also, Alexander the Great was frequently depicted with ram's horns on his head. As if to symbolically mark the passing of an age, images of bull slayings became prominent during this era, as in the Mithraic religion of Persia or in the Old Testament story of Moses chiding the Israelites for their lingering devotion to a golden calf (a Taurus image).

But as with every age, outer manifestations like these are all symbols for *inner* changes in the collective psyche. As such, the widespread images of military conquests and fire during this Age can be seen as echoes of an inner awakening of egoic self-awareness occurring for many across the globe.

For instance, modern psychology tells us that one of the chief functions of a developed ego is its ability to organize and control the otherwise chaotic and unruly energies of the psyche. The effort by the great empires of this time to conquer and consolidate outlying "barbaric" cultures and bring them under centralized control can be seen as synchronistically mirroring an inner consolidation of the human ego taking place during that age.[3] In a similar way, the rise of monotheistic religions among the Jews and Egyptians during this time reflects an egoic awakening through the consolidation of many gods into one. Considering that one of the key phrases commonly associated by astrologers with Aries is "I AM!" it is intriguing that one of the religions of this time, Judaism, worshipped a God by the name of "I AM!"

The Age of Pisces: The Water Element (1 A.D. to 2000 A.D.)

Among the manifestations of the Piscean Age was the rise of a global religion centering primarily on symbols of water: baptism, walking on water, changing water into wine, and so forth. Indeed, for the student of astrological symbolism, Christianity offers a mother lode of correspondences in connection with Pisces. For example, Christian scripture speaks extensively of fishermen, wine, helping the downtrodden and outcasts of society, and the washing of feet—all traditional symbols of Pisces. One of the defining miracles of Christ's ministry was the feeding of the multitude with two fishes and five loaves of bread. More subtly, the eating of fish on Friday by Catholics is linked by some to the fact that Friday is governed by Venus, the planet that is "exalted" (i.e., attains its optimal expression) in Pisces.

Were such correspondences intentional on the part of the Church fathers, or was their emergence purely synchronistic? Scholars disagree on this point, so we may never know for sure. But either way, we can study these symbols for what they reveal to us about the archetypal dynamics of the time. Viewed as a whole, they tell us that humanity was learning to relate to the divine and the world-at-large through a more *emotional* filter. In its more constructive aspect, this brought about a newfound element of compassion and faith in society, especially within Christian society. We see the emergence of a spiritual sensibility that spoke of "turning the other cheek" rather than the smiting of one's enemies. This was a shift from *Roma* to *Amor,* one might say.

In a more negative vein, this same emphasis on emotionality ushered in a spirit of dogmatism and persecution in the emerging religions. Pisces is intensely concerned with matters of faith. However, taken to extremes, this can lead to zealotry, self-righteousness, and the urge to establish absolute guidelines for all to follow. At its worst, the Piscean Age was an era of religious intolerance, when large populations were expected to show unquestioning allegiance to a monolithic belief system, as exhibited in much of Christianity and Islam during this time.

One of the more striking Piscean symbols found in Christianity is its central image—the crucifixion. It is sobering to consider that for nearly two thousand years now, Western culture has defined itself largely in terms of an image of a man nailed to a cross, tortured, and murdered in a most gruesome manner. Yet viewed archetypally, this singular seed-image contains the best and worst of the Piscean legacy. On a negative level, the crucifixion expresses dark Piscean qualities such as self-pity, masochism, guilt, and martyrdom. These reflect the self-dissolving principle of water, but directed in a more destructive, self-abnegating way.

In some respects, we might well call the Piscean Age the ultimate age of neurosis. For example, this was an era when many felt that suffering and guilt were somehow synonymous with spirituality. This is precisely the sort of delusion that arises when the ego is unhealthy or ungrounded, and thus finds itself sucked back into the more corrosive, ego-dissolving emotions of the soul.

The crucifixion has a more positive interpretation, too. As esotericists know, Pisces symbolically relates to the transcendence of the ego and the surrendering of personal interests in service of a higher ideal. As the last sign in the zodiac (determined by the sun's counter-clockwise movement), Pisces is that final stage in the soul's evolution where the boundaries of personality have begun to dissolve and the soul merges with the cosmic ocean of existence. This is what the crucifixion means in its highest sense: the principle of sacrifice, worship, profound devotion. It is the water element at its most refined. A few examples of this higher aspect of Pisces are St. Francis of Assisi, or the ideals of chivalry and courtly love, with their ethos of self-sacrifice and idealism, that arose during the medieval era.

The Age of Aries brought an awakening of the outwardly directed ego, but the more feminine Piscean Age brought about a newfound sense of interiority or inwardness. In religious terms, this was most evident in the emerging Christian emphasis on moral reflectivity, or *conscience*, the flip side of which was the emergence of a new mood of guilt throughout Western society. Prior to Christianity, one rarely finds a sense of conscience or "sin" as we now think of it. By way of example, the earlier Greeks saw their relationship to the gods in more mechanical and external terms than we do now. When crimes were committed, one atoned for them not because of an inner sense of guilt so much as the belief that one had accrued a "stain" of sorts which could be removed through an appropriate sacrifice (Dickinson 1966).

Outwardly, this new sense of interiority was mirrored in the rise of architectural features like the dome and arch, so critical to the Islamic mosque and structures like the Pantheon in Rome. This interiority was visible as well as in the introduction of pupils into the eyes of Roman statues early in the Age; examine the ancient busts of early Romans and the Greeks and one finds that their eyes have no pupils. As symbols, artistic shifts like these signaled a new world of emotions opening up during the early Christian era, a development which would eventually make possible the later birth of modern psychology.[4]

The Age of Aquarius: The Air Element (2100 A.D. to 4200 A.D.)

The most frequently asked question concerning the Aquarian Age is this: When does it begin? That is a bit like determining when the dawn starts. Is it when the morning sky first starts glowing, long before the actual sunrise? Or is it when the sun appears over the horizon? The same problem applies to understanding the timing of the Great Ages. An Age doesn't begin on a single day or year; it unfolds gradually over many centuries. Consequently, even if the Aquarian Age may not fully begin in earnest for several centuries yet (most estimates suggest somewhere between 2100 and 2800 A.D.), throughout this book we will consider many examples which suggest its symbols are already appearing in our world. The Internet and space travel are two instances we will be looking at in greater depth.

The deeper meaning of the Age can be understood by studying the underlying element involved. In the case of Aquarius, the influence of air is dominant. This is reflected in a literal way with the startling rise of aviation technologies over the last two centuries; humans are increasingly learning how to master the air realm, not only through aviation but in the construction of ever-taller buildings which allow us to live higher up off the ground. The media employs metaphors that reflect this elemental shift. A show is "on the air," or a broadcaster is "taking to the airwaves."

As with our other ages, such outer symbols are but reflections of an inner shift taking place throughout our culture, one that relates to an awakening of *mind* in the evolution of human consciousness. Understood symbolically, air is the medium through which we communicate our thoughts and ideas, and is the element most associated with rationality and thinking. What this means is that the Aquarian Age will undoubtedly witness major advances in humanity's intellectual growth, though admittedly at widely varying levels of sophistication. Terms like the "information superhighway" and the "information revolution" are two examples of how the impending Aquarian influence has already begun to propel our world toward more mental values and modes of experience. The modern separation of church and state is further evidence of the disengaging of our rational minds from the dogmatic and emotional concerns of the Piscean Age.

An essential key to understanding the meaning of Aquarius lies in something hinted at earlier, namely, that each of the different elements repeats itself three times over during the course of the zodiac. Consequently, there are three earth signs, three water, three fire, and three air. In each expression of a different element, we see that elemental principle in subtly different ways. To illustrate this, let us focus here on the trio of air signs: Gemini, Libra, and Aquarius.

The Three Phases of the Air Element

Given the progressive nature of the zodiac, each of these signs reflects the workings of mind in broader and more impersonal ways. For instance, in Gemini rationality expresses itself in its most personal form, through the workings of the everyday mind and ordinary forms of communication. In Libra, the rationality of the air element manifests in more interpersonal ways, with a mentality that is directed toward interactions with others in wider social contexts. An example of this is a teacher standing before a class, or a salesman dealing with clients.

In Aquarius, however, we see the element of air-rationality expressing itself through the most impersonal contexts possible, toward ever greater collectives, perhaps even the cosmos. For that reason, Aquarius might be described as the principle of cosmic rationality or cosmic mind, the ability to perceive or make connections of the most abstract and cosmic sort. Aquarius isn't simply concerned with ideas and theoretical relations; it is concerned with ideas and relationships that are global or universal in scope.

For this reason, the Aquarian Age will undoubtedly be concerned with knowledge of the broadest and most collective sort. A perfect example of this is modern science. Rather than focus its attention on a scientist's own ideas and feelings, science attempts to uncover those laws or principles which would apply everywhere, and everywhen. Already we see this impersonality expressing itself in the way many people are involved with social connections and networks extending over vast distances, as through the Internet or TV. Such technologies allow people across the world to communicate with one another, but in more cerebral ways.

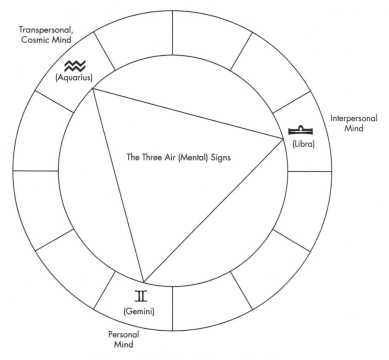

Transpersonal,
Cosmic Mind

(Aquarius)

Interpersonal
Mind

(Libra)

The Three Air (Mental) Signs

(Gemini)

Personal
Mind

Figure 1-4. The Three Air Signs

The zodiac contains three separate air signs, each of which reflects the workings of the mind in increasingly expansive ways. In Gemini, we see rationality at its most personal and everyday, as might be exemplified by an ordinary conversation with a casual friend or sibling. In Libra, we find the workings of mind turning to slightly more impersonal concerns now; for example, think of a teacher lecturing to a class or a store clerk speaking to a customer, where the ideas involved are somewhat more informal and unemotional in nature. Finally, in Aquarius we see mind at its most impersonal and cosmic, where ideas have become largely divorced of emotional, subjective elements. A perfect example of Aquarian rationality would be science, which attempts to uncover universal truths underlying our world.

This shifting orientation toward the Aquarian expression of air is no doubt behind the growing fascination we see with outer space and its exploration, as reflected in films like *Star Wars* or *2001: A Space Odyssey,* and TV shows like *Star Trek.* Works like these capture the emerging spirit of "longing for the stars" that is so intrinsic to Aquarius. Later in the book, we will explore these and other aspects of the Aquarian paradigm-shift in more detail.

Transitional Symbols on the Brink of Aquarius

With one foot in the Piscean Age behind us and another in the Aquarian Age before us, we find ourselves caught between radically contrasting, and sometimes conflicting, value systems. If the Great Ages represent a Shakespearean drama of cosmic proportions, then we have stepped onstage precisely at the point between acts, as it were, when the old props and backdrops have begun to be replaced by new ones. One result of living in this liminal in-between state is the rise of various transitional forms—developments that are symbolic hybrids of the Piscean and Aquarian energies. Here are a few examples of these from recent times.

Televangelism: What happens when old-school Piscean-style Christianity meets up with Aquarian Age-style media technology? One result is the distinctly modern phenomenon called televangelism, in which preachers employ the fruits of global technology for spreading the gospel of salvation to even larger audiences than ever before.

The Abortion Debate: As one age comes up against another, there can be a violent clashing of values and ideologies from both sides of the divide. A vivid example of this is the modern controversy over abortion. On the one hand, there are the largely Christian-based "pro-life" advocates who represent the forces of the Piscean Age with their expression of sympathy for the helpless unborn. On the other hand, we see the "pro-choice" advocates representing the forces of Aquarius, who champion the rights of individuals to decide their own fates. Over the years, there has been little compromise between the views of these two camps, and there is little hope for change in sight, but with good reason. They arise out of two fundamentally different paradigms, two radically different ways of seeing and evaluating the world—as it were, one from the last Great Age and one from the next.

The Storming of the Bastille: Sometimes single events from history can serve as symbolic benchmarks in the transition between eras. One of the earliest and most dramatic examples of this was the storming of the Bastille on July 14, 1789, a pivotal event in the French Revolution. On this date, French radicals overtook and opened up the famed prison which had been holding political prisoners, and released those few who remained. In astrological symbolism, prisons are associated with Pisces, while the principles of freedom and revolution are associated with Aquarius. The opening up of a prison and release of its prisoners was a symbolic landmark in the move from the old authoritarian order to a more freedom-oriented one.[5]

Alcoholics Anonymous: For astrologers, one of the more negative symbols long associated with Pisces has been the addiction to alcohol and other intoxicants. In the case of Alcoholics Anonymous, we see an example of people coming together specifically to break free from their addiction to alcohol, nicely symbolizing the effort to undo our bondage to Piscean-Age consciousness, through the support of a nondenominational group (typical of Aquarius). At the same time, AA still has one foot planted in the values of that receding Age as evidenced by its emphasis on the need to *surrender* to a higher power ("Let go and let God"), leading some to charge that this is in fact a modern secular religion with its own brand of commandments (the "twelve steps"). For better or worse, AA is a hybrid creation that blends the values of both Piscean and Aquarian Ages.

Transition Symbols in Cinema: Throughout this book, we will see many examples of how the cinema is a rich source of symbolic clues for understanding the transition taking place in our society. Take Peter Weir's 1998 movie *The Truman Show,* based on a script by Andrew Niccoll. This ingenious film tells the story of Truman Burbank (played by Jim Carrey) and his attempts to break free of a media-permeated world in which he has spent his life as the unwitting subject. Lording over this world is a powerful artist named Christof (Ed Harris), who has choreographed the circumstances of Truman's life from birth onward as part of a vast performance piece known to all except Truman himself.

Throughout most of the movie, Truman is shown living in a world bounded by water (Pisces); each time he attempts to escape from this world, he is lured back with the promise of alcohol (a Piscean symbol). He eventually learns to overcome these temptations and succeeds in escaping from this water-bound world into an air-based one (Aquarius). The movie climaxes with the protagonist walking on water and literally stepping into the sky. Note the name of the God-like figure he is shown trying to break free of within that water-bound world: *Christof,* or, *of Christ,* another symbol of the Piscean era.

Transitional Symbols in Literature: The transition to the Aquarian Age has expressed itself within the forms of modern literature as well. For instance, the passage from one age to another sometimes expresses itself in mythic symbols that depict a hero slaying (or rejecting) a creature symbolically associated with the prior age, such as Moses casting out the golden calf. In relatively modern times, a similar pattern can be found in books like Herman Melville's *Moby Dick.* Here we see a figure in the open air (Ahab) attempting to slay a creature of the sea, symbolizing transcendence over the water realm (Pisces). Additionally, if the whaling industry is taken as a symbol for modern industrial civilization generally, then Melville's tale underscores the shift from a more emotional and intuitive age to the more technological and business-minded one of Aquarius.[6]

The Pilgrims' Immigration to America: Whether we know it or not, we are all pushed or pulled to some degree by the imperatives of our age. We act out the necessities of a broader drama. As a case in point, the attempt by pilgrims to escape religious persecution in the old world in order to find religious freedom in the new one expressed a shift from the more dogmatic and persecution-oriented Piscean era to the freedom-oriented Aquarian one. Little could they have realized how they were also setting the stage for a collective drama whose implications would extend far into the future and influence the geopolitical direction of an entire planet, the subject of the next chapter.

<u>2</u>

America, Democracy, and All That Jazz: Birthing the Aquarian Spirit

Of all the symbols for the coming Age which have begun surfacing in recent centuries, there is one which arguably stands head and shoulders above all the others in both importance and scope. It is neither a person nor a single historical event, but rather a grand development of a far broader sort: the emergence of the American nation. Gertrude Stein once remarked that "America is the oldest country in the world because she was the first country into the twentieth century." We might alter that statement slightly to read, "America is the oldest country in the world because she was the first country into the Aquarian Age." Without a doubt, the United States is the cutting edge of the Aquarian Age. Within its history, institutions, and social customs we find a multitude of subtle clues of the themes and trends of the coming Age.[1]

The Birth of a Nation

What is it exactly that suggests a connection between America and Aquarius (aside from a vague linguistic resemblance)? For one, there is the synchronicity of its birth: the United States achieved independence in tandem with the discovery of Uranus—the planet most associated with the sign Aquarius. The astronomer William Herschel sighted this planet in 1781, the same year the British general Cornwallis surrendered at Yorktown, the end of the Revolutionary War. Astronomers would eventually learn that Uranus is unique among all the bodies in our solar system in that it is tipped sideways on its axis, by a factor of ninety-eight degrees. This is a reflection, some might say, of the revolutionary meaning of this planet and in turn the revolutionary nature of America itself.

Then there is the symbolism of the American flag. It is noteworthy that the United States was the first nation on Earth to display stars on its flag. As mentioned in the last chapter, Aquarian symbolism involves the sky and stars. Their presence on the U.S. flag may portend the more upward, galactic thrust of America's destiny, which may, on one level, pertain to its role as a leader in aviation and space travel.

Note how there were originally thirteen stars on the American flag, ostensibly a reference to the thirteen founding colonies, but with potentially deeper implications. As the American-born yogi Goswami Kriyananda once put it, only a mystic would consciously use the number thirteen in any major undertaking. Numerologically, thirteen is the number of revolutionary change, in that it represents a break with the established order, symbolized by twelve. The presence of thirteen at America's birth signals the emergence of a global force that will break with the past in forging a new future for humanity—whether for constructive or destructive ends remains to be seen.

It is intriguing that some of the founding fathers harbored this sense of destiny regarding their fledgling nation. This sense was implied on the Great Seal of the United States with its Latin inscription *Novus Ordo Seclorum,* variously translated as "the new order of the ages" or "the new secular order." Even before it had achieved independence, many had come to believe America would be the crucible for a new kind of society. For instance, some believe that Francis Bacon was directly inspired by this idea of a new society when writing his unfinished work *The New Atlantis.* Nor was this simply a theoretical project with him. Having been given the task of distributing land grants in the New World by the King of England, Bacon apportioned property according to a larger plan, intent on planting seeds for a spiritualized secret society on these shores.

In the same spirit, Benjamin Franklin promoted the dream of this "higher society" not only through his involvement with the independence movement, but by printing American editions of the Masonic writings of his time. When in France, Franklin is known to have received initiation into several esoteric orders, and he was made a member of the Rosicrucian

Brotherhood. Franklin's metaphysical interests are also evident in the fact that he was an astrologer, having published astrological planetary almanacs during his life.

Perhaps the most distinctly Aquarian feature of the emerging American nation was its overriding concern for freedom. Through most of its history, humanity has labored under oppressive social, political, or religious systems of one type or another. For many, America thus became the realization of millennial dreams of liberty and the possibility of achieving a better life. Steven Spielberg's film *Saving Private Ryan* effectively conveys a sense of how oceans of blood have been spilled through history to secure the ordinary freedoms we now take for granted.

Within the broad course of world history, America was the embodiment of those efforts, serving as the beacon for the emerging Aquarian era. Carl Jung once remarked, "There is no morality without freedom," and the emergence of a free society would signal an important advance in the spiritual growth of the human race. In an essay published in 1999, syndicated columnist Georgie Anne Geyer addressed the striking influence of America on the twentieth century, suggesting how its greatest export may actually be the dream of freedom itself:

> Think of where we were at the beginning of this century. The great masses of mankind still lived in rigid structures, from clans and tribes to caste systems so inexorable that no one outside the elites could ever dream of changing their status. We still lived in a world of empires: The British, with fully a fourth of mankind under their sway, but also the Austro-Hungarian, the Ottoman, and the French. Colonialism was the rule in much of Africa, the Middle East and Asia. . . . In the 35 years that I have been covering all parts of the world, I have found . . . that the seduction of America in this century is to be found in the less-glamorous idea that every man and woman everywhere, regardless of status of birth or gender or color, *could develop into a fully self-realizing individual* [emphasis added] (Geyer 1999).

If we peer behind the surface of the American dream, we find that it was the result of three developmental streams that converged during the 1700s: political (democracy); monetary (modern capitalism); and technological (the Industrial Revolution). Through a closer examination of each of these, we can understand the American psyche better and shed light on formative trends of the coming age.

The Paradox of Democracy

Strictly speaking, America was not the first democracy on the planet. One finds variations of representative government among the Greeks, English, Scandinavians, Swiss, and Native Americans in earlier times. Yet on American soil, democracy would develop to a degree never before seen in the world, and would influence the geopolitical balance of the planet for centuries to come.

Democracy transfers power from a ruling elite or aristocracy to the people themselves; a government from the "bottom up" rather than the "top down." If one hoped to find a metaphor that might convey the spirit of this governmental system, a good choice is that uniquely American art form, jazz. In contrast with more Piscean-age art forms like the Gregorian chant or the symphony orchestra, in which individual creativity was largely subsumed toward some higher ideal or authority, the jazz band represents a system where each player is regarded as an equal. Though there is always some musical framework to be followed, the musicians have considerable leeway to creatively express their visions.

That is a description that could just as well be used to describe the American political system. In American democracy, each state and each citizen is allowed a certain latitude within the general boundaries set down by the "sheet music" of American life—the U.S. Constitution. Like jazz, the United States has exhibited a degree of flexibility in its institutions that allows it to change in step with its people and the times.

Yet there is a great paradox at the heart of democracy which in turn mirrors one of the defining paradoxes of the Aquarian Age. I'm referring here to the curious way democracy emphasizes the individual and the collective simultaneously. For example, take the concept of individualism, which lies at the heart of democracy. We take it for granted now, but the word itself— "individual"—is a recent addition to our language, having been in common usage for only several centuries now. Within this simple linguistic invention lies an important shift in the global consciousness, one inspired partly by the spiritual teachings of an earlier time.

In his book, *Freedom: Alchemy for a Voluntary Society,* Gnostic scholar Stephan Hoeller points out how American democracy was influenced not only by the political systems of the ancient Greeks (and, some have argued, the Native American Iroquois Confederacy), but by an ancient body of mystical writings originating in Alexandrian Egypt commonly termed the Hermetic teachings (Hoeller 1992). Central to this body of thought was a sense of the innate divinity of individuals.

This was a view that offered a stark contrast to the Biblical doctrine of original sin that had extended its influence during the Piscean Age, and which held that individuals were inherently *unworthy*, redeemable only through external intermediaries. Since the Renaissance, the Hermetic teachings have influenced a growing number of thinkers, eventually including the founding fathers themselves, some of whom were members of esoteric fraternities. This renewed sense of our inherent divinity provided further momentum to the growing spirit of individualism, and resulted in a political philosophy that honored and encouraged the "inalienable right" of each person to engineer his or her own destinies, rather than be determined by monarchs or emperors.

But at the same time that it emphasizes the individual, democracy paradoxically stresses the development of a new kind of *group* consciousness as well. After all, democracy doesn't simply extol a philosophy of "every man for himself," a rampant individualism where each person goes off in their own direction. That is anarchy. Instead, it encourages an alliance of free-thinking individuals who pursue their dreams in concert with one another, joined by laws designed to ensure our mutual freedoms.

In *Leaves of Grass*, Walt Whitman touched on this paradox when he wrote, "One's-self I sing, a simple separate person/Yet utter the word Democratic, the word En-Masse." In its own way, America perfectly embodied this side of the equation, with its own unique brand of group consciousness. For example, upon visiting America in the early nineteenth century, Alexis de Tocqueville remarked how Americans of all ages and conditions are constantly forming associations of one type or another, whether for constructing churches or sending missionaries to far-off lands. Also consider the role that Masonic fraternities played in the founding of the United States, as both George Washington and Benjamin Franklin were Masons.

This Aquarian group orientation is reflected also in the corporate, conglomerate-minded side of American life. Indeed America might be described as something of a conglomerate entity, comprised of joined states. I once heard someone remark that the U.S. is a bit of an oddity among nations in that it doesn't have a proper name of its own; "America" is the name of the continent, not the nation, and could just as easily apply to South or North America. The term "United States" is more of a functional title that describes its conglomerate status, as compared to a true name like Spain or Italy. One might even note the acronym which is formed by the opening letters of United States: *US*. This is echoed by the collective emphasis of those famous opening words of the preamble to the Constitution which say, "We the people . . ."

But here is the paradox: with the new power granted each individual, the individual has, in another sense, become proportionally less powerful. For when every person has input into the governing process, it is much harder for any one person to exert far-reaching influence in the world. For example, in a traditional monarchy it was possible for one person to change things in a sweeping way, for either good or ill. But in a democracy, every decision and action must be ratified by the entire voting body; consequently, no single leader can truly exert the kind of control over the direction of society any longer. So at the same time there has been an empowering of the individual will, we have simultaneously witnessed a neutering of the same.

This is precisely the paradox underlying Aquarius. There has always been controversy over the true priorities of this sign, in terms of whether Aquarius governs individualism or group consciousness. The fact is it relates to both, if for no other reason than that the individual is always defined by the collective, and the collective always defined by its individuals. Reconciling these polarities will undoubtedly be one of the challenges in the coming age. For example, to what extent should the rights and needs of the individual override those of the collective? To what extent should the welfare of the group override that of individuals? What is the proper balance to be struck between these extremes?

There are great risks when either extreme goes too far in a democracy. When individualism is taken to extremes, it leads to isolationism, selfishness, or anarchy. When the collective is overemphasized, it can lead to mob rule as in the case of the French Revolution, where the abstract ideal of "the people" and the "collective good" far outweighed the rights of individuals, who were regarded as dispensable.[2] Again, the jazz model offers a useful metaphor in helping us envision an appropriate balance, by illustrating how each member of an ensemble can enjoy a certain autonomy and creativity. This is precisely the balance between individual and group rights that the founding fathers sought to strike in writing the Bill of Rights.

Capitalism and the Entrepreneurial Spirit

As Americans came to discover, political freedoms were integrally linked with economic freedoms; consequently, the second major stream feeding into the American spirit was the advent of modern capitalism. For millennia,

monetary wealth resided primarily in the hands of either the state or a controlling elite. What capitalism introduced was an economic system that
allowed ordinary people to pull themselves up by the bootstraps, to engineer
their own financial destiny. Capitalism gave us the entrepreneurial model.

Here, too, the image of the jazz ensemble provides us with a metaphor,
translated into economic terms. By contrast, a monetary system like communism could be likened to the Piscean Age example of the Gregorian choir,
since each person's contribution is pooled toward a collective concern.
Capitalism is like jazz in that each person has the freedom to earn and spend
money in the way he chooses within reasonable limits. Ideally, capitalism
balances the interests between individuals and the group, while allowing for
a certain improvisatory flexibility throughout the system.

It is noteworthy that the book that came to define modern capitalism,
Adam Smith's *Inquiry into the Nature and Causes of the Wealth of Nations,*
was synchronistically published in 1776, the same year as America's
Declaration of Independence. This influential volume suggested the importance of minimizing regulatory controls by the state over the economy, advo-
cating instead that it run free and regulate itself. Here was another expression
of the emerging Aquarian shift of power from "above" to "below," by allowing the economy to operate almost entirely by forces of supply and demand,
regulated not by governments or restrictions but by consumers. Note, too,
that the first bank to receive a charter in America, the Bank of North
America, was established the same year as the discovery of Uranus in 1781.

Within the comparatively classless society American democracy had
made possible, this economic revolution would eventually have profound
repercussions. Whereas the rigid class structures and economic systems of
Europe had constrained individuals to occupy narrow rungs on the social
ladder, American capitalism allowed each person a new power and mobility. This was the classic "rags-to-riches" scenario dramatized in the novels
of Horatio Alger. Rather than a political milieu in which individuals were
nurtured and guided by their clan or state, the new democracy, aligned with
capitalism, signaled humanity's "step out of the garden" in the way it permitted individuals to assume greater control over their destinies.

There were both positive and negative results of this socioeconomic revolution, which give us further clues to the coming Aquarian revolution. At best, the
spirit of competition fostered by capitalism encouraged a climate of creativity,
technological innovation, and personal empowerment that wasn't possible in
most other economic climates. By contrast, think of life under Russian commu-

nism for the better part of the twentieth century and the effects that heavy-handed bureaucracies and the ethos of personal sacrifice had on individual creativity within that system. One tends to find a greater spirit of vitality within capitalistic societies than in systems like these. As a precursor of the times ahead, this link between vitality and freedom may suggest that the Aquarian Age may likewise witness a similar spirit of vitality and entrepreneurial creativity.

The downside here has been the spirit of greed and materialism that generally accompanies capitalistic systems, as graphically illustrated by the transformation of America into a business itself. As the saying goes, the business of America is business. It's interesting that we don't call our leader "his holiness" or "your majesty," but the chief executive—how very secular and functional it has become. The Pandora's Box of capitalism seems to be that when humans are given unlimited opportunities for acquisition, acquisition all too easily becomes the driving force of life itself. The sheer force of capitalism is such that it can often pull the collective consciousness down to a level of purely material concerns. Plutarch decried this danger back in ancient Athens, where capitalism led to a kind of moneymania; and this type of materialism may become a major challenge of the coming age.

Moreover, there are also the effects of the "lowest common denominator" problem, i.e., what succeeds in a consumer-driven society is what usually appeals to the largest number of people. More often than not, that's an inferior quality product. Thus, we wind up with McDonald's hamburgers spreading across the planet rather than fine French cuisine, for the simple reason that they appeal to greater numbers of people and are more affordable. In a capitalist economy, subtler or more beautiful products created by individual craftsmen can easily be driven out by more generic products designed with the bottom line in mind.

Just as democracy had its own paradox, so does capitalism. The success of the entrepreneurial system insures that smaller entrepreneurs will tend to get overshadowed by larger, more successful ones. For instance, imagine a lone businessman who starts out with a single store and then parlays it into a chain of stores nationwide; in turn, the chain threatens the livelihood of smaller mom-and-pop stores across the nation, each one of them run or owned by an entrepreneur like our original businessman.

We find this same tension between the individual and the collective playing itself out on the planetary level as well through the continuing drama of "globalization." This term refers to the way multinational businesses have begun extending their influence across the planet, frequently threatening regional interests along the way. Here too, the key to a healthy compromise may lie in the jazz model, in how to strike a balance between the whole and the parts, between multinational interests and regional economies. As for which way is it likely to swing in the centuries to come, the only thing we can say with certainty is that it's likely there will be an ongoing teeter-tottering between both extremes, rather than any one system winning dominance once and for all.

The Technological Stream: The Industrial Revolution

The third major stream feeding into the emerging American nation was the Industrial Revolution. This was the great shift that occurred during the eighteenth century and changed the economic model from an agricultural, home-centered, and handicraft-based economy to one characterized by machinery and industrial production. Instead of the local artisan or farmer supplying goods, the new source of products and employment became the factory. Though this trend took place over several decades, some of its most important developments coincided closely with the discovery of Uranus. For instance, 1781 was the year James Watt invented the first steam engine which converted steam power to rotary motion.

While the birthplace of this revolution is commonly ascribed to England, it was in America where the forces of industrialization were most powerfully coupled with those of capitalism, quickly making it the most powerful nation on Earth. As such, the industrial revolution provided yet another key ingredient in the making of the American Dream. For example, think of the role played in American society by the advent of the assembly line, of steam power, the cotton industry, automobiles, cars, telecommunications, transportation—the list goes on.

Here is another manifestation of the Aquarian mythos. The machine represents one of the prime symbols for Aquarius's emphasis on air-sign rationality. More properly, the machine symbolizes the forces of mind as applied to the domain of matter (a point we will explore in greater detail in chapter 5). Though there had been machines of one sort or another throughout history, suddenly in the 1700s they were embraced with a passion that was unprecedented. Something new was in the air, affecting how people regarded themselves and their world.

Take philosophy. In 1779, two years before the discovery of Uranus, philosopher David Hume made his now-famous comment about the universe being "one great machine." In addition to solving age-old problems of manual labor, machines were a fascination on many fronts. Automatons—

early "robots" designed to mimic humans or animals in remarkable ways—became the rage throughout Europe during the eighteenth century. Note, too, that several of our founding fathers were notable inventors, including Jefferson and Franklin.

In connection with the rise of industry came the emergence of the factory system. Aquarius governs mass forms of creativity, where many people join together in the creative process, and this is what the factory system introduced: a radically new system in which people who had previously worked in isolation found themselves working side-by-side with scores of other workers. The factory workplace model was accompanied by the introduction of the assembly line that made possible the creation of large numbers of identical items at low cost. Previously, great care and craftsmanship had gone into making ordinary objects, but with mass production, the process shifted from an emphasis on personal creativity to a more impersonal and functional form of creativity—where uniform parts with no unique identifying characteristics were stamped out *en masse*.

Industrialization shows us a very different side of Aquarian creativity than that which is expressed by the jazz band, in terms of its emphasis on part versus whole. Whereas jazz draws together individuals without sacrificing personal creativity, the assembly line is an impersonal setup where individuality is subsumed to the greater system. Since its inception, the image of the assembly line has been used by social critics as a metaphor for the negative effects of modern society on our lives. Echoing Charlie Chaplin's image from *Modern Times,* we have *all* become cogs or "interchangeable parts" within a great machine, the argument goes. With the rise of multinational corporations and the global economy, the principle of the "assembly line" extended throughout our world in many ways, such as with chain stores and franchise restaurants, to cite just two examples. Thanks to a fast-food business like McDonald's, we see regional or national cuisines replaced by uniform foodstuffs, the same wherever one goes.

We might hold in mind the jazz ideal here, too, as offering a balance between part and whole, individual and system. Just when we think products and workers around the world are becoming more depersonalized and standardized, there are clues to suggest that consumers may be craving a more personalized, creative touch with their products through specially tailored items and services. As applied to the factory system, the jazz model would challenge us to find a way of allowing workers to express their personal creativity while also meeting the demands of the mass market. We may well discover that creativity in the workplace boosts, rather than diminishes, profits.

America—Awakening a New Style of Mind

The three streams of democracy, capitalism, and industrialism came together to form the American experience and its unique sense of freedom. Yet look deeper and we find that they stem from a broader shift taking place in global consciousness—the emergence of a new kind of *mind* within our world.

For millennia, the majority of humans had seen their world in largely prerational terms essentially through an emotional "filter" of consciousness. But beginning in the seventeenth and eighteenth centuries, a new spirit began emerging which led many to view their world in the light of reason. That is, assumptions and beliefs about the world, long taken for granted, were now being questioned and subjected to logical analysis. For the astrologer, of course, this mental awakening is perhaps best understood in terms of the *air* archetype associated with the emerging Aquarian consciousness. The important point is that each of the three developments expressed and encouraged a certain rationality in the human experience, a certain style of mind. Though this trend surfaced in a number of countries, including Holland and England, it found its clearest expression in America, whose youthfulness provided a blank slate on which the new mind could take shape and develop, relatively unburdened by tradition.

It was a style of mind with a distinctively *utilitarian* quality to it. For instance, America has long been a fountainhead of ideas and innovations most often marked by practicality. This has been evidenced not only by its myriad technologies, but by its approach toward philosophy; for example, the Pragmatists and Christian Scientists. One of the things that struck the French commentator Tocqueville about America was its utilitarian bent; Americans, he said, habitually preferred the useful over the beautiful, even preferred that the beautiful be useful. Having a product be unique or elegant was not as important as having something that simply *did the job*—and did it *cheaply!* All those fancy frills and flourishes so characteristic of the Piscean Age were brushed aside in favor of more streamlined functionality. "Usefulness over sentiment" might well be the motto for America and the Aquarian Age.

The Shadow Side of Aquarian Rationality

As with every new advance in human consciousness, there is also a darker side to this new style of rationality. True, it held the promise of bright new potentials in many areas of the human experience, yet it proved problematic in the basic area of human emotion. As astrologers realize, the air-sign personality is often out of touch with its own feelings and instincts to the degree that these can become unruly forces beyond one's rational control. As astrologer Liz Greene puts it:

> Air is the element which is most typically human, the furthest removed from instinctual nature. . . . Could it be that the airy type . . . has a rather infantile approach to the world of feeling? Could it be that he *must* appear detached, controlled and reasonable because he is really terrified of what might be boiling away down in the depths?
>
> Some airy people are only too aware of the uncomfortable autonomy of their feeling function, and treat it as though it were some kind of dark beast which occasionally escapes through oversight, but on good days remains behind bars so as not to disturb the smooth order of rational life (Greene 1978).

In some ways this description of the pitfalls associated with air signs sheds light on some of the distinctive trends we see taking shape in society these days, especially in America. Think of an Aquarian president like Ronald Reagan. He may have been a perfectly nice fellow in private, yet in his public policies he seemed largely out of touch with the problems of average Americans, let alone the underprivileged and homeless. Then there was Reagan's lack of concern over environmental issues; he mirrored the same sort of utilitarian insensitivity that has allowed modern-day businessmen to despoil Mother Nature for more than two hundred years, because to them the only value of nature has been economic.

But most insidious of all is the "unintentional cruelty" Greene goes on to describe. It is here that rationality can become a destructive force, if developed to an unhealthy extreme, to what Greene calls the "dark beast" syndrome. In a certain sense, one could say that *each* of the three air signs is at war with itself, in terms of the conflict between emotions and rationality.

This could describe the conflict at the heart of the American personality. Since the beginning, the American psyche has been in a state of civil war with itself, in its difficulty in coming to grips with the darker, more instinctual side of its emotions. One needn't look any farther than America's problematic attitudes to sexuality and guns for illustrations. Though many nations have experienced civil wars, America's battle between the North and South has become such a defining element of its character and cultural mythology that it's reasonable to think it reflects a conflict raging at the core of its being. But the essential point is this: This conflict may prefigure the central psychological challenge of the coming air age.

The stakes are high, for, to the extent that air-rationality doesn't come to terms with these energies, there is the danger it may find itself overwhelmed by forces rising up from below. Notice how this archetypal predicament lies at the heart of virtually all of America's popular mythologies, from earliest times up through the present. For instance, take what has generally been called the "greatest of all American novels," *Moby Dick.* In Ahab's battle with the great whale, we not only see an archetypal battle between the past and future Ages, but a graphic description of the psychological conflict between "above" and "below." Seen in this way, the complete destruction of both the *Pequod* and Ahab by the great whale speaks to the challenges of trying to subdue those emotional forces in too forceful a fashion. Published in 1852, Melville's great tale may even be read as foreshadowing the Civil War, the tragic conflict that would tear at America's heart less than a decade later. Ahab equates to Abraham Lincoln, who would likewise perish while trying to subdue a great force from down under.

In the now-classic 1950s science fiction film *Forbidden Planet,* we find a similar idea in its story of a distant planet that once housed a highly advanced race of beings called the Krell. This now-extinct civilization met its destruction at the hands of its own unresolved subconscious energies— what the film's characters refer to as "monsters from the Id"! Though they had evolved to a high degree in purely mental ways, they failed to realize the dangers posed by not dealing with the more animalistic sides of their natures, and they were ultimately consumed by that side as a result.

In an analogous way, this archetypal conflict is mirrored in America's perennial fascination with mobsters and the criminal underworld. Take what some have called the greatest American film since *Citizen Kane,* namely Francis Ford Coppola's *The Godfather* series. We find the same lure of the shadowy underside, clothed in the imagery of gangsters and underworld fraternities. The lesson could be stated this way: to the extent that we do not harmoniously deal with the Aquarian energy in an aboveboard fashion, we may find ourselves drawn to its inharmonious, inverted, subterranean form.

The Lincoln/Kennedy Parallels

This psychological conflict may also help to explain one of the great coincidences of modern history—the parallels between the Lincoln/Kennedy assassinations. Since Kennedy's death in 1963, various observers have noted the unusual string of similarities that link these key events a century apart. Some of these include the following:

- Both were involved in civil rights for Blacks.

- Both of their wives lost children while living in the White House.

- Both were assassinated on a Friday in the presence of their wives.

- Abraham Lincoln was elected to Congress in 1846; John F. Kennedy was elected to Congress in 1946.

- Lincoln was elected President in 1860, Kennedy in 1960.

- Lincoln was killed in Ford's Theater, while Kennedy died while riding in a Lincoln convertible made by the Ford Motor Company.

- Both served their country in war—Kennedy in WWII, Lincoln in the Black Hawk War.

- The names Lincoln and Kennedy have seven letters each.

- Kennedy had a secretary named Lincoln, while Lincoln had a secretary named Kennedy.

- Both presidents were succeeded by vice-presidents named Johnson who were southern democrats and former senators.

- Andrew Johnson, who succeeded Lincoln, was born in 1808.

- Lyndon Johnson, who succeeded Kennedy, was born in 1908.

- John Wilkes Booth, who assassinated Lincoln, was born in 1839. Lee Harvey Oswald, who allegedly assassinated Kennedy, was born in 1939.

- Booth and Oswald were both shot before they could stand trial.

- The names John Wilkes Booth and Lee Harvey Oswald each have fifteen letters.

- Booth shot Lincoln in a theater and fled to a warehouse; Oswald shot Kennedy from a warehouse and fled to a theater.

Over the years, skeptics have generally discounted these coincidences, saying that one could find parallels between *any* two figures in history if one tried hard enough. Yet when I have seen this attempted, the results invariably appear far more contrived to my mind than those found in the Lincoln/Kennedy case. This set of parallels holds genuine synchronistic resonance.

But what do they *mean?* Through the years, different writers have weighed in on the matter, but to my mind, the answer hinges on a little-noted coincidence: both of these figures were air signs (Lincoln an Aquarius, Kennedy a Gemini). Add to this the fact that both individuals were killed by forces from "below"—whether that be southerners, Castro, underworld figures, or covert forces of some other sort. (In the case of Kennedy, of course, there is still heated discussion over whether Lee Harvey Oswald even was involved in the assassination. Though in either event, he remains a symbolic figurehead in the debate.)

Whomever you tag as the villain in either assassination, we are left one commonality: in both cases, two air-sign presidents were taken down from "below." This may be a synchronistic warning about both America and the coming Aquarian age. It cautions us against the dangers of living too exclusively in the realm of mentality, while cultivating a spirit of positivity and "can-do" optimism that fails to fully address the darker aspects of human nature. Sooner or later, the subterranean forces, if not adequately addressed, will rise up and exact their toll, whether this takes the form of violence, sexual problems, or a general malaise. Jungians would describe this in terms of being overpowered by the Shadow, that darker side of human nature that constitutes our personal "underworld."

This is the message conveyed by that disturbing, yet uniquely American film, David Lynch's *Blue Velvet.* Though upsetting to many viewers, Lynch's masterwork expresses this inherent tension in the American experience insightfully. The story opens in a seemingly average town in America, with its white picket fences and chirping birds. Before long, there are hints of something dark beneath the surface, starting with a scene in which the viewer is taken visually beneath a suburban lawn to witness slithering, crawly critters normally hidden from view.

Then into this seemingly perfect American town arrives a naive young man who finds himself gradually drawn into the seamy underworld of this community. The film follows his progression through this darker world as he gradually learns to adjust to these violent and sometimes sexual forces. Note the name of the character who serves as our young protagonist's guide to the underworld throughout the film: *Booth*. At one point in the film, the name "Lincoln" prominently appears on a sign for no apparent reason. Whether or not director David Lynch knew what he was doing in weaving these symbols into his story, he was tapping into something fundamental about the American psyche.[3]

Healing the Split between "North" and "South"

How shall we resolve this problem of the "Civil War" between the "North" and "South" in our collective soul? Psychologically, one answer involves learning to come to grips, fully and honestly, with those emotional forces that lie "beneath" us. I'm referring to all those energies we might normally find unpleasant in our lives, especially those which disturb our puritanical tendencies. Among Americans, these forces seem to include nearly any experience centering on sexuality and anger.

It is encouraging to see the changes that have taken place in America over recent decades, in terms of the way Americans tend to be more honest about the "shadow" aspect of life than they were during hypocritical times like the 1950s. This is a contrast brilliantly addressed in the 1998 film *Pleasantville*, which illustrates the way society has not fallen into a state of moral decline so much as it has become more emotionally complex in its perspectives on life. (I take up the implications of this film in more detail in my discussion of the shuttle disaster in chapter 12.)

In more external ways, this healing process is also directly connected to our ability to express compassion for society's dispossessed, such as minorities, the homeless, or the needy, the figures we most readily project our unresolved "shadow" energies onto. This doesn't mean providing more handouts, but devising workable solutions to help these individuals improve their lives.

As dark a film as *Blue Velvet* was, it's important to note that it concludes on a symbolically hopeful note, a scene of a bird holding a worm in its mouth. The symbolic pairing of the bird and the serpent is one with deep mythic roots. Their pairing at this concluding point of the movie, after being shown as separate images earlier in the film, heralds the possibility for a uniting of "lower" and "higher," of "heaven" and "earth" within ourselves—the balancing of our spiritual consciousness with our emotional and physical instincts. Despite the more troubling aspects of Lynch's work (as in its frequent depiction of women as victims), it offers an insightful meditation on our modern psychic struggle as we head into the next Great Age.

Yet to grasp the larger picture involved here, we need to step back farther and see America's emergence within its historical context. For better or worse, the drama of American history is the drama of the coming Great Age; but how does this national saga connect with the broader set of developments that have been unfolding since the end of the eighteenth century? That will be the focus of the next chapter.

3

Windows to the Future: Glimpsing the Cutting Edge of Long-Range Trends

A Great Age doesn't arrive all at once but unfolds gradually over many decades and centuries, and each passing year unveils another nuance of meaning within the emerging order. Like the incoming tide, the Ages make their presences felt in pronounced waves—periods when the symbols and energies of the new order break into consciousness with heightened force. These periods offer us valuable windows to the future through which we can discern the emerging trends of the coming age.

Such periods can vary enormously in length, lasting anywhere from a single day to several decades in all, but each one tends to highlight a different facet of the emerging mythos. For instance, one period may call attention to the technological possibilities of the future, while another might underscore artistic directions taking shape. What determines the character and quality of each window? Astrology can provide some clues.

For example, when Uranus (the planet most associated with Aquarius and its technologies) comes into "contact" with Saturn (the planet associated with tradition and structures), we might see reforms taking place in our political structures or even architectural styles. On the other hand, when Uranus comes into contact with Jupiter (a planet associated with cultural and philosophical values), we might see breakthroughs in artistic or religious areas.

In this chapter, we will reflect on some of the notable "future windows" which have appeared during the last two centuries, and which have helped to lay the foundations for the coming era. Though these are not the only such windows from these years, they bear directly on the topics in this book. During each of these periods we will concentrate on those events which played a special role in furthering the Aquarian revolutions of thought we are focusing on in this book. Like omens, these developments can be seen as the cutting edge of longer-range trends that will play themselves out for centuries to come, and that we will return to in later chapters.

"First Light"—1775 to 1793

In the last chapter, we looked at some of the political developments associated with our first major window onto the Aquarian Age—the late eighteenth century. Beginning with the "shot heard round the world" at Lexington in 1775 and running up through the turbulent climax of the French Revolution, this time frame sounded the primary themes of the centuries to follow. Astrologically, there were several factors responsible for this. In addition to the epochal discovery of Uranus in 1781, this period featured two major conjunctions (zero-degree alignments) between Jupiter and Uranus (in 1775 and 1789, respectively). There was also the major polarity involving Pluto and Uranus which culminated in 1793. Simply interpreted, these configurations, involving powerful planets of change, suggested that a spirit of revolution was in the air.

In addition to those developments already covered in the last chapter—industrialism, democracy, and capitalism—this period also saw the initiation of several other major trends. For instance, the young Ludwig van Beethoven had his first works published during this period. The late 1770s and early 1780s was a time when Franz Mesmer's theories of animal magnetism attracted great attention. Though now largely discredited, this development planted the seeds for modern-day psychology and introduced the use of hypnosis (later employed by figures like Charcot and Freud). Also important were Mesmer's psychosomatic views on health. The 1700s in general were a time of powerful esoteric fraternities like the Freemasons and Rosicrucians, both of whom exerted enormous influence on the political and cultural affairs of the era.

One important way to understand the meaning of any age is to carefully study its governing symbol. For example, we saw how the sign Taurus is associated with the image of a bull—an apt expression of the earth principle and its down-to-earth concerns. Aquarius is associated with the image of a human being. What does this mean for the coming age?

One interpretation is that this will become an era of the *anthropos*, when humanity itself becomes a worthy object of study, when we will progressively be turning our attention upon ourselves as a species. One early example of this was the publication of Immanuel Kant's *Critique of Pure Reason* in 1781, the same year Uranus was discovered. In this hugely influential work, Kant heralded a turning away of human thought from metaphysical speculations about unseen realities back to the human mind itself and the immediacy of human understanding. This turning away would eventually serve as the springboard for later developments in epistemology, phenomenology, and existential thought, all of which focused attention on various aspects of the human experience.

The human-orientation of the emerging Aquarian sensibility at this time was also reflected in a new developing spirit of humanitarianism in society, as epitomized by the publication in 1777 of John Howard's *The State of Prisons in England and Wales,* a book on penal reform, and in Thomas Clarkson's 1787 essay on slavery, "A Summary View of the Slave Trade and of the Probable Consequences of Its Abolition." Though earlier eras had seen isolated acts of humanitarianism take place, it was invariably within a different context. St. Francis had wanted to sanctify poverty, not abolish it; the old "Poor Laws" had never been designed to abolish poverty but to prevent the poor from becoming a nuisance. As historian Kenneth Clark has noted, the antislavery movement of the late 1700s was to be the first large-scale expression of humanity's awakened conscience and of the serious desire to improve the human condition (Clark 1969).

The 1860s—Emancipation and Evolution

Because of its slow movement, a planet like Uranus can take a full 84 years to make a complete circuit around the sky from any given starting point (as seen from the vantage point of the Earth). Thus it was during the mid-1800s that Uranus returned to the same zodiacal position it occupied during the 1770s and '80s, the period of America's Revolutionary War and this planet's original discovery. For astrologers, this meant that the mid-1800s were a reassertion and reformulation of those themes and qualities which had first taken form during this earlier period. Amplified by a major grouping of planets that occurred in 1861, all lineups of this sort served as important symbolic triggers of cultural change throughout society.

Whenever the "tectonic plates" of a departing Age come up against those of an emerging one, the result can sometimes be "earthquakes" of a most dramatic sort, the most tragic sort being war. Throughout history, warfare has been a prime vehicle through which the changing symbols of the times first emerge into the collective consciousness.[1] A key example of this from the nineteenth century was the American Civil War.

Like all great battles, this was, at its most basic, an archetypal conflict, involving a clash of different values and symbols. On the one hand, the Confederate South expressed the interests of the waning Piscean Age, not only in its adherence to slavery, but its comparatively "romantic" way of life (idealized in the film *Gone With the Wind*). On the other hand, the armies of the Union North, spearheaded by Aquarian Abraham Lincoln, embodied the interests of the emerging Aquarian consciousness, not only with its concern for equality and emancipation but its more industrially orientated values. Synchronistically, perhaps, across the world in 1861, the long-oppressed serfs of Russia were being granted their freedom.

This political revolution closely coincided with another "war" being waged on the scientific front. With the publication in 1859 of Charles Darwin's *On the Origin of Species,* there occurred a decisive conflict between two different views of humanity's essential nature. It was the traditional, religious view (Pisces) versus the secular view of science (Aquarius). In the vanguard of this battle was Charles Darwin, a man born on the very same day and year as Abraham Lincoln. In contradiction to the prevailing religious viewpoint, Darwin suggested that humans weren't created out of thin air by some divine being, but evolved as a result of mechanistic processes. By suggesting that we, too, might simply be material entities like everything else, Darwin served to dispel our long-cherished notions of ourselves as privileged creations in a divinely infused world.

In the arts, a futuristic vision of the world was taking shape through the popular works of Aquarian Jules Verne, who by 1865 was writing of spaceships and projectile trains to the moon. Henry Ford, the man who revolutionized the modern world with the mass-produced automobile, was born in 1863. In music, the modern trend toward harmonic complexity found its chief powerful proponent during this period in Richard Wagner.

What some have called the first truly "modern" novel, *Madame Bovary,* was published in 1857, and in 1865, Lewis Carroll published *Alice in*

Wonderland, a work that grows more contemporary with each passing generation. In 1861, Charles Baudelaire published *Les Fleurs du Mal,* a collection of poetry that in turn paved the way for the later revolutions in modern literature and the linguistic complexities of writers like James Joyce.

During the mid-nineteenth century, spirituality, too, was undergoing major changes, in part as a direct result of Spiritualist phenomena first reported in upstate New York during 1848. Throughout Europe and America, and eventually reaching all the way into Abraham Lincoln's White House, men and women from all walks of life sought the counsel of mediums (what we now call channelers) in hope of obtaining valuable messages from "the other side," that is, from the "dead." It proved to be a transitional phase in the movement toward a more democratized religious sensibility, by offering individuals a more personalized (though still mediated) contact with the spiritual realms than Christianity, with its even greater reliance on intermediaries like Church, priesthood, and Jesus himself. Interestingly, the Spiritualist movement also played a role in the emergence of modern psychology, with psychologists like Carl Jung having begun their careers with a study of the mediumship phenomenon.

The 1890s—the Modern Imagination Awakens

For astrologers, the most significant planetary configurations are those involving the slower-moving planets of our solar system. Because such patterns can last so long, their influence is powerful, and the cosmic sweep of their orbits suggests a more global, generational influence than exists with the faster-moving planets. During the early 1890s, the two slowest-moving planets of our solar system, Neptune and Pluto, came together in a tight alignment. Occurring only once every 500 years, the rarity of this celestial fusion made this one of the most powerful of recent cosmic triggers in the transition from the Piscean to the Aquarian Age.

The unique qualities of these two planets are visible in many aspects of this period. For example, Neptune is decidedly ethereal and otherworldly in emphasis, while Pluto embodies a more sensual quality—the very qualities we find conjoined in the music of Debussy, the sinewy, serpentine motifs of Art Nouveau (generally regarded as having begun around 1890), and the artwork of painters like Jean Delville *(The Treasures of Satan, Orpheus),* Frederick Leighton *(Flaming June),* and even the intricate glass vases of Tiffany. Like some strange new perfume imported from afar, a powerful mood of exoticism permeated the air during these years which opened minds to a new world of *feelings*.

Viewed in the context of the shifting ages, the cultural manifestations of this period take on added significance. With any major celestial alignment, there is a closing-off of old themes and an opening-up of new ones within society. When this happens so close to the cusp of an emerging Great Age, as it did with the Pluto/Neptune alignment of 1891 and 1892, such configurations become all the more powerful as catalysts of change.

This means that the significance of this period is twofold, expressing qualities of both the passing and emerging ages. We find the vestigial qualities of Pisces within the spirit of "decadence" and disintegration that flourished at the nineteenth century's end, a period broadly referred to by historians as the *fin de siècle* (end of the age). This manifested in such ways as widespread drug use, a fascination with Oriental themes and motifs, and a burgeoning interest in mystical subjects. Here was Piscean romanticism at its most extravagant, reflective, and sometimes self-destructive. Symbolically, it is notable that the late nineteenth century was characterized by a profusion of water imagery in all the arts, ranging from Melville's *Moby Dick* at mid-century to the works of impressionistic composers and artists like Debussy and Monet, and even in the visions of dead or drowning women so beloved by pre-Raphaelite painters of the era.

At its most negative, this waning Piscean mood is visible in artworks like Edward Munch's *The Scream* (1895), and the publication of Bram Stoker's *Dracula*. Begun in 1890 and published on May 26th, 1897, this story of vampirism encapsulated the spirit of Piscean-Age romanticism at its most nefarious.[2] The general sense of an old order passing away was also evident in the ebbing influence of Native American culture during this time, a trend that reached its watershed in the tragic massacre of men, women, and children at Wounded Knee in 1890 (euphemistically called the last great Indian "battle" of the era).

On the other hand, alongside these retroactive trends were a series of futuristic developments that heralded Aquarian directions. These included the invention of wireless telegraphy in 1891, the electrification of society, the development of the automobile and aviation, the rise of financial tycoons like Rockefeller and Carnegie, the emergence of cinema, and the birth of modern subatomic physics with the discovery of the electron in 1897. In 1895, H. G. Wells published his futuristic novel *The Time Machine*. Modern-day psychology had its birth with the publication of William James'

Principles of Psychology in 1890, while Freud's *The Interpretation of Dreams* was published in late 1899. In 1892, the final, authorized version of Whitman's *Leaves of Grass* was published, and Nietzsche published the fourth and final part of his pivotal work, *Also Sprach Zarathustra*—these two works prefigured modern sensibilities in key respects, as we will come to see.

Perhaps most fascinating of all were those historic developments which combined opposing trends into one. Like the Roman god Janus with two faces, one looking forward and one backward, the 1890s gave rise to prominent hybrid forms that fused the themes and motifs of the Piscean and Aquarian Ages. It is often said that the seeds of a new era are always born out of the decaying forms of the older one; that could well be said about the developments of the late nineteenth century. As one example of this, let us consider the work of that figure who became the tonal prophet of the musical revolutions yet to come—Claude Debussy.

Born during the previous "window" of the 1860s, Debussy combined Piscean and Aquarian motifs in his revolutionary musical stylings. On the one hand, they brought to a grand summation all the romantic yearnings of the Piscean Age, with their swirling emotions, shimmering surfaces, and organically undulating rhythms. Indeed, one of his most famous orchestral pieces was titled *La Mer,* which means, appropriately, the sea. Astrologically, it is significant that two of Debussy's most acclaimed pieces were begun in coordination with the Pluto/Neptune conjunction of the period: his orchestral suite, *Afternoon of a Faun* (started in 1892) and his impressionist opera *Pelléas et Mélisande* (begun in 1893).

While deeply Piscean in many respects, Debussy's music proved to be the Trojan Horse in which the seeds of a future tonal revolution would be ushered into Western consciousness. Inspired by Javanese gamelan music heard at a Parisian exposition, he dispensed with fixed musical keys and decentralized the traditional melody line into cascading webs of musical impressions. Debussy advanced the harmonic experiments of Beethoven and Wagner several critical steps farther, and in so doing transformed the direction of modern music. At the time, many found Debussy's music barely comprehensible in its strangeness; yet it would serve as the springboard for later pioneers like Igor Stravinsky, Arnold Schoenberg, Anton Webern, and Alban Berg. Truly, the musical complexities and cross-cultural experimentations of the Aquarian Age can be said to have begun with the tonal experimentations of Claude Debussy.[3]

The 1890s were also a time that saw the streams of gospel, blues, and ragtime music coalesce in New Orleans to form the beginnings of jazz. As we saw in the last chapter, jazz emerged as one of the supreme metaphors for the Aquarian Age, through its vitally democratic character and dynamic, improvisational qualities. Born out of the suffering and religiosity forged in the crucible of slavery, it drew on emotional streams rooted in the Piscean Age, yet transformed these energies into an artistic vehicle that helped to usher in Aquarian values in artistic ways.

In religion and spirituality, this juxtaposition of Piscean and Aquarian qualities is also visible in the rise of several key mystical groups during this period. These included the Golden Dawn, a magical fraternity founded in 1888 (and which featured such prominent members as Aleister Crowley and W. B. Yeats); a major revival of Rosicrucianism; and the expanding popularity of the Theosophical Society, spurred on by the publication of H. P. Blavatsky's *The Secret Doctrine* in 1888. In their concern with mysticism, these groups were Piscean in essential symbolism, yet they were Aquarian in their intellectual sophistication and liberal tolerance of diverse viewpoints. Chicago's Parliament of World Religions in 1893 further underscored this ecumenical trend by demonstrating how different religions could coexist harmoniously under the same roof, even literally. Arguably the pivotal event of this gathering was the introduction of Swami Vivekananda to enthusiastic audiences, an event widely viewed now as the turning point in the meeting of East and West.

Importantly, these same years also saw the birth of such influential twentieth century spiritual and creative figures as occultist Dion Fortune (1891); author, J.R.R. Tolkien (1892); philosopher Pierre Teilhard de Chardin (1881); yogi Paramahansa Yogananda (1893); novelist Aldous Huxley (1894); spiritual teacher J. Krishnamurti (1895); futurist Buckminster Fuller (1895); and astrologer Dane Rudhyar (1895).

The Roaring '20s

If the nineteenth century was the last fully Piscean century of our time, then the twentieth century could properly be called the first fully Aquarian century. During this century, the decks were cleared of old agendas, and the business of the new Aquarian dispensation was set into motion. Beginning with startling revolutions in science and art at the century's inception, many people sensed something new in the air, something both exhilarating and frightening. This transformation was evident in the physics theories of Max Planck and Albert Einstein, the cubist experiments of Pablo Picasso and Georges Braque, and the captivating cinema of George Melies, Edwin Porter, and D. W. Griffith.

But it was also lurking in the deadly technologies of World War I, which single-handedly managed to wash away whatever lingering vestiges of Piscean Age romanticism might have remained for many in the world—or, as Robert Graves said of this conflict's impact, "Goodbye to all that." All of these revolutions and more came to a furious climax within the cultural and scientific revolutions that we call the "Roaring '20s."

This period shared many qualities with the earlier "windows," foremost among them being a powerful concern for freedom. We find the crusade for personal rights extended in further ways, such that during the 1920s, this trend encompassed the lives of women. This extension was due in great part to the ratification of the Nineteenth Amendment in 1920, giving women the right to vote. The year 1920 was also the time that Margaret Sanger founded the National Birth Control League. Interracial concerns experienced a step forward with the freer mingling of blacks and whites at some musical clubs and venues. While the Revolutionary and Civil Wars had been concerned with political and economic freedoms, the 1920s—the age of speakeasies, flappers, and bootleggers—saw a growing trend toward social and artistic freedom in new and sometimes unexpected directions.

The clash between religion and science that characterized the evolutionary debates of the 1860s was echoed in the Scopes Trial of 1925. The 1920s were a revolutionary period for science, with advances in quantum physics and breakthroughs in astronomy. Two major discoveries stand out: in 1925, Edwin Hubble showed that our galaxy was but one in a vast cosmos of "island universes," and in 1929, he introduced the "Big Bang" theory of cosmology, with his discovery that all visible galaxies seem to be rushing apart from one another. The era of space travel had its beginning on March 16, 1926, with the first successful rocket experiments by Robert Goddard.

If jazz was born during the 1890s, it was in the 1920s that it blossomed into the art form we are familiar with today. This was the era of Louis Armstrong, Fletcher Henderson, and King Oliver; it was a time when Prohibition led to a proliferation of jazz clubs and speakeasies around the nation. It was an era that even saw the emergence of orchestral works inspired by this new art form, such as George Gershwin's *Rhapsody in Blue,* composed in 1924. During the 1920s, the innovations of jazz also began to merge with that other pioneering musical stream from the 1890s: impressionism.

Until that point, jazz's most distinctive feature had been its combination of syncopated rhythms and group improvisation. But figures like Duke Ellington would transform the field by introducing into jazz the complex tonalities and shifting key signatures pioneered by Debussy. In fact, the developing relationship between jazz and French Impressionist music turned out to be a two-way street. When Maurice Ravel came to New York and met with George Gershwin, he surprised his host by asking not to see the local orchestral halls, but the jazz clubs, an influence reflected in his later compositions. The influence of Scott Joplin's ragtime style is apparent even in Debussy's *Golliwog's Cakewalk* of 1908. Over ensuing decades, the result of this fusion of musical streams would pave the way for the radical stylings of pioneers like Dizzy Gillespie, Thelonious Monk, Charles Mingus, and Miles Davis.

The popularity of jazz in the 1920s was closely linked to another profoundly Aquarian trend of the time, namely, the rise of modern media. This was an era when radios and phonographs were becoming fixtures in nearly every household across the country. This proliferation of media technology had many lasting results, among them the birth of modern celebrity culture and the notion of the media hero. Foremost among these was that daring young pilot, Charles Lindbergh (an Aquarian by birth). Radio introduced other hallmarks of contemporary life, such as modern advertising and consumerism; the first commercial broadcast was transmitted across the *airwaves* in 1920. Once corporations discovered the untapped potential of media to sell their wares, they feverishly set out to find new and improved ways to manipulate mass tastes. This is a point I will return to later on.

Media would have a profoundly democratizing influence on modern culture because of its unique ability to draw together people from all walks of life. With few exceptions (such as the Renaissance), societies had historically maintained a clear demarcation between "high" and "low" culture, between the upper and lower classes. Prior to radio and near the turn of the century, working men and women couldn't *afford* to attend fashionable theaters or concert halls even if they wanted to. Conversely, the rich elite tended to avoid the honky-tonks and clubs where the new music was being played.

But modern technologies like radio and the phonograph went far to erase that distinction by encouraging both high- and lowbrows to tune in to the same programs. As a result, music and drama from both ends of the artistic spectrum were going out over the airwaves to the masses. Directly because of this, the 1920s were a time when popular culture was rapidly becoming a dominant force in society. It would prove to be yet another manifestation of the Aquarian surge toward democratization (some might even say homogenization) that had begun two centuries earlier.

Cinema was also reaching a new maturity as an art during this decade, through the work of geniuses like Sergei Eisenstein, Fritz Lang, F. W. Murnau, and Carl Dreyer. In literature, a major revolution in style exploded into consciousness with the publication of James Joyce's *Ulysses* in 1922. Building on the innovations of the nineteenth century symbolist writers, this Irish Aquarian opened the door to later experiments in modern literature in ways that reflected the qualities of the Aquarian Age and its emphasis on intellectual complexity, humanitarianism, and cross-cultural references, to name three.

The 1960s—The Triumph of Popular Culture

During the 1960s, fans of popular music across the world turned on their radios to hear these lyrics: "This is the dawning of the Age of Aquarius." Whether or not the composers of this song had any inkling as to what these words meant, it provided an apt refrain for a period many came to believe was a turning point in the emergence of Aquarian sensibilities.

Astrologically, there were some good reasons for entertaining this thought. In early February of 1962, for instance, there was the rare lineup of seven planets in Aquarius. As mentioned earlier, planetary lineups like these are among the most significant engines of change in the transition from one age to another. That also holds true for the cojoining of Pluto and Uranus that occurred in 1965 and 1966. Patterns like these point to a period of exceptional social ferment and futuristic yearnings. These were further punctuated by the alignment of Jupiter and Uranus that occurred at the end of the decade, in 1969—an unusual planetary combination that brought us the summer of Woodstock and humanity's first steps on the moon.

As with our other future windows, the primary thrust of this period was in the direction of freedom. By contrast, the Revolutionary War had conferred freedom primarily on white males; the Civil War had opened the door for Blacks; the 1920s allowed voting rights to women; and the 1960s built upon these in important ways.

For Blacks, this was the decade of Selma, Civil Rights reforms, Malcolm X, Martin Luther King, and Huey Newton. For women, it was the era of the women's movement, the publication of Betty Friedan's *The Feminine Mystique* (1963), and the introduction of birth control pills. For the youth culture, it was a time of unprecedented influence and social engagement. And, for society as a whole, it was a period when average men and women were pushing the envelope in all forms of self-expression, from fashion and religion to sex. Politically, a spirit of unrest had begun sweeping the planet in areas as diverse as China, Nigeria, Czechoslovakia, Ireland, America, France, and the Middle East.

Like the 1920s, the 1960s were a time when electronic media were changing people's lives in dramatic ways. Marshall McLuhan now proclaimed that the "medium was the message." In the sciences, this was a period of widespread change and innovation. The year 1962 saw the publication of T. S. Kuhn's now-classic *The Structure of Scientific Revolutions,* a controversial work that offered a new way of looking at scientific knowledge. In 1964, physicist John Bell's theory of "non-locality" was published; it was a model suggesting that all phenomena in the universe were fundamentally connected even if they were physically separate and at a great distance, contrary to everyday appearances. Subatomic physics underwent radical innovations, too, with the introduction of quark theory in 1963. Modern-day chaos theory took shape that same year with the publication of Edward Lorenz's work on the "butterfly effect."

In technology, it was a revolutionary period on many fronts. In 1962, the modern telecommunications industry was transformed with the launching of the first active communications satellite, Telstar. That same year, the Cuban missile crisis showed how dangerous a world armed with nuclear weapons could be, as we found ourselves at the brink of global incineration. Computer technology was undergoing major strides during this time; for example, 1962 was the year Doug Engelbart published his pivotal essay "Augmenting Human Intellect," widely viewed as a turning point in the development of artificial intelligence. In 1969, the United States Department of Defense set up ARPANET, the precursor to the Internet. The laser was developed into a functioning technology during the 1960s, which in turn made further developments in many other fields possible, such as the invention of holography.

The 1960s would become the decade most identified with the "space age." In 1961, Soviet cosmonaut Yuri Gagarin became the first man in space, with American astronauts soon following in his wake. John Glenn's famous flight into space occurred in February 1962. Bringing it all to a climax would be humanity's first trip to the moon, which unfolded literally within hours of a major astrological configuration that had futuristic overtones (Jupiter joining forces with Uranus). The TV show *Star Trek* aired its first episode on September 8, 1966, and Stanley Kubrick's classic sci-fi film *2001: A Space Odyssey* hit theaters in 1968.

The 1960s saw an explosion of artistic creativity in ways similar to the 1920s and 1890s, but hot-wired by advanced media technology and psychedelic drugs like LSD. Similar in many ways to the Roaring '20s, the 1960s became a boom era for popular art, a time when the lines between high and low culture were blurred further than ever before. In rock music, it was a decade that played host to many brilliant performers, including the Rolling Stones, Jimi Hendrix, Frank Zappa and the Mothers of Invention, the Beach Boys, and Joni Mitchell—to name a few. But front and center were two pioneering influences that fueled most of that decade's excitement: the Beatles and Bob Dylan.

The Beatles landed in America on February 9, 1964, bringing with them a revolution in fashion, music, and social attitudes. In their own way, the Beatles embodied the jazzlike ideal. Here were four clearly defined individuals, each with his own unique style and personality, all pooled to create a harmonious whole. Throughout their career, the Beatles became a vanguard of Aquarian sensibilities, both musically and socially, but certain events in their relatively brief career would become benchmarks in the transition from the old era to the new one.

One example of this was a controversial remark made by John Lennon to a British reporter in 1966 (shortly after the final Pluto/Uranus conjunction of that year) that the Beatles had become "more popular than Jesus." Though never intended as a denunciation of Christianity, it triggered a firestorm of righteous indignation everywhere, with Fundamentalists smashing their Beatles records and denouncing the group as a force for evil. As with all major events that provoke a strong emotional reaction, deeper chords were being struck. As a symbolic manifestation of the times, this scandal became yet another transitional event in the shift from Pisces to Aquarius, as a previously religious worldview found itself eclipsed by a popular, secular one.

From the other side of the Atlantic there arose another pioneering influence of the era, singer-songwriter Bob Dylan. Significantly, his first album was released the same month as the multiplanet lineup in Aquarius in early 1962. Just months later, the Beatles' career shifted into high gear; they would sign on with Decca records and producer George Martin. Dylan offered somewhat more intellectual fare than the Beatles, with his songs of humanitarian passion and civil rights activism. In the spirit of earlier symbolists like Melville, Baudelaire, and Joyce, Dylan's lyrics would eventually assume a complexity and depth never before seen in popular music, while offstage championing a fiercely individualistic attitude with his iconoclastic lifestyle and odd appearance.

Like the Beatles, Dylan's career was also punctuated by transitional events that embodied the shifting values operative between Great Ages. The most conspicuous was Dylan's going electric in tandem with alignment of Pluto and Uranus at mid-decade. Pluto conjuncted Uranus from late 1965 to June of 1966—a planetary combination often described by astrologers as being "explosive" or "electric" in quality. Dylan played electrically in public for the first time during July of 1965, then toured with his rock-and-roll band through Europe during the spring of 1966. Clearly, he was riding the wave of cultural change.

Indeed, it is striking how both the Beatles and Dylan reached their creative peaks with this planetary alignment. In 1965, the Beatles released their breakthrough album *Rubber Soul,* while 1966 saw the release of *Revolver,* now considered by many critics to be their most innovative work, surpassing even *Sgt. Pepper's Lonely Hearts Club Band* in brilliance. Additionally, 1965-1966 was the period during which Dylan released three albums now considered his greatest, *Bringing It All Back Home, Highway 61 Revisited,* and *Blonde on Blonde*—astonishingly, all in the span of a little over a year. Perhaps underscoring the fact of their attunement to the coming air-age, many of the key figures in this musical revolution were air-signs, including Paul McCartney, John Lennon, Bob Dylan, and the Beach Boys' Brian Wilson.

The 1990s—The Rise of the Internet

For astrologers, the 1990s were notable for another major alignment of outer planets, this time involving Uranus and Neptune. Culminating in 1993, this was the first time these two planets had come together in this way since 1821 (yet another window in its own right). Any major planetary configuration can serve as a cosmic trigger in the unfolding of an advancing Age, but what made this configuration in 1993 significant was how those planets were associated with the outgoing and incoming Ages. Neptune is the ruler of Pisces, and Uranus is the ruler of Aquarius. This suggests that the events of this period held special importance in signaling the passage from the old order to the new one.

In politics, Bill Clinton entered office in 1992, marking the first time Washington would be run by Baby Boomers raised on the rock-and-roll music of the 1960s. The 1990s saw the Aquarian political thrust toward freedom taking on greater momentum, a trend that actually began during the epochal year 1989. That was when we obtained our first close-up of Neptune through *Voyager II*; it was also the year this planet cojoined with Saturn (the planet of "endings"), providing yet another symbol of "closure" for Piscean themes. Within days of that exact configuration, the Berlin Wall came down—a dramatic expression of the decline of that most Piscean of economic systems, communism. The fall of the Berlin Wall helped prepare the way for the surge toward democratic reform that swept Eastern Europe and various third-world countries in the years to follow. The 1990s would be a time when the concern over rights expanded to include such disenfranchised groups as the disabled, gays, children, animals, and even the environment itself.

It was a decade of important technological developments, including the unveiling of sophisticated new weaponry during the Gulf War, breakthroughs in cloning and longevity research, the introduction of Viagra, and the launching of the Hubble telescope, which became fully activated in 1993. But the high-tech development with arguably the greatest impact proved to be the Internet. First inaugurated in its modern form in 1989, the Internet exploded into worldwide consciousness during the twelve-months following the Uranus/Neptune conjunction of 1993. The result was, of course, a complete transformation of the telecommunications field. Aside from its impact on business, the Internet made possible a democratization of information, one that has often been compared to the invention of the printing press five centuries earlier. Anyone with access to the Internet can now obtain volumes of data at a moment's notice.

On a social level, this innovation further helped to crystallize what Marshall McLuhan had called the "Global Village"—a world in which geographical boundaries were being erased by technology and distant peoples were now neighbors. As the world's remaining totalitarian states realized, there were profound political repercussions of this technology, since it allowed people to bypass normal lines of communication and share information. Like television and radio, the Internet quickly became a catalyst for democratic reform throughout the world.

The early influence of the Aquarian Age has already brought about a shift from a mindset dominated by Judeo-Christian religious values to one dominated by secular and worldly interests. This transition has not always been a smooth one. Take the case of the U.S. government's siege of the Branch Davidian complex in Waco, Texas, on April 19, 1993. This was an event closely coinciding with the conjunction of Neptune and Uranus, the planetary rulers of Pisces and Aquarius, respectively. Government agents used heavy-handed methods to harass and ultimately destroy a Christian religious compound led by David Koresh. Whether one sees this event as a necessary curbing of religious extremism or as an unjust repression of religious freedoms by an overbearing state, this tragedy offers a sobering reminder of how heavy-handed the ascent of one age over a previous one can sometimes be.

In less conventional contexts, however, the 1990s were a time of considerable spiritual ferment, as befits the more adventurous tendencies of the Uranus/Neptune conjunction. Throughout the decade, many previously obscure esoteric or philosophical ideas began to filter into the popular consciousness. Books such as Sogyal Rinpoche's *Tibetan Book of Living and Dying* (1992), Thomas Moore's *Care of the Soul* (1992), Jack Kornfield's *A Path With Heart* (1993), Ken Wilber's *Sex, Ecology, Spirituality* (1995), and popular works of fiction like James Redfield's runaway bestseller *The Celestine Prophecy* (1994) appeared in the marketplace.[4] Noteworthy, too, was the hundredth anniversary of the Parliament of World Religions in Chicago in 1993, which, like its predecessor, sought to bring together men and women from around the world to exchange ideas and pool energies toward the realization of common goals.

As happens during all configurations involving the outer planets, the Uranus/Neptune configuration of the 1990s brought about a "piercing of the veil," in that our collective sensibilities began opening up to exotic new influences. This lure of the exotic or offbeat no doubt foreshadows the avant-garde, unusual aspects of the Aquarian Age itself. This manifested partly as a growing fascination with subjects normally considered fringe, such as UFOs, paranormal research, and anomalous phenomena in general.

For example, this decade saw the rise of alternative radio talk shows like Art Bell and TV shows like *Sightings* and *The X-Files* (which premiered in

1993). The phenomenon of crop circles achieved worldwide notoriety at this time, as did the mystery of the 1947 Roswell crash in New Mexico. Just as the 1960s had given birth to the original *Star Trek* series, the 1990s saw its worthy successors in the series *Star Trek: The Next Generation,* and the cult favorite *Babylon 5.* Even closer to the fringe, this was the decade that American and European researchers attempted to find ways of using technology for contacting the deceased—work that received qualified acknowledgment by none other than the Institute of Noetic Sciences.

In the arts, this trend toward exoticism produced a cross-cultural blending of aesthetic streams from countries around the world, similar to what took place previously during our previous windows. In music, the popularity of artists like Enya, Dead Can Dance, Deep Forest, and Enigma spearheaded a growing trend which came to be known as world music. One could go into some of the most conservative music stores and find recordings of African tribal sounds fused with those of New York techno artists, or Latin American rhythms combined with artists from Sweden.

In the classical field, 1993 and 1994 were years when music lovers around the U.S. were suddenly gripped by the compulsion to purchase a hauntingly ethereal recording by an obscure composer, the *Symphony No. 3* by Henryk Górecki. But it was also a time when alternative rock moved to the forefront of popular tastes with the emergence of "grunge" music, a style spearheaded by bands like Nirvana and Smashing Pumpkins.

Since Uranus governs technology and Neptune rules the imagination, it's fitting that this decade was a time when humanity found new ways of utilizing computers to help birth its wildest fantasies. In so doing, they may have provided us with a sneak preview of what lies ahead in the high-tech world of Aquarian entertainment. This included breakthroughs in both virtual reality and computer-generated art. On the cinematic front, this marriage of technology with the human imagination gave rise to astonishing advances in special effects, a trend which began in 1989 with James Cameron's film *The Abyss,* and which came to its fruition with Steven Spielberg's *Jurassic Park* in 1993.

In general, the Uranus/Neptune influence made this decade one of impressive creative work in both film and television: in TV, for example, it gave us such shows as *Twin Peaks, The Simpsons, Seinfield, My So-called Life, Northern Exposure, The Larry Sanders Show,* and the aforementioned *The X-Files.*

In cinema, the stylistic innovations of relatively unknown experimental filmmakers like Stan Brakhage *(Dog Star Man)* in the 1960s were now becoming commonplace elements of TV ads, rock videos, and movies, through the work of directors like Oliver Stone, Martin Scorcese, and David Fincher. The 1990s was a period of many memorable movies, including *Exotica, JFK, The Sixth Sense, Schindler's List, City of Lost Children, Fallen Angels, Pulp Fiction, The Shawshank Redemption, Groundhog Day, The Piano, Kundun, The Emperor and the Assassin,* and *Raise the Red Lantern,* to name a few. In particular, the latter half of this decade ushered in numerous visionary works that hinted at deeper implications for the coming age, including *Dark City, Gattaca, The Truman Show, Pleasantville,* and *The Matrix.* Over the course of this book, we will return to examine in more detail what these visionary films have to say about the shape of the coming age.

Neptune Unbound—The Transfiguration of Piscean Consciousness

When an old age gives way to a new one, what happens to the archetypal energies of that earlier time? As the Aquarian Age continues to ascend in influence during the coming centuries, will the receding Piscean consciousness and its manifestations vanish from sight, never to be seen again?

If history is any indication, the answer is not quite so simple. One possibility is that the forms of the older era will linger on in vestigial ways for thousands of years beyond their presumed shelf life. For instance, Judaism is by all accounts a religious phenomenon associated with the symbolism of the Aries Age; yet despite nearly being expunged in 79 A.D., it continues to thrive today as a living tradition, and this is thousands of years after the Age of Aries. Another scenario that can take place at the close of an Age is that the energies and forms of the era mutate in subtle ways and get transfigured within the context of the new era. Here again, Judaism offers a good illustration. Not only did it continue to exist on its own, but it spawned a powerful, and distinctly Piscean offshoot, Christianity. While Christianity shared many of Judaism's values and customs, it put a new spin on the themes of that older tradition.

So what new offshoots will the Piscean Age spawn during the coming Aquarian Age? Some important clues can be found within the various historical developments we have been looking at throughout this chapter. For instance, the more closely we look at the trends and developments of the late nineteenth century, the more it becomes apparent this period represented a grand closing crescendo for many of the energies of the Piscean Age. This is a phenomenon recalling cultural historian William Irwin Thompson's notion of the "sunset effect," that final blaze of glory which occurs at the end of an era or civilization.

Yet we also discover that the manifestations of that same period, while Piscean, appear stripped now of their strictly *religious* connotations. Consider Debussy: His music voices a Piscean-style consciousness, as reflected in its watery sensibilities and mystical otherworldliness, yet it is distinctly secular and nonreligious in character, bordering even on the pagan at times *(Afternoon of a Faun)*. In other words, those Piscean energies were transformed now into something different, more Aquarian.

For much of the last two thousand years, the boundless energies of the human imagination were almost entirely channeled into specifically religious ends. Artistic creativity was regarded as a fundamentally spiritual phenomenon to be employed in the service of a higher power. While this resulted in many remarkable artworks through the centuries—the Age of Pisces could be seen as an unparalleled era of great art and music—it also had a constricting effect in the way it forced artists to always set their sights in the clouds, as it were. In turn, this meant bypassing other possibilities closer to home, such as searching out the aesthetic potentials in the base realm of everyday life.

With the advancing Aquarian Age, however, we are beginning to see the Piscean impulse *unhinged* from transcendental goals, free to run in new directions. The inspirational impulse is still there, but shorn of the dogmatic trappings and constraints that bound it for two thousand years—indeed, for almost all of history. The result? Everything that is both best and worst in modern culture.

In spirituality, this trend expressed itself in a direction toward liberalized, nonsectarian forms of religious thought during the late nineteenth century. This was exemplified by the Parliament of World Religions and the rise of the Theosophical Society, to cite two cases. More broadly, it's visible in the widespread yearning for *mystery* that gripped the Western imagination in the mid- to late-nineteenth century, and which manifested as a fascination with tales of disembodied beings, subterranean realms, and ancient ruins. An early pioneer in this vein had been the American writer Edgar Allan Poe, whose work evoked emotional depths and shadowy atmospheres that were entirely new to most audiences. This was especially apparent in countries like France, where the works of Poe not only inspired Baudelaire and Mallarme, but musical composers like Debussy. Likewise, musicians like Richard Wagner and pre-Raphaelite painters like Dante Gabriel Rosetti and William Holman Hunt demonstrated how one could draw on mythic and quasi-religious themes while avoiding allegiance to dogma.

Of course, this freeing-up of the Piscean impulse had its problematic side. While the human imagination was no longer bound in a strict way to religious concerns, that freedom hardly eliminated the need for transcendental ecstasy. Consequently, the nineteenth century saw the rise of a widespread urge for release through whatever means could be obtained. As noted, this had its mystical expressions, but its destructive effects were also dramatic. One was the drug epidemics that afflicted Europe and America during the late nineteenth century, with growing numbers of people turning to cocaine, absinthe, and opium to fill this need for escape. It was this same impulse that also caused artists like Paul Gauguin to abandon their families for the South Pacific islands.

However, this displacement of the transcendental impulse took some unexpected twists as well, one of which was the rise of an entirely new art form which would sweep the world in short order—modern cinema.

4

The Omens of Cinema: Insights from an Entirely New Art Form

On December 28, 1895, in the basement of the Grand Cafe in Paris, Auguste and Louis Lumiere premiered a series of short films before an audience of several dozen curious spectators. It was a historic moment, in that this was the first time that motion pictures had been projected before a paying audience. The show lasted just 20 minutes, but the effect was electrifying. Soon people began lining up outside the cafe to see the Lumieres' amazing black-and-white movies of ordinary scenes, and within twelve months, the Lumieres' *cinematographe* device had been exhibited in numerous countries, even Australia.[1]

Strangely, the Lumieres regarded their device as having little future. But not everyone shared this sentiment. When the Lumieres toured Moscow in 1896, the famed Russian novelist Maxim Gorky wrote of the strange, even disturbing impact this device had on the imagination, and he hinted at the far-reaching implications this medium might someday hold for the communication arts.

Of course, Gorky was right, and the Lumieres were wrong. In the blink of an eye, historically speaking, this invention was transformed from a novelty seen by a curious few to a major cultural force that affected the world. By the 1950s, movie studios had been erected in every major nation, films were employed for everything from public education to military training. By 1995, one hundred years after that first screening in Paris, an estimated one billion people were watching the televised Academy Awards ceremony in Los Angeles, an event celebrating the art, technology, and business of film-making. In a sense, novelist Gore Vidal put his finger on the mark when he said that Hollywood had become the cultural capital of our world.

There have been many remarkable inventions in recent history, but what explains the astonishing *emotional* appeal this medium has held for so many across the world, propelling it to the forefront of popular culture? Clearly, something deep was at work here which connected the Hollywood mythos to fundamental levels of the human psyche, but what was it? What relevance does this technology have for the Aquarian Age? To answer these questions, we need to first step back and understand cinema's (and television's) historical context.

The Medium Is the Message

Since time immemorial, humans have expressed an abiding hunger for the fantastic—the world of imagination and make-believe that is the stuff of our dreams. To paraphrase poet Robinson Jeffers, we yearn for visions that will fool us out of our limits and transport us beyond the constraints of ordinary space and time. It may be mere escapism, or it may be a reflection of a longing for transcendence and meaning in life. Whatever the explanation, it mirrors a hunger of the soul, ignored only at great peril. Like oxygen for a deep-sea diver, our craving for the fantastic and the ecstatic seems directly related to the maintenance of our psychic well-being, as individuals and as a society.

Toward this end, men and women have turned to any number of methods and forms through the centuries, from ingesting mind-altering substances to performing elaborate rituals and religious rites. It was this need that inspired our earliest cave gatherings in which participants undertook their initiatory ceremonies; it was this need that provided the impetus for the sacred dramas of the Greeks, dedicated to the god Dionysus; and this need was the driving force behind the storytelling and myth-making traditions of every culture around the world, allowing listeners to be transported into realms that existed "once upon a time."

As the influence of organized religion began to decline in the seventeenth and eighteenth centuries, men and women found themselves searching for new or different vehicles through which to satisfy this need in the way religion once had. Throughout much of Europe, this search gave birth to a powerful thirst for the numinous and awe-inspiring image, something forcefully denied to people by the iconoclastic Protestant reformation. For instance, precisely as European society was becoming more scientific and rational, there arose that most extravagant and imaginative art form, opera. This strange new creation offered a heady fusion of imagery, music, action, and words that prefigured today's modern musicals, even rock videos. With its multisensory richness, opera's rise to popularity in the eighteenth century provided a counterbalance to the dry rationalism of the Enlightenment, with its exclusive emphasis upon the *word*.

Despite the popularity of opera and other art forms, the gnawing hunger persisted. For instance, while opera would be transformed into a brilliant art form by geniuses like Mozart and Wagner, it wasn't to everyone's tastes, nor was it widely accessible. Much the same could be said about theater, which frequently had the disadvantage of lacking musical accompaniment. The development of the novel in the eighteenth and nineteenth centuries engaged the interior lives of readers, yet lacked the dynamism of sound and image. All the while, science was continuing to strip away what few mysteries remained concerning our world, as religion continued losing ground as an acceptable means of ecstatic release. By the late nineteenth century, the mood could be described as one of quiet desperation.

It was into this vacuum that cinema arose. Film drew upon the other art forms which had preceded it, including literature, theater, poetry, music, and painting. Its birth coincided closely with the powerful planetary configurations of the early 1890s, celestial patterns which had the effect of piercing through the membrane of our collective psyche and allowing an entirely new art form to enter into the world. Cinema proved to be like a spigot into the collective unconscious, through which flowed a rush of images that gave expression to the highest and lowest aspects of the imagination.[2] In no time at all, movie theaters evolved from the nickelodeons to the grand palaces of the silent era, with an opulence and mystique recalling the old cathedrals. Like the church, here was a new place where people could congregate in large, cavernous rooms replete with pipe organs, to solemnly partake in ritual communion with the revealed mysteries upon an elevated altar (stage).

Cinema was not merely the first new art form to appear in recorded history; it was destined to become the quintessential Aquarian Age art form. Why? For one, it was the first art in history to be dependent completely on electricity; one can dance, paint, sing, or write books without electrical power, but one cannot create cinema. Its Aquarian features were also visible in its democratic nature, by offering affordable entertainment for all classes of society. For example, in New York City around 1900, newly arrived immigrants unable to afford the concert hall or theater could see the newest films for pennies.

The cinema also revealed its Aquarian characteristics in the way that it soon became the first fully "corporatized" art form in history, created on assembly lines not unlike cars churning out of a factory for purposes of profit. Like any other manufactured item, every print of a film was identical in every respect to every other copy, down to the single frame. Unlike traditional religious rituals, in which every performance might differ in subtle ways from every other performance (depending on the time or the place of its enactment), one could always be assured that a film viewed in Spokane would be identical to the same film viewed in Schenectady.[3] What it all meant was this: the psychic wellspring that had nourished society for millennia suddenly found itself a new medium through which to express its urges, transformed by the context of a technological society.

The Dual Visions of Cinema

Or at least that's a simple description of events, for what became apparent from the very start was that the imaginal vision conveyed by cinema actually possessed two distinctly different faces. Yes, there was the more fantasy-based aspect of filmmaking that had its roots in the religious and dramatic traditions of history. Here was cinema with its more Piscean face, concerned largely with imaginary realities and otherworldly yearnings, and which unashamedly sought to transport viewers out beyond the here-and-now. By all accounts, the first great pioneer of this more subjective stream was the French filmmaker George Melies and his *A Trip to the Moon.*

On the other hand, there was also a distinctly Aquarian face of cinema taking shape, what might be called the documentarian aspect. In contrast to the more subjective and fantasy-based mode of cinema, this aspect of filmmaking offered something comparatively new with its attempt to capture the world more objectively and realistically, unaided by props and elaborate sets. The great early pioneers of this approach were the Lumiere brothers, whose moving images of workers leaving factories, and trains arriving at stations sought to hold a mirror up to reality in a sober-eyed fashion, bringing us *back* to the here-and-now. This traces its roots to such developments as the telegraph, newspapers, even scientific tradition itself, with their secular concern for raw information.

In the century since the birth of cinema, these two stylistic streams would cross-pollinate as filmmakers found ways of drawing upon *both* stylistic directions at once. Examples of this include the works of filmmakers like John Cassevetes *(Shadows)*, Richard Lester *(Hard Day's Night)*, Oliver Stone *(JFK, Natural Born Killers)*, Orson Welles *(Citizen Kane)*, and the entire French "New Wave" movement.

What might all this mean symbolically for the Aquarian Age? One interpretation is that this vision reflects a fundamental duality in the Aquarian imagination itself. Perhaps our psyches are becoming similarly engaged in a dance between these opposing trends. There will always be the need of the more traditional Piscean-style imagination, that craves the fantastic and seeks to be transported outside itself. Yet we are also seeing a powerful craving for more realistic fare that reflects the secular spirit of the emerging Aquarian consciousness, as reflected not only in documentary films but the phenomenon of network news. As we will see over the next few chapters, this stream will prove to be particularly important for understanding other aspects of the Aquarian experience.

Cinematic Signs of the Times

Let us turn now to the images and themes provided by the films themselves. Like all art forms, the cinema is a mirror of the shifting Zeitgeist. At its most prosaic, this seems to be nothing more than a matter of art reflecting life, in the same way that changing hemlines can reflect the wavering tastes of a fickle public. Yet at other times, there seems to be a more *synchronistic* element at work, such as when a film is released that coincides in uncanny ways with historic developments taking place at the same time. For instance, the premiere of *The China Syndrome* coincided within days of the nuclear accident at the Three Mile Island power plant in Pennsylvania in 1979. The synchronistic element might take the form of several films being released around the same time, independently of one another, yet which all feature similar storylines: *The Matrix* and *The Thirteenth Floor*, both released in 1999 are examples. In these cases, astrology is a useful tool in offering insight into the archetypal dynamics at work that reflect themselves in every aspect of our culture.

Especially fascinating, though, are those instances where an artwork seems to point the way to our future. As mentioned before, artists can pick up on trends long before they become reality. One thinks here of Jules Verne writing in the nineteenth century about humans someday flying to the moon and building their launchpad in Florida; this was where it would eventually be constructed a century later. Or Verne's prediction of the escape velocity space travelers would need to break free of Earth's gravity; this also turned out to be close to the actual figure. What about satirist Jonathan Swift, who in 1726 speculated about the two moons of Mars before they were discovered, even describing their orbital characteristics in detailed ways, which 151 years later were borne out to be essentially true?

Cases like these seem to suggest that artists can occasionally hit upon insights regarding future trends. But how can we tell which works are fantasy and which are prophetic? Aside from the palpable quality of genius that imbues certain works, astrologers have an edge in this regard, since they can study the horoscopes of the artists or even their artworks. This sometimes shows how in-tune these individuals and their creations are with Aquarian currents.

With these points in mind, I will be drawing throughout this book on an assortment of films that hold portents for the times ahead. As examples of this approach, let us briefly consider four films that bear directly on the shift from Pisces to Aquarius.

The Abyss (1989): The Shift from Water to Air

As we will see over the course of this book, there are many ways to approach the symbolism contained in any movie. In the case of James Cameron's film *The Abyss,* the approach I find useful involves looking to an important astronomical development which occurred at the time of this film's initial release: the *Voyager II* mission past Neptune. First launched in 1977, the *Voyager II* spacecraft was designed to take close-up photos of most of the outer planets in our solar system. Scheduled to fly past Uranus in 1986, this spacecraft would make its closest approach to Neptune on August 24, 1989, and provide us with our first detailed look at this distant planet.

As the time of the fly-by approached, I began watching for events that might in any way reflect, synchronistically, the archetypal properties of this planet. But because of Neptune's symbolic association with Pisces, I began to wonder whether I'd see developments that somehow summarized the themes of the receding Piscean Age.

As it turned out, nearly all of 1989 was colored by a conspicuously Neptunian mood on many fronts. At its most negative, this time saw a mounting sense of dread throughout the West as a result of the escalating drug crisis occurring in both North and South America. Seemingly every day prior to the fly-by we saw ever-more horrific stories coming out of South America of drug cartels wreaking havoc through political assassinations and public bombings. On the actual day of the fly-by, August 24, drug lords in the region formally declared war on the Colombian government. This development was so grave that President George Bush asked the American networks for air time to make a televised speech addressing this situation. Clearly, this was showing us the darker side of Neptune's addictive and escapist tendencies played out on a global stage.

I noticed several other key developments which seemed to reflect the Neptunian/Piscean energy of the time in both positive and negative ways. These included the installation of a new leader in Poland on the day of the fly-by, an event that was the first nail in the coffin of Western Communism. Considering that modern Communism had begun in tandem with Neptune's discovery (Neptune was discovered in 1846; Marx's *Communist Manifesto* was published in 1848), the change of power in Poland almost seemed to herald a wrapping up of a trend which had started a century and a half earlier. Another striking news story during this time was the stunning image of Christian preacher Jim Bakker having a full-blown emotional breakdown in public as he was led away in handcuffs from a federal courthouse. Here, too, one might perceive another sign of the waning Piscean Age influence, aligned so closely with Christianity.

But the Neptunian mood of the period was especially conspicuous in the films of that period, particularly Cameron's special-effects epic *The Abyss*, having gone into nationwide release on August 9 shortly before the fly-by. This film takes place, appropriately, largely underwater, and centers on the problems that arise when a nuclear warhead winds up near the ocean floor following a submarine disaster. The movie concludes with a haunting sequence in which the male protagonist (Ed Harris) offers his life for the sake of humanity, plunging down thousands of feet to the ocean's bottom to defuse a bomb. Having accomplished this task and out of oxygen, he unexpectedly finds himself rescued by alien creatures, who take him into their underwater ship to recover.

In an unusual isolation chamber, he experiences a dramatic transition: having adapted earlier in the story to underwater existence by inhaling an oxygenated liquid that one breathes like regular air, he now undergoes a "rebirth" as he shifts from a water-breathing state to an air-breathing one, with alien intelligences looking on. Arguably the dramatic climax of the film, the moment is strongly reminiscent of childbirth itself, as he coughs liquid out of his lungs and struggles to regain his footing. As it turns out, his renewal is parallel to that of humanity itself; for it is through his selflessness that all humans on Earth are saved from destruction. In the film's "director's cut," this point is reinforced by the appearance of a huge tidal wave that threatens to overwhelm the world's coastlines, but which is turned back at the last moment by the aliens in response to this one man's humanitarianism.

Of the many elements in this movie which captured the Neptunian mood of the period, I focus on one in particular: that climactic elemental transformation. Similar to the ending of *The Truman Show,* our protagonist makes a pivotal shift from a water-based state to an air-based one, with Ed Harris's character struggling to expel water from his lungs and breathe oxygen again. Though he is actually reverting to an air-breathing state, this transition is given greater power by its placement in the film, and its suggested parallels with childbirth. As if to underscore the importance of this symbolism, the film concludes with the image of a gigantic alien spacecraft rising up out of the ocean—another expression of the shift from the water to the air element.

In light of this movie's timing in relation to *Voyager II*'s sojourn past Neptune, these scenes are yet another marker of society's transition from Pisces to Aquarius, and its movement from an emotionality-based era to an rationality-based one. We have come to the end of the line, so to speak, in terms of dealing with the concerns and lessons of an earlier age, and we are beginning to turn our attention now to a very different set of issues and lessons. Not to say that the Piscean age ended in 1989, any more than it did in the 1960s, or the 1890s. The influence of the Piscean Age will no doubt continue for many centuries to come, but there will continue to be certain key pivot points in that larger transition where the dynamics of change are amplified in dramatic ways, as decaying layers of that earlier age are shaved away. Our close-up view of Neptune in 1989, along with the other astrological patterns in effect that year, provide an example of such a pivot point.[4]

Star Wars (1977): Futuristic Art

Love it or hate it, there's no denying George Lucas tapped into something deep in the global psyche with the release of his first *Star Wars* film in

1977. An overnight sensation, the film treated audiences to sights and sounds they had never experienced before, while creating a new cinematic vocabulary that would impact movie-making for decades to come. As someone I know remarked at the time, watching the film for the first time was almost like stepping into an entirely different world that had its own inhabitants, atmospheres, and even logic.

Part of the reason for its enormous appeal, of course, was the skillful way Lucas incorporated the timeless themes of traditional myth into his story, retelling the classic hero's quest of a young man who comes of age, apprentices with a master, and surmounts a great challenge. What made it all so timely, however, was how Lucas succeeded in reframing all these elements in terms of space-age technology and values, making these ideas fresh in a way few other modern artists had been able to do. As such, he crafted a truly Aquarian vision, and gave us the sense that we were somehow glimpsing our impending "destiny in the stars," as well as the prospect of an interplanetary society. The sheer novelty of its vision pushed the envelope of our collective imaginings one step further.

But almost as important as the film's content was the skillful way it utilized new developments in film technology, and this was another way in which Lucas proved to be ahead of his time. Through its use of computers and sophisticated new techniques, he opened our eyes to a new range of images and effects, thus paving the way for a new generation of pioneers in the entertainment fields. Directly as a result of *Star Wars,* Lucas founded Industrial Light and Magic—a fittingly Aquarian name, we will see—a special effects house widely regarded as the leader in its field, which has since devised special effects for countless TV shows and films, including *Jurassic Park, Terminator II,* and *The Abyss.*

However, *Star Wars* also underscored the less pleasant ways in which the worlds of art and consumerism were becoming fused in the new culture. To help recoup the possible financial losses of this first film, Lucas had undertaken an elaborate campaign of marketing tie-ins and merchandise spin-offs that set a trend which would influence hundreds of later films. More than any other film prior to it, *Star Wars* helped blur the line between art and commerce. Here, too, we see a possible sign regarding humanity's future, in the precarious dance between corporate interests and artistic integrity that may challenge us in the millennia ahead.

Further important clues into this film's significance might be gleaned from looking at Lucas's horoscope, specifically in terms of how it reflects his attunement to futuristic trends. Astrologically speaking, there are many things one can look to if one wants to see a person's attunement to Aquarian themes and symbols. The most obvious is the position and quality of Uranus in their horoscope. In the case of George Lucas, Uranus was positioned in early Gemini at the moment of his birth on May 14, 1944. Why is this important? Because this is the same zodiacal point Uranus inhabited when the Declaration of Independence was signed, on July 4, 1776. As astrologers describe it, Lucas was born precisely during America's "second Uranus return"—the point when this planet had completed its second complete journey around the zodiac from its position in 1776.

What does this mean? Simply, since Uranus is the planet most associated by astrologers with all futuristic and technological concerns, it tells us that Lucas is plugged directly into the innovative and high-tech sensibilities of the American psyche. As one example, note that Lucas's first major blockbuster *(American Graffiti)* was essentially an homage to America and its technologies. This film centered as much on souped-up automobiles and radios as it did on the actors.

But let's take this agreement a step further. As we've been discussing, America is a microcosm for the Aquarian Age. Indeed, if one had to pick a single horoscope to represent the birth chart for the Aquarian Age, one could do worse than choose the horoscope of America itself. Uranus makes a full circuit around the zodiac every eighty-four years, and each time it returns to this "home point" it ushers in a new wave of innovation and complexity relating both to America and the coming Age. As we noted, George Lucas was born precisely as Uranus was making its *second* full swing back to this point, at 8 degrees of Gemini. Because of the link between America and Aquarius, this means that Lucas is deeply in touch not only with American tastes, but the emerging currents of the Aquarian Age. With his own Uranus plugged directly into that "home" position it occupied within America's chart (not far from the zodiacal degree it inhabited when Uranus was discovered several years later, in 1781), Lucas had his finger on the pulse of the themes, symbols, and values that would figure in humanity's future destiny.

From the start, Lucas's work reveals a recurring interest in futuristic possibilities. His first theatrically released film, *THX 1138*, offered a bleak look at the challenges of technology and individualism in the future. Several years later, *Star Wars* established his reputation as an artistically-minded futurist and a technology-minded businessman.

It is curious the way *Star Wars'* storyline mirrors the themes and struggles of the Revolutionary War itself; for example, in both cases, we find ourselves looking at rag-tag groups of frontier-style rebels going up against far more organized and powerful empires, spearheaded by great tyrants: Darth Vader and King George, respectively. In both cases, the overriding concern is attaining *freedom.*

Could it be that this is an omen for our future? If so, then America's destiny might foreshadow that of the Aquarian Age in some way; perhaps Lucas's film and the Revolutionary War both are precursors of coming trends, in their mutual emphasis on obtaining freedom and achieving independence from depersonalized systems of any sort, governmental, corporate, or technological.

After studying George Lucas's horoscope, I wondered what other individuals might have been born during periods when Uranus returned to its "home" point in Gemini (as found in both the United States horoscope of 1776 and Uranus's own discovery horoscope of 1781). Might these individuals likewise exhibit "futuristic" interests or involvement with Aquarian themes?

Here are a few of the names I found during its first return to Gemini in the 1860s:

Alfred North Whitehead	Feb. 15, 1860	Uranus at 8 Gemini
Alan Leo	Aug. 7, 1860	Uranus at 11 Gemini
Rudolf Steiner	Feb. 27, 1861	Uranus at 8 Gemini
Laurie Dickson	1861	unknown
George Melies	Dec. 8, 1861	Uranus at 14 Gemini
Claude Debussy	Aug. 22, 1862	Uranus at 20 Gemini
Auguste Lumiere	Oct 19, 1862	Uranus at 20 Gemini
Vivekananda	Jan. 12, 1863	Uranus in 17 Gemini
William Randolph Hearst	April 29, 1863	Uranus at 18 Gemini
Henry Ford	July 23, 1863	Uranus at 23 Gemini
Richard Strauss	June 11, 1864	Uranus at 24 Gemini
Louis Lumiere	Oct. 5, 1864	Uranus at 29 Gemini
William Butler Yeats	June 13, 1865	Uranus at 29 Gemini

While it's still too early to assess the full impact of Uranus's subsequent return to Gemini in the late 1940s—there are undoubtedly many more individuals to emerge from this period—the early results are already intriguing. Among the notable figures born during this time were:

David Lynch	Jan. 20, 1946	Uranus at 13 Gemini

Highly personal film director, whose TV series "Twin Peaks" became a cultural phenomena during the early 1990s

Bill Clinton	Aug. 19, 1946	Uranus at 21 Gemini

Former U.S. president and subject of unprecedented media scrutiny during his term in office

David Bowie	Jan. 8, 1947	Uranus at 18 Gemini

Musical and fashion trend-setter extraordinaire whose first major musical hit centered on an astronaut lost in space ("Space Oddity") and whose first major acting role was as an alien in *The Man Who Fell to Earth*

David Letterman	April 12, 1947	Uranus at 18 Gemini

Trend-setting talk show host and all-around iconoclast

Laurie Anderson	June 5, 1947	Uranus at 21 Gemini

Musican and performance artist whose work in both media incorporates technology in novel ways

Art Bell	June 17, 1947	Uranus at 14 Gemini

Late-night radio personality specializing in "alternative" topics (UFOs, paranormal research, quantum physics, etc.)

Arnold Schwarzenegger	July 30, 1947	Uranus at 24 Gemini

Actor whose greatest success has been in futuristic films like *Total Recall* and *The Terminator*, in which he played a robot from the future

Oliver Stone	Sept. 14, 1946	Uranus at 21 Gemini

Brilliant filmmaker with an eye toward controversial themes and cutting-edge editing techniques (e.g., *JFK, Born on the Fourth of July*)

Steven Spielberg	Dec. 18, 1947	Uranus at 14 Gemini

Cinematic genius and visual futurist extraordinaire (*Close Encounters, A.I., Minority Report*)

Aside from examples like these, the late 1940s were instrumental for a number of broader revolutionary developments across the world.

This era saw:

- the birth of the CIA (1947);

- the rise of the world's largest democracy (through India's independence, 1947);

- the emergence of modern Israel (1948);

- the publication of Norbert Weiner's *Cybernetics* (1948);

- the theoretical discovery of holography by Dennis Gabor (1948);

- the development of the modern computer (ENIAC, the first all-electronic computer, introduced on February 15th, 1946—Uranus positioned at 13 Gemini);

- the United States government's subjection of its own citizens to lethal doses of plutonium as part of a large-scale radiation experiment (1945 to 1947); and

- the so-called "Roswell incident" in New Mexico (Uranus at 23 Gemini, near its discovery point)—an event that, if real, would have signaled a huge leap in our technological knowledge (July 1947).

The Matrix (1999): Aquarian Myth

The same year George Lucas jumped back into the fray with his prequel, *Star Wars: Episode I—The Phantom Menace,* a smaller-budget production also appeared on the scene and went on to become a worldwide block-buster. Enigmatically titled *The Matrix,* it told the story of a group of cyber-rebels living in a world where "reality" proved to be nothing more than a computer-generated facsimile. In this world, life is a struggle to break free of the hypnotic grip of an artificial reality. With its combination of stylish camera work, effective storytelling, and tightly choreographed action sequences, *The Matrix* struck audiences with its novelty and stylistic fresh-ness, reminiscent of the first *Star Wars.* In a time when many felt that noth-ing new could be done with special effects, here was a film with surprisingly new images and experiences. The coinciding of Lucas's *Phantom Menace* and the release of brothers Andy and Larry Wachowski's *The Matrix* within months of one another seemed fitting, as if to signal a passing of the torch from one generation to the next. In the minds of some, the emerging *Matrix* series held the promise of being the new generation's *Star Wars*.[5]

As the nineteenth century ethnologist Adolph Bastian pointed out, any mythology can be studied in terms of either its "elementary ideas," those universal themes and symbols it shares in common with mythologies everywhere, or its "ethnic ideas," the local inflections and cultural modifications given those universal elements. On the first of these levels, that of universal meanings, the story of *The Matrix* touches on many of the same timeless themes found in mythic traditions, including the heroic quest, death and resurrection, awakening out of illusion, and the archetype of the wise sage. In fact, it has much in common in these respects with *Star Wars*, even its central characters bear a resemblance to one another: Luke Skywalker = Neo; Obi-Wan Kenobi = Morpheus; Princess Leia = Trinity; Darth Vader = Agent Smith.

But in terms of that unique spin it put on those timeless themes and archetypes, *The Matrix* differs from Lucas's vision in several notable ways, and consequently offers a different window on the trends of the Aquarian Age. For example, while Lucas's storyline emphasized the interstellar angle, *The Matrix* focused more on earthbound technologies, computers, learning chips, and virtual reality. In turn, it underscored a different set of issues from *Star Wars*, such as the growing mind-body disassociation brought about by technology, the problem of mind manipulation on a mass scale, and the challenge of distinguishing illusion from reality in a technology-saturated age.

In stylistic feel, too, *The Matrix* was distinctly different from *Star Wars*, and to that extent offered a somewhat different insight into the emerging qualities of the next Age. As some critics remarked in 1999, the newest *Star Wars* installment almost seemed stale by comparison to the hipper, edgier *The Matrix*. For all his genius, Lucas's version of the future world seemed more rooted in the sentiments and values of Piscean-Age consciousness, with its lush landscapes, flowing robes, and sweeping orchestral music. *The Matrix*, with its punkier edge, could prove to be truer to the spirit of the electrified Aquarian Age than that conveyed by Lucas's vision.

Citizen Kane (1941)

Citizen Kane has been hailed by critics everywhere, and inspired generations of directors and screenwriters. What was it, exactly, that made this film so special? There was, of course, the audacity of its invention, the way it broke so many rules of movie-making. There was the broad scope of its story, which spanned decades and employed scores of different settings. Its unusual narrative style was startling, in the way it jumped back and forth through time in the most unexpected ways. Most of all, there was the beauty of its images, the way each shot was framed with the care of a Vermeer painting.

Since it premiered, the influence of *Citizen Kane* on other filmmakers has been so pervasive that it is hard for us now to imagine how it might have seemed to audiences in 1941, when its innovations were still fresh. But a small sense of that initial excitement can be glimpsed by reading some of the early reviews that greeted it on its release, such as this comment from critic Jesse Zunser:

> It is an astounding experience to watch Orson Welles, 25-year-old Boy Genius of the Western World, in the process of creating on the screen one of the awesome products of his fertile imagination. You come away limp, much as if you had turned into Broadway and suddenly beheld Niagara Falls towering behind the Paramount Building, the Matterhorn looming over Bryant Park, and the Grand Canyon yawning down the middle of Times Square (Kael 1994).

Having studied this film for 30 years, I've grown increasingly convinced that it is a Rosetta Stone for the coming Aquarian Age. What could a film about the rise and fall of a newspaper publisher have to do with our future? To an extent, great genius is *always* prophetic in the way it taps into a deep strata of the collective unconscious, and draws on developing archetypal trends before they have surfaced into general consciousness. As the film most frequently lauded as "the greatest ever made," Welles' masterwork invites closer scrutiny for its clues on impending trends.

For the astrologer, there are other reasons to believe this film might hold long-range significance, such as the remarkable planetary patterns that accompanied its release, which all suggested an Aquarian trajectory. *Citizen Kane* premiered in New York on May 1, 1941, and had its West Coast premiere one week later.[6] That week alone saw *four* major astrological configurations take place, all directly or indirectly involving Uranus, the planetary ruler of Aquarius.[7] We will return many times to this remarkable film, so I will only touch on a few essential points of interest.

To begin with, consider its technical and stylistic innovations. Though *Citizen Kane* certainly wasn't the first to employ some of the techniques it is often credited with (such as low camera angles or deep-focus photography, in which scenes are shot to convey the greatest depth of field possible), it brought them together with a virtuosity that was groundbreaking. Welles' film comprised an encyclopedia of all those innovations that had been developed up to that point, while introducing a few new ones as well. On both counts, it prefigured the direction modern cinema would take for decades— perhaps even centuries—to come.

Among these techniques we might mention the following: the fish-eye lens; overlapping dialogue; "point-of-view" imagery; a film-within-a-film; high contrast photography; hand-held cameras; ultra-realism; gothic romanticism; the "jump cut"; the "long take"; artfully crafted dissolves and superimpositions; and contrapuntal sound editing. I often find myself looking at some modern film, and realizing that a seemingly new idea or technique it offers had already been employed by Welles in 1941. As one example, I was recently watching the 1992 Chinese film *Raise the Red Lantern* and noticed the ingenious way the director never shows the audience the face of its lead male character; later on, it dawned on me that Welles had already done this in 1941, by never showing the face of its central reporter searching for the clue to "Rosebud."

Citizen Kane's subject matter foreshadows certain important trends of the Aquarian Age, centering on such themes as materialism, personal isolation, and the empty pursuit of pleasure—all dangers on the road ahead. Another important aspect is its theme of the media and the power of its owners to manipulate the masses ("The public will think what I *tell* them to think!" Kane bellows in one scene).

But there are subtler Aquarian clues in this film, such as its striking approach to time. Rather than tell its story in a conventional A, B, C manner, *Citizen Kane* takes a cut-and-paste approach, scrambling its episodes to form an unexpected story arc. For example, Welles starts the film at the *end* of its subject's life, then jumps back and forth through time, giving us a jigsaw-puzzle portrait of the character's life and personality. Technically speaking, Welles wasn't the first to do this; that honor generally goes to William K. Howard's 1933 film, *The Power and the Glory* (scripted, incidentally, by an old friend of Welles' from Illinois, Preston Sturgess). But here, too, while Welles wasn't necessarily the first, it was the brilliance with which he employed this approach that made *Citizen Kane* so unique and ultimately so influential.

In the decades to follow, scores of other films would follow in *Citizen Kane*'s footsteps, experimenting with time in new ways, such as Stanley Kubrick's *The Killing*, Quentin Tarantino's *Reservoir Dogs* and *Pulp Fiction*, Oliver Stone's *JFK*, Francis Coppola's *The Godfather Part II*, Steven Soderbergh's *Out of Sight* and *The Limey*, Francois Girard's *The Red Violin*, Tim Blake Nelson's *Eye of God*, the Wachowski brothers' *The Matrix*, and Christopher Nolan's *Memento*.

Taken as an Aquarian sign of the times, what does Welles' inspired stylistic trend mean? Traditional esoteric sources place time under the rulership of Saturn. As the symbolic ruler over factors like authority, gravity, materiality, and traditional structures of all types, the radical reshuffling of time found in films like *Citizen Kane* could be heralding a fundamental change in our long-held perspectives toward the material world, as well as our attitudes toward tradition and authority. Welles decentralized the linear narrative and scattered it in many directions—perhaps this complexity of style foreshadows a new complexity in our thinking.

But perhaps it has a more literal significance in foreshadowing a shift in our understanding of the physical plane (Saturn) and the principles of time and gravity. If so, then this stylistic trend would hint at a time when we could learn to master these natural forces. Could it be that we will eventually discover how to manipulate time just as Welles did in his art? Only this much we can say for sure: time and gravity have been the focus of increasing scrutiny among scientists for many years already, and the prospect of further major breakthroughs in these areas is plausible.

As enormous as cinema's impact had been, it would soon be eclipsed by the appearance of another technology on the scene with even greater reach and variety. Though sharing certain elements in common with the older form, it introduced a new set of variables into the equation, and in so doing expressed the spirit of the Aquarian Age in an even more concentrated way. This shall be the focus of our next chapter.

5

Television, Cyberspace, and the Global Brain

Former newsman Walter Cronkite once called it the most powerful force on Earth. It has influenced the worlds of fashion and the arts, shaped our lifestyles, and transformed the nature of political discourse forever. Through it, we can peer into the far corners of our planet and even into deep space— all with the flick of a switch. Yet it is small enough to be carried by most people, and cheap enough for families in most nations to afford.

What is it? Television, of course. Cinema brought the startling phenomenon of moving pictures to our local neighborhoods, but TV suddenly provided ordinary people with their own miniature "movie theaters" in the privacy of their homes. It shared certain features with the cinema, for instance, its dual vision, with fantasy-based or escapist programming and reality-based, documentarian fare (e.g., news broadcasts, public television, and "reality-TV" shows). What's more, TV would serve as the prime vehicle for the display of feature-length films, bringing them to a wider audience than they could reach only through theaters. Even better, TV has shown itself to be a window onto the constantly shifting landscape of our collective unconscious.

But there were key differences between these media. For one, television had a decidedly masculine feel to it, employing an electron "gun" that shot its colder light into viewers' eyes in a more aggressive way, as contrasted with the more feminine reflectivity of film's "silver screen." Some even claimed its imagery acted on the brain differently, with a more hypnotic entrainment of consciousness than that experienced while watching films (Mander 1978). While cinema had its roots in the traditions of sacred theater and religious ritual, TV possessed a more secular ambience, shearing away further layers of mystery and magic from our creative image-making. Cinema gave us *gods,* but TV seemed more adept at giving us *celebrities;* that is, whomever appeared on the silver screen suddenly became larger than life, while figures presented on TV became *smaller* than life. In a sense, television became the latest step in the gradual collapse and desacralization of our cultural symbols to result from the shift between Pisces and Aquarius.

TV in the Information Age

If every technology reflects its age, what does television tell us about ours? As a cipher to the Aquarian consciousness, let's begin by considering its role in the emerging information age. Despite a heavy emphasis on fantasy-based programming, TV's greatest impact on the geopolitical stage has been its unique capacity for conveying *information*—political, cultural, religious, sociological, and scientific. In the course of a single day, an average TV viewer flipping channels could learn more about the world than the average human living in medieval Europe might have learned in a lifetime. As an information medium, TV traces its roots less through theater and sacred drama and more through radio and telegraph. It appropriated the documentary stream begun with cinematic forms like the newsreel, then created its own branch of news programming with the option of twenty-four-hour news channels for the deeply curious. Television is thus a key expression of the impending "air" age, with its concern for information, networking, and communication.[1] In a way that we now take for granted, it has broadened the horizons of viewers across the planet by making us aware of values and ideas we might never have encountered otherwise.

Of course, the Internet took this Aquarian democratization of knowledge a crucial step further by granting individuals access to oceans of data with unprecedented ease and control. Imagine if thirty years ago someone had told you that some day every person on the planet could possess the equivalent of a reference librarian living in their home who could search for information on any subject at any hour. "Absurd!" you would have said, yet that is essentially what the Internet has provided to us.

Information which had previously been the guarded property of an elite few is now available with astonishingly little effort. Someone wanting to learn the secrets of Tibetan Buddhism need no longer trek through ice-covered Himalayan passes; now they can obtain it by logging onto a website. Our minds are being opened in unimagined ways as we head into the next age, and will no doubt continue to open even more over the centuries to come.

The question is, what will be the *quality* of this mental expansion? Will media encourage an expansion of our knowledge that gives short shrift to our emotional lives? For that matter, to what degree will these new technologies enhance our capacity for real *thinking*?

I'm reminded of an episode of that hilarious TV show, *The Simpsons*, in which the older daughter, Lisa, as part of a scheme she is hatching, is trying to get her parents to stop watching TV. She unplugs the TV set while they are watching it, and says, "Why don't we listen to the radio for a while instead?" They sit there for a moment in silence, then her father, Homer, impatiently chimes in, "Well . . . put *something* on . . . I'm starting to *think*. . . ." That hits the mark. Compared to reading a book or having a stimulating discussion, television seems to engage the mind in a more passive way.

As cultural critic Jerry Mander has pointed out, the transfixed gaze of your average television viewer seems akin to that exhibited by a hypnotized person. The greater interactivity of the Internet remedies this problem to a degree, yet it still raises serious questions of both *quality* and *depth*, due not only to its often superficial content, but the narrow range of its sensory engagement. So when it is proclaimed that the Aquarian Age could be a profoundly mental one, there is no guarantee this will assume a more sophisticated form, as far as the masses are concerned.

The New Telecommunity

The emergence of a worldwide media grid is proving to have far-reaching social consequences as well, and these also mirror the concerns of Aquarian consciousness. In traditional times, a person's group was generally thought of as being their family, circle of friends, or local community and religious affiliations. But television and Cyberspace have linked us up in such a way that we now find ourselves joined to people we never knew before. This is the new Telecommunity, and it is a chief manifestation of the emerging Aquarian world.

Years ago, Marshall McLuhan coined the term "global village" to describe the coming society he predicted, and his prediction has already proven itself true in many ways. As a result of telecommunications, *everyone* has become our neighbor, and it becomes increasingly difficult for us to think of ourselves as separate from each other; our sense of personal identity is more and more linked to all of humanity.

At its most constructive, this reality has made possible an exciting cross-pollination of minds from around the world in fields such as philosophy, science, and the arts. Unlike the classical academy which was situated in a single geographical location like Athens or Alexandria, telecommunications decentralizes the locus of knowledge such that anyone, anywhere, can partake of it.

If there is a dark side to this phenomenon, it is perhaps its strangely *impersonal* character. Television indeed has the ability to link up billions of people across the world at the same exact moment while simultaneously allowing each of them to remain isolated from one another, with no physical or emotional contact. That might be seen as an apt description of Aquarius itself, which deals with more impersonal forms of social connection, and is constantly concerning itself with the tension between collectivism and individualism.

Like the lead character in *Citizen Kane*, we, too, may find ourselves increasingly spread out over the world by means of telecommunications, yet increasingly insulated from others in emotional ways, buffered from this contact by those very technologies. If we are not careful, the Aquarian Age could prove to be a time when we know more about people living in Borneo than about our own next-door neighbors.

The Global Brain

For some, the developing global network hints at something certain writers have referred to as the "global brain"—a large-scale mental entity that involves the workings of many individual minds in concert. As mentioned earlier, the sign Aquarius relates to a form of *collective* rationality, with a concern for *mass* thought-patterns and *universal* ideas and values. Modern media is one expression of this.

Had one been looking down on Earth during the last fifty years, it would have seemed as though a vast neural web were spreading out across the planet, with tentacles extending in all directions, and electrical impulses racing across synaptic centers. Significantly, a major factor in this worldwide revolution was the introduction of the telecommunications satellite, which provided us with an orbiting network of relay stations whereby signals could traverse the globe instantaneously. This was a development that began in the months immediately following the Aquarius lineup of early 1962, with the launching of *Telstar*. The Internet has accelerated this process exponentially. As writer and lecturer Terence McKenna once described it, the Internet is "a multisensored dynamic organism that lives on information" (McKenna 1998). Indeed, there are times when one could get the impression that the new telecommunications grid might have a mind of its own.

In a related vein, some have begun drawing comparisons between this new group mind associated with telecommunications and Pierre Teilhard de Chardin's theory of the Noosphere—a collective mind-field which Teilhard de Chardin saw as evolving out of humanity like an invisible mental atmosphere over the Earth (1959). As such, the telecommunications network spanning our world might be described as the "exoskeleton" of Teilhard de Chardin's Noosphere.

Remote Control: The Media and Mass Manipulation

But what are the implications of this new group mind? Is this a constructive or destructive development in terms of its impact on individuals? True, it allows us to link ourselves with the collective intelligence in a way never before experienced—but what does it mean for our spiritual lives?

When Neil Armstrong took his first steps on the moon in 1969, some speculated that it signaled the true birth of the Aquarian Age. Why? Because as Stephen Levine articulated it, it represented "the one-pointed consciousness of the whole world on a single happenstance" (Levine 1974). In some ways, that meshes well with the collective mind orientation of Aquarius. But we should be clear about what this attention means, for there is a big difference between an entire world consciously aligned to a single constructive thought and a world focused on a more meaningless or even destructive image.

For instance, what if that "single happenstance" happens to be a beer commercial? Or an image of a dictator broadcasting over state-run TV? Suddenly, the notion of everyone being "of one mind" doesn't seem so appealing, recalling *Star Trek*'s concept of the Borg: the alien race in which individuals are numbers in a hive mind, with no individuality. This is

Aquarian "interconnectedness" with a vengeance. (It is funny the way the Borg's square-shaped spacecraft even resemble a badly wired TV set.)

In and of itself, the Aquarian collective mind is neither an entirely good or bad thing, since it can be directed either way. The possible dangers here are formidable, in terms of how easily individuals can get swept up in the eddies and currents of the collective mind-field. Of particular concern here is how the media-supported group mind could, in the wrong hands, be intentionally used toward negative ends, thereby giving new meaning to the term "remote control." Is there symbolic significance to the fact that humanity's first televised broadcast powerful enough to reach into space featured the image of Adolf Hitler during the Munich Olympics of 1936 (a fact touched upon in Carl Sagan's story *Contact*)? Could this possibly be underscoring the inherent totalitarianism of this medium? By way of contrast, imagine an entire world focused on the thought of *healing* someone, or engaged in prayer for world peace.

The problem of media manipulation is also a central leitmotif of the film *Citizen Kane*, with its depiction of Kane as a "molder of mass opinion"; or Kane's telling remarks that he is "something of an expert on what people will think." Most notorious was his line (inspired by a real-life statement attributed to William Randolph Hearst) that "if the headlines are big enough, the news is big enough!" The lesson we might draw here is this: If we wish to remain free of the powerful eddies and currents of the Aquarian group mind, it is imperative that we take the time to better understand the forces underlying it. How do we do that? One way is by carefully studying the powers behind media. Who or what is pulling the strings? I propose we focus on three principal players: the government, the "herd mentality," and big business.

Government: In the old days, it was a simple matter for totalitarian governments, à la Orwell's Big Brother, to control the minds of their citizenry through media. But with the proliferation of the Internet and cable channels these days, it is harder now for the state to control *all* the channels of information in a society now. However, this doesn't mean big government is out of the picture entirely, for there are still plenty of ways for a government to influence the attitudes and opinions of a population.

One effective way to shape public opinion is by infiltrating key media outlets. During the 1970s, for instance, many were shocked to learn that agencies like the CIA had long cultivated connections with reporters in top news organizations around the U.S., including CBS and *The New York Times*

(Bernstein 1977). Though ostensibly done for news-gathering purposes, it was obvious that such operatives could just as easily insure the proper spin was placed on sensitive stories when necessary. Want to influence public opinion on some important issue? What better way than to have your own agents reporting it!

Another effective way of influencing public opinion is by means of strategically released disinformation. As shown in films like *Wag the Dog,* where attention is diverted from a breaking White House scandal with news of a phony overseas war, one can muddy the waters on any important issue by leaking bad or misleading data. Of course, there is always old-fashioned secrecy—after all, people can't protest policies or actions they don't know about.

Then there are more insidious theories concerning mind-control technologies supposedly developed by the American and Russian governments, designed to influence individuals or entire populations. Of course, science fiction writers and right-wing alarmists have long warned of the time when we'll all be fitted with microchip implants that allow our every movement to be monitored. Aside from speculative possibilities like these, what *is* certain is the extent to which our governments are capable of high-tech surveillance using satellites or other monitoring devices.

Though long dismissed as paranoid fantasies, the existence of global intelligence operations like "Echelon" (utilized by the NSA) and "Carnivore" (utilized by the FBI) have been confirmed in recent years. These are state-of-the-art surveillance technologies purportedly capable of monitoring much, if not all, electronic communications around the world at any given moment. These systems were rationalized on the grounds of combating terrorism, but it's not hard to imagine how they could be abused—a scenario portrayed in the 1998 film *Enemy of the State.* It may be that the most valued commodity in the Aquarian Age will be information, but in a negative sense, information could lead to the most insidious form of mass control of all, since those who control the flow of information in a society could control the lives of its citizenry.

The Herd Mentality: Have you ever felt yourself compelled to watch a TV show because everyone else was watching it? Or found yourself swept up in a mass anxiety over a much-hyped crisis, such as the Y2K problem or a new conflict breaking in the Middle East? If so, then you've experienced the power of the herd mentality. To an extent, humans have always been creatures of their times, borne along on the winds of popular sentiment.

With the rise of mass media, however, the power of this influence for better or worse has been amplified to an unprecedented degree.

Consider the way mass tastes drive television programming. TV is a heavily democratic media, in that what makes it onto the small screen is what the viewing public wants. But rather than cast our ballots at a voting booth, we register our opinions through the products we purchase or the shows we watch, duly monitored by the ratings companies. In some ways, this has its perks. For instance, I'd rather watch programming determined by mass opinion than the dictates of a ruling politburo. The trade-off here is that what generally winds up being broadcast through the media is what appeals to the broadest possible audience, and, more often than not, that's junk.

In a society where art is determined by popular decree, the bad tends to drive out the good, the result being that the group mind is drawn down to the level of the lowest common denominator. Alexis de Tocqueville once remarked that without wealthy patrons, artists in a democracy would find themselves forced to cheapen their work to survive. That's a problem only too evident in the high-stakes world of modern media.

On this level, then, the potential dangers of mass mind-manipulation may lie less with covert governmental agencies than in our own collective mediocrity. One might say that consumer-driven media is the one form of totalitarianism we seem willing to support, or as media critic Mark Crispin Miller once put it, "Big Brother is you, watching!" (Miller 1988).

Big Business: We come to perhaps the biggest mover and shaker in the shaping of the Aquarian mind: big business. As far as media is concerned, we are aware of its more obvious presence through paid advertisements and product sponsorships. Over the years, businesses have spent billions learning how best to influence the buying habits of the public, and as someone who once worked briefly in an advertising firm upon leaving college, I'm aware of how companies use images, words, and music to lull consumers into purchasing items they never realized they needed so badly.

But more worrisome are the subtler ways in which big business can influence our attitudes through the media. For instance, what happens when corporations start buying up the media networks? Though there are scores of channels now available to the average TV viewer, these are owned by an increasingly small handful of large conglomerates like Sony, Time-Warner, Disney, or by billionaires like Rupert Murdoch. The trend seems to be that greater numbers of media outlets are being concentrated into fewer hands.

What's so terrible about this? When so many media channels are controlled by so few interests, there's a greater likelihood that news coverage will be skewed in favor of those interests. Unlike the thirty-second commercial that trumpets its presence front and center for all to see, the powers of manipulation can now become virtually invisible. Say a large energy-based conglomerate buys up a major media network; will you trust the accuracy of any reporting conducted by that network on stories relating to alternative energy research? It's not hard to imagine how a world economy run by a few large multinationals could shape the public's perception of world events. In such a case, the drift of media programming no longer falls under the simple heading of supply and demand, but becomes a conscious redirecting of public tastes by the few. If government in earlier times was an institution of solitary rulers lording over submissive masses, the more decentralized Age of Aquarius could be a time in which the world is governed by a global alliance of corporate boards.

For students of cultural mythology, there are important implications here for our understanding of modern culture. For thousands of years, the stories that shaped and reflected our culture were usually handed down by families, schools, or religious institutions. But as media commentator George Gerbner has pointed out, the stories which shape our lives now are handed down to us largely by big business, through such vehicles as TV shows, movies, and books—in almost all cases produced by large conglomerates (Gerbner 1998).

The implications are sobering: the tales our children are being raised on now issue from corporate boards, in the interests of their bottom line. These entities have become the new lawgivers in our society, and our values and visions are bestowed upon us now from atop corporate Mount Sinais in remote boardrooms high in the city skyscrapers. In a way, it's as if our lives have been hijacked by corporations, a condition reflected in the popular mythologies of modern cinema.

In *The Truman Show,* the lead character is depicted as the first person in history to have been legally adopted by a corporation. In *Citizen Kane,* the title character is depicted as having been adopted at an early age by a bank, after vast natural resources are found on his family's property. On one level, Kane's life is a metaphor for what has happened to America itself: having begun as a frontier culture, the discovery and exploitation of vast natural resources rapidly transformed it into a world financial power that eventually took the American dream in a very different direction from what had been intended by the founding fathers. On a more human level, that outcome may be indicative of what is happening to everyone now, in that each of us is being "adopted" by corporate interests to the extent that we allow ourselves to be entranced by our era's consumerist values.

Enter the Internet

These, then, are some of the formidable powers in the shaping influence of mass media in our lives. In recent years, though, a new element has been introduced into this mix, extending the powers of conventional media in surprising new ways: the Internet. A unique blend of television, telephone, telegraph, and the computer, the Internet has created an electronic grid that links individuals and collectives across the world instantaneously.

Some see the Internet as a precursor for an even more extensive development in our future, the emergence of a vast electronic network where people, appliances, businesses, databanks, and even pets are connected in a wireless invisible web. This would constitute the Aquarian network at its most extravagant and, some would say, its most disturbing. Yet even in its infancy, the Internet is revealing effects that are far-reaching in scope, and shed further light on the implications of the Aquarian Age.

For one, it has opened new lines of communication to anyone with access to a computer. Ordinary people can not only access vast amounts of data now, but disseminate their own ideas to a worldwide audience. One result of this has been a freeing up of people's imaginations. Writing in the online magazine *Salon,* author and columnist Camille Paglia once described the Internet as "human imagination unleashed in all its perverse glory" (Paglia 2000). By providing yet another expression of humanity's collective unconscious, we have witnessed an eruption of unbridled fantasy into public life that is even more dramatic than what TV and cinema made possible. Who can say what further creations await us in the great pool of our collective imagination?

Perhaps the most vital element introduced by this technology has been the independence it offers its users. By providing a way for individuals to democratically plug in and out of the telecommunications matrix at will, it shifts the reins of information control back into the hands of ordinary men and women.

In the arts, for example, the Internet subverts the trend toward corporatized creativity in all fields by allowing artists to bypass the corporate system and display their works before a worldwide audience. Politically, the Internet has made possible the linking up of previously disparate forces in a way that has proven difficult for governments to completely regulate. The Internet has also offered a forum for previously disenfranchised or alternative voices in the world community; this is a development that could alter the political climate in unforeseen ways for centuries to come. In short, the Internet has introduced a more jazzlike dynamic into the global telecommunications mix by opening the system to more *interactive* participation on the part of individuals.

The downside here is that this same technology can be easily used by subversives, political foes, or hackers for disrupting the social order. Likewise, the Internet provides a ready forum for anyone wanting to know how to create bombs, for pedophiles who wish to prey on unsuspecting children, or for bootleggers who wish to illegally transmit or copy intellectual properties. Psychologically, the Internet has amplified the sense of isolation begun with television and the radio by allowing people to interact with the world entirely through their modem. In April 2000, the Archbishop of York attacked the Internet as having enormous potential for evil in the way it encourages people to relate to others strictly through technology. Another perspective on the Internet comes from a reader of *Time Magazine,* writing in a letter-to-the-editor:

> The difference between corporate dominance of media and online do-it-yourselfers is the difference between oligarchy and anarchy. Sure, we may no longer be inundated with Hollywood and Madison Avenue products like the Monkees, the Spice Girls, and the *Phantom Menace,* but we will get an avalanche of what is essentially vanity publishing—work by people who in earlier times would have been told to come back to the editor or producer when they had developed their talent and skill to a minimum standard (Case 2000).

The pressing question on many people's minds concerning this new technology seems to be this: Can the Internet retain its independence in the face of growing attempts to control the flow of information by both business and government?

The Techno-Ecology of the Mass Mind

Without a doubt, media represents one of the great metaphors for the emerging Aquarian Age, and as such provides a rich cipher into the dynamics of the unfolding mass mind. We've looked at a few of the implications associated with modern media in this chapter, yet we've also seen how there are in fact many different types of media and telecommunications technology, and that each one holds a different implication for the emerging collective consciousness. For example, there are vast differences between the Internet and a television station run by a totalitarian government. In the first case, there is a great deal of interactivity and autonomy available to the individual, while in the latter there is almost none.

How do we begin to make sense of all these variations on the theme of media as omens for our future? Could it be that some come closer to the Aquarian spirit than others?

I propose that *all* these variations and forms hold some meaning for the coming Age, when viewed as shadings in a spectrum of possibilities. By way of analogy, the Piscean Age did not bring us one variety of religious manifestation, but many, from Meister Eckhart to Torquemada. So why should we expect the coming age to be any different, any less complex? In this way, all these different forms of telecommunications technology illustrate the shifting dynamics or ecology between the group and the individual in the coming age. As systems theory demonstrates, the basis of any system is the relation of the whole to the part, whether that be neurological, societal, biological, or governmental in nature. That basic model may be applied to our understanding of media, too.

For example, at the one extreme we have those media environments where the system dominates the individual to an overpowering degree, as exemplified by a single TV station in a totalitarian country. Here, individuals have no real choice or input into the programming, and are simply passive recipients to the greater system. At the other extreme, we have the computer hacker who uses his skills to destroy (or reform) the larger network. Here, the system is at the mercy of the empowered individual.

But in between these two extremes are those media environments where the average person enjoys a certain amount of interactivity with the system, as with an ordinary Internet or e-mail user. This stage is roughly equivalent to the jazz dynamic described earlier, since it more closely balances the interests of the group and the individual.

Which of these models comes closest to representing the dynamics of the Aquarian Age? It's more probable we will see an ebb and flow among *all* these stages, in varying degrees of emphasis (see appendix 2). In other words, there will be times when society and its technologies could be an oppressive force in the lives of individuals, and there will be times when we'll see renegade individuals or groups trying to disrupt the larger system. Then there's the possibility we will see a harmonious balancing of the interests of individuals and the larger system. But as we'll also discover, this multiphase range of possibilities holds implications far beyond the role of media in the Aquarian Age.

The Glorious Flatland—A Broadening or Shrinking of Horizons?

Long before the fall of the Iron Curtain, I heard a lecture by a Russian citizen who had been traveling through the United States on an extended tour. He offered his frank assessments of American attitudes, and provided what struck me as a surprisingly even-handed account of this nation's strengths and weaknesses. Among other things, he remarked that Americans struck him as possessed of a sense of curiosity a mile wide but an inch deep.

True enough, but this same point might hold relevance for the Aquarian Age, too. For while the coming era may bring about an unprecedented broadening of our horizons, intellectually and scientifically, there is the chance it will do so at the expense of our inner lives.

Think of your stereotypical computer nerd, who spends hours a day surfing the web or involved in Internet chat rooms, yet who has little real contact with actual human beings. His mind is expanding, true, yet something is missing in terms of the psychological growth and social skills that attend ordinary interpersonal contact. As our relationships with others and the natural world become increasingly mediated by technology, we may find ourselves experiencing a flattening of our emotional lives, as we come to know the world through inorganic machines, monitored from a state of relative isolation.

How are we to explain these paradoxical tendencies between the expansive and the constrictive properties we've been discussing? One answer lies in understanding the connection between the Great Ages and the esoteric model of the chakras. Having studied this system for twenty-five years, I am consistently amazed at how well it explains a range of symbols associated with the Great Ages and the Aquarian times to come.

Astrology and the Chakras

In Hindu yogic philosophy, the theory of the chakras is defined as a psycho-spiritual model of personality based on the influence of subtle energy centers throughout the body. Tradition holds there are thousands of such centers scattered throughout the body, but seven or eight of these along the spine are considered the most important in terms of influence.

Each of these centers is associated with one or more areas of psychological concern, ranging from the earthiest drive for survival up to the highest urge toward spiritual transcendence. This isn't a hierarchy in terms of good or bad, since every center has its constructive and destructive expressions, its appropriate place in any lifestyle. Rather, spiritual life is about finding a healthy *balance* among the chakras.

According to one school of thought, there is a close relationship between the symbols of astrology and chakras.[1] As the philosopher Origen wrote, "Thou hast inside these a little Sun, and Moon, and even the stars. . . ." So it is with the chakras. As without, so within, the esoteric tradition tells us. In this way, the positions and relationships of the planets at one's moment of birth can be studied as a precise mirror of the energies within our chakras—providing one knows how to interpret them (see figure 6-1).

The Inner "Solar System"

Each of the primary chakras relates to a planet from traditional astronomy. According to systems like Kriya yoga, these are from bottom to top: Saturn = base chakra; Jupiter = second chakra; Mars = third chakra; Venus = heart chakra; Mercury = throat chakra; Moon = chakra at back of head; and Sun = chakra at middle of forehead, or "third eye." (The so-called crown chakra atop the head has no planetary equivalent, and for that reason is omitted here.) Hence, each chakra can be understood in terms of the qualities of its corresponding planet. For example, the root chakra can be related to Saturn and this

Figure 6-1. The Chakras and the Planets

According to some schools of esoteric thought, the planetary symbols of traditional astrology correspond to specific chakras or subtle energy centers associated with the body. (The chakra at the top of the head, called in Sanskrit
Sahasrara, represents a point beyond ordinary consciousness, and therefore has
no planetary equivalent.)

planet's concern for worldly responsibilities, achievement, and materiality.
Likewise, the fourth chakra at the level of the heart expresses the qualities of
Venus, with its concern with love, harmony, and pleasure.

However, each chakra possesses two secondary states of consciousness
that exist on the right and left side of its central, balanced expression. On the
one side, we find a more *masculine* expression of that chakra's energy, reflecting a more rational and external manifestation of its archetypal principle. On
the other side, there is a more *feminine* expression of that chakra, more emotional and internal in its manifestation.

While the core energy of the chakras can be related to the seven traditional
planets, these peripheral states to the right and left of each chakra can be associated with the twelve zodiacal signs, in a precise and orderly way. To show
this relationship between the auxiliary states and the zodiacal signs, simply

spin the conventional zodiac around until Leo and Cancer are positioned at the very top, at which point the correlation is obvious (see figure 6-2).

Figure 6-2. The "Inner Zodiac"
The twelve signs of the zodiac correspond symbolically with the peripheral energies alongside the chakras. This relationship can be seen by spinning the zodiac around until Cancer and Leo are positioned at the top of the zodiacal wheel. According to this arrangement, Aquarius equates to one side of the root or first chakra—the level of consciousness concerned with materiality and the Earth plane.

According to this arrangement, Aquarius is the masculine aspect of the root (Saturn) chakra, while Capricorn is its feminine expression. Sagittarius is the masculine aspect of the second (Jupiter) chakra, while Pisces is its feminine aspect. Aries is the masculine aspect of the third (Mars) chakra, and Scorpio is its feminine, internalized expression. Libra is the masculine aspect of the heart (Venus) chakra, while Taurus is its feminine aspect chakra. Virgo is the feminine aspect of the throat (Mercury) chakra, while Gemini is the masculine expression of that chakra. Leo is the masculine aspect of the chakra at the level of the forehead (associated with the sun), while Cancer is associated with the feminine polarity of this chakra. Let's see how this system relates to an understanding of the Great Ages.[2]

In simple terms, this correspondence suggests through the signs that the shifting of the ages reflects a corresponding shifting of energies within our "collective chakras"—our collective psychological states. When the Age of Aries was in effect, there was an emphasis within the collective psyche on third-chakra matters: the awakening of ego, a thrust for power, widespread military campaigns, the founding of empires, etc. With the rise of the Piscean Age, there occurred a shift toward second chakra concerns, which included a greater emphasis on questions of belief, dogma, and devotion.

What does it mean that we are moving into an age ruled by Aquarius? As the transposition of the air element onto the root chakra, it suggests a period in which we are going to see the principle of rationality applied to understand and master the physical plane. This means that the coming Age could be a time of enormous mental expansion with a strong utilitarian slant (as touched upon in chapter 2). Contrast this with an air sign like Gemini, which is also very mental in its focus but far more Platonic in nature, in the sense of being more concerned with the investigation or entertaining of pure ideas.

But Aquarius takes the principle of mentality and applies it to earthly matters, which is why this sign is related to activities like engineering, science, invention, social reform, and business. These are all rational pursuits with physical applications. It also helps to explain why the machine is such a vital symbol in understanding the Aquarian mythos, since it embodies these dual principles to perfection. Compare a machine with a rock: The rock represents unformed matter, but a computer represents matter modified by human intelligence. It expresses air rationality and root chakra materiality together.

Uncle Sam—Icon for the New Age?

This connection between Aquarius and the root chakra can help us explain other long-standing questions about this sign and the coming age. Prior to the discovery of Uranus, for instance, the sign of Aquarius had always been associated with the planet Saturn. This has mystified many modern astrologers since these two planets are apparently so different from each other. Saturn is more restrictive and "leaden" in nature, while Uranus (and Aquarius) is lighter-than-air in its qualities. So how could these seemingly contrary planets be joint rulers of the same zodiacal sign?

The chakra connection I've pointed to here may help solve this problem. For while they may seem to be totally different on their surface, these two planets share a few traits related to the concerns of the root chakra. For example,

consider the way both planets are intensely concerned with science and matters of time. Both are concerned with structures, though with Uranus those
may be more technological, social, or intellectual in nature, as in the case of
someone who works with a media network or a large association. In the case
of Saturn, those structures tend to be more political or material in nature, as
in the case of someone who works as an administrator or architect.

One symbol that aptly expresses this paradoxical fusion of qualities is
Uncle Sam. This political icon for the U.S., when viewed esoterically, can also
be seen as a symbol for the coming age. Uncle Sam's clothing, in jarring patterns and clashing colors, is the very embodiment of Aquarian oddball eccen-
tricity, yet the figure underneath those forms is classically Saturnine in
nature—tall, lanky, grim in visage, with a goatee to boot. Symbolically, it says
this: Behind the face of Aquarius lurks Saturn!

This has several implications for the coming age. A downbeat interpretation would be that hidden in the so-called freedoms of the Aquarian Age
lie the same old tyrannies. Dress them up anyway you like—as democracy,
technological conveniences, or financial opportunities—but the age-old
forces of power and greed are still there as dangers if we are not careful. This
certainly has been one of the lessons America has had to learn over the
course of its short history, as it continues to grapple with the problems of
big government, big business, and a latent imperialistic streak.

A more positive interpretation of this symbol is that true Aquarian freedom must be built on the bedrock of law and order—on *limits.* If you have
been to a third-world country where law enforcement is lax, or seen a community where policemen don't take their jobs seriously, you know how necessary limits are for maintaining liberty and in part why American society
has been so successful. As many have pointed out, one way or another we
are a nation of laws. That may be a lesson for our future as well, in terms
of our learning to strike the balance between liberty and restriction, anarchy
and totalitarianism. Read symbolically, the figure of Uncle Sam embodies all
these potentials, both constructive and destructive.

The Reign of Quantity

There are other ways in which this root chakra emphasis has begun
making its presence felt. One has been the rise of economics as a dominant
force in our world. Who would have dreamt five centuries ago that, one day,
economic systems would elicit the sort of rabid support once associated

exclusively with the world's religions? Yet that is precisely what happened during the twentieth century in the global clash between communism and capitalism, to cite the key example.

In a broader sense, this root chakra emphasis has led to a culture which nearly worships money as one of its principal "gods." The tallest structures in our time now are no longer religious ones, but corporate headquarters. This materialistic shift has been dramatized in films such as *Citizen Kane* and Oliver Stone's *Wall Street*. It's even reflected in the changing fashions of our era. For instance, compare the styles of European royal courts during the sixteenth century, say, with the more functional business suits of modern-day presidents and prime ministers.

We further see evidence of this root chakra consciousness in the growing emphasis on *quantity* over *quality* in many areas of modern life. A movie or TV show is judged now less by how good it is but by its ratings, by how many viewers it attracted. Assembly line workers are generally judged less by the competence of their efforts than their output. Our intellectual worth is assessed in terms of percentage points on standardized I.Q. tests that ignore vast areas of creativity in other areas of experience.

An Obsession with Time

In this same vein, the Saturnine emphasis of the root chakra manifests in our increasing obsession with time. Within the sciences, researchers have succeeded in measuring exceedingly small increments of time, while cosmologists have measured the age of the universe using billion-year increments. Einstein fundamentally changed our view of time by showing that it was elastic, that it could stand still were we able to reach the speed of light. Quantum physics uncovered other strange properties of time, including its ability to move forward and backward.

We saw in the last chapter how a key feature of modern cinema has been its ability to manipulate time, not only through editing and montage but techniques like slow-motion, reverse-motion, time-lapse, and the freeze-frame. In writing, the ability to work with time inspired many of literature's modern works, including Laurence Durrell's *Alexandria Quartet*, Marcel Proust's *Remembrance of Things Past*, H. G. Wells' *The Time Machine*, and Ambrose Bierce's *Occurrence at Owl Creek Bridge*.

But for many of us, perhaps the most conspicuous effect of this trend has been the way our lives have become so thoroughly *ordered by time*. While it's true many traditional societies patterned their lives according to cycles of time, such as the passing seasons or the rising and setting of celestial bodies, there are significant differences in the ways we live with time. For earlier cultures, calendars and clocks generally possessed an organic fluidity that reflected the ebb and flow of nature herself. Depending on one's viewpoint, we have been freed from the tyranny or virtues of nature's cycles, having replaced these with a uniform set of artificial timetables. Whether it is fall or winter, the bank clerk leaves for work at the same time each day. Regardless of variations in time zones, one can plan a conference call to parties at the far ends of the earth down to the precise second, due to synchronized timepieces.

Our lives are shaped by our obsession with time, whether that be for catching trains, punching in at work, or watching our favorite television show. In some ways, the preeminent symbol for coming age is turning out to be the clock—digital, of course. In the coming age, humans seem determined to either become the masters of time, or its willing prisoners.

"Boxed-In" Reality

A somewhat different way to approach the astrology/chakra connection has to do with the geometrical symbols associated with each of the chakras. For the ancient yogis, each chakra level was associated with a particular shape. The root chakra is associated with the square, its fourfold angularity signifying the earthy solidity and limitation of material-plane consciousness (see figure 6-3).

With this as a starting point, it is possible to draw any number of intriguing correlations with current trends in culture. For instance, look at how the grid pattern has come to dominate our cities, with their rows upon rows of square buildings lined up for miles on end. This angular grid pattern is even echoed in the wiring of our computer chips, which resembles the layout of a modern city in certain ways (something hinted at in the closing scene of the early computerized film *Tron*). In cinema, Stanley Kubrick's film *2001: A Space Odyssey* depicts the great mystery of our future, not as a sphere, a triangle, or a star, but an elongated slab; while TV's Dr. Who traveled throughout time and space in a TARDIS, a box-like device that looked like a telephone booth. In *Star Trek: The Next Generation*, the alien race called the Borg traveled through the universe in a spaceship in the shape of a cube.

Numerically, the square shape might be equated with modern science's obsession with four basic forces of the universe—electromagnetic, gravitational, weak nuclear, and strong nuclear. Genetic science views all biologi-

Figure 6-3. The Chakras and Their Geometrical Shapes

According to esoteric yoga, the first five chakras are associated with specific geometrical shapes, in reflection of their elemental nature. The root chakra is equated with the square, expressing the element of earth; the second chakra is symbolized by an upward-pointing crescent, expressing the element of water; the third chakra is symbolized by a downward-pointing triangle, expressing the element of fire; the fourth chakra at the heart level is symbolized by two interlocking triangles, expressing the element of air; the fifth chakra is symbolized by a circle inside a triangle, expressing the element of ether. (The higher chakras above this point have no geometrical equivalents.)

cal variations in terms of four molecular bases, the G, A, C, and T pairs of a DNA molecule. Jungian therapy speaks of four basic personality types—feeling, thinking, intuitive, and sensate. In popular culture, the archetypal musical group of modern times, the Beatles, had four performers.

Examples such as the Borg ship may echo the negative side of this trend, such as the way we seem to increasingly live our lives in a box. Think of how much time we spend viewing our world through square or rectangular windows, car windshields, computer screens, house windows, or television sets. Symbolically, the root chakra is associated with the fact of physical embodiment, so perhaps it is fitting that just as we find ourselves entering an age ruled by the root chakra, we also find ourselves increasingly encased in shells and boxes of one sort or another.

At its worst, some would say our lives are *spiritually* collapsing to box-like proportions. Is it possible that the coming age will witness a kind of "cosmic winter" in which our world is characterized by superficiality and coldness? In his book *Flatland: A Romance of Many Dimensions* (1880), E. A. Abbot offered the tale of beings who live in a two-dimensional world. For some, that image of "Flatland" has been a metaphor for our materialistic worldview, so dominated by the secular forces of business and science.

Yet as I have been stressing throughout this book, there are always two sides to every story. The root chakra symbolism of the coming age will no doubt have its constructive applications, too. Let us turn our attention to some of these.

The New Realism

Within the arts, the emerging root chakra influence can be seen in the increasing trend toward realism and worldliness that has characterized so many avenues of creative expression in recent history, and which has transformed the way we see the world. Though this has given rise to its share of bad art, it has also been responsible for much of what is distinctive and even great about modern culture. Take musical movements like blues, jazz, and rock-and-roll, all of which have had their moments of unbridled genius. What distinguishes each of these from traditional, religion-based art forms is their devotion to everyday concerns and emotions as a starting point, rather than to faith in some otherworldly realm of gods and angels.

Yet the influence of this trend has been evident in many areas of Western culture over the last few centuries. We see indirect traces of it in the late seventeenth century emergence of rococo art, when creativity began divorcing itself from religious concerns, and orienting itself toward a more art-for-art's-sake approach. Another early expression of this sensibility was in seventeenth century Holland, home to painters like Jan Vermeer and Franz Hals; it was also the birthplace of the camera and modern-day capitalism.

More recently, realism is visible in such twentieth century forms as the newsreel, film documentary, and television news. All of these reflect a common interest in nuts-and-bolts facts and details. In its own way, even the abstract art movement reflects a shift away from Piscean-Age emotionality toward root chakra consciousness, as evidenced in Picasso's proclamation that "I must break free of beauty and sentimentality!" In their own way, Andy Warhol's paintings of soup cans and Marcel Duchamp's "ready-mades" (everyday items exhibited as sculptures) reflect the shift of our collective consciousness to the concerns of the root chakra.

In cinema, the influence of realism underlies the works of directors like Erich Von Stroheim *(Greed)*, John Cassevetes *(Shadows)*, and Vittorio de Sica *(The Bicycle Thief).*[3] In literature and drama, it is in the works of the realist writers like Alexandre Dumas, Emile Augier, and Henrik Ibsen, and naturalist writers like Emile Zola and August Strindberg. We see it in the earthiness of Ernest Hemingway, and in the social realism of nineteenth century painters like Jean-François Millet and Gustave Courbet. When Baudelaire waxed poetic of prostitutes and the decadent side of life, he was giving voice to this shifting trend of consciousness toward root chakra matters. All in their own ways, these figures aspired toward finding unique beauty and lyricism in those areas of experience traditionally considered mundane or profane.

Similarly, American poet Walt Whitman devoted his life to celebrating what Paul Zweig called "the mystery of ordinariness" (Callow 1992). Consider these lines from *Leaves of Grass,* where Whitman praises the raw beauty of the big city with its bustling masses:

> Give me Broadway, with the soldiers marching—give me the
> sound of the trumpets and drums!
> . . . .
> Give me the shores and wharves heavy-fringed with black ships!
> O such for me! O an intense life, full to repletion and varied!
> The life of the theatre, bar-room, huge hotel, for me!
>
> (Whitman 2000)

The New "Down-to-Earth" Spirituality

The root chakra influence has made an important contribution to modern spirituality as well. Look at the growing trend toward more "grounded," or down-to-earth, forms of spirituality. During the Piscean Age, for instance, it was enough in many circles to simply believe in otherworldly realities or to put one's faith in disembodied saviors or lofty ideals, such as the promise of future salvation or eternity in paradise. By contrast, Aquarian spirituality seems to usher in a more utilitarian approach that, at best, is oriented toward the application of spiritual principles to everyday life. Rather than ask "Is there a God in Heaven?" Aquarian spirituality says, "How can we bring God into everyday life?"

This marriage of Heaven and Earth is already visible in some of the mythologies in popular culture, such as "angels coming down to Earth." Movies like *Wings of Desire* and its American remake *City of Angels* are about heavenly beings choosing to take human form to experience the joys and sorrows of earthly life. Considering that angels are one of the primary symbols of Aquarius, this symbolically points toward the progressive descent of spiritual energy into the root chakra in the coming age.

In fact, the angel motif has been cropping up in many different ways lately. For instance, popular television talk show host Oprah Winfrey (an Aquarian) has devoted many of her shows in recent years to discussing practical forms of spirituality. In the late 1990s, Oprah founded a grass-roots humanitarian campaign called the Angel Network, but she was referring not to disembodied beings, but ordinary humans who have devoted themselves to taking on the spiritual work of "angels," as it were, through charitable acts in the world. Another prominent Aquarian aligned with this project is actor Paul Newman, who has also devoted much of his adult life to humanitarian causes that bridge business and media with charitable actions. These examples may be harbingers of the broader trend toward practical spirituality which embodies the best of Aquarian consciousness.

James Joyce's *Ulysses*—A Myth for Our Times?

What clues might we draw from Aquarian James Joyce's *Ulysses*, what some critics have called the greatest novel of the twentieth century? Its story centers on the life of an ordinary person, Leopold Bloom, as he makes his way through Dublin over the course a single ordinary day. For students of the deeper meaning of the Aquarian Age, there are many useful messages to be drawn from Joyce's multilayered text.

One message concerns what some students regard as this book's underlying theme of tolerance and brotherhood. This was exemplified by a key passage set in a hospital waiting room midway through the book. Stephen Daedalus suddenly feels great compassion for his elder, Leopold Bloom, just as Bloom in turn feels compassion for a young man who has been struck down by a soldier in the street. The scene is accompanied by the sound of a newborn baby's cry and a great thunderclap, signaling the end of a long-standing drought in the region—synchronistic reflections, as it were, of the importance of this encounter in the lives of both men. It is a turning point for both Bloom and Daedalus, who at this moment become bonded in a spirit of sympathetic fellowship (Joyce 1967). Through touches like these, Joyce gave voice to the spiritual tenor of the coming age, with its message of everyday humanitarianism, which offers a stark contrast to the other-worldly ruminations found in Piscean-Age writers like Dante or Milton.

There is also a deeply Aquarian message in Joyce's choice of mundane settings for his story, and in the strange title he gave his book. On its surface, the word *Ulysses* points to the Homeric hero who had to make his way home to Ithaca following the Trojan War. Why choose so mythic a title for a book set in modern times? Joyce is telling us there is far more than meets the eye in his seemingly prosaic tale. In the mundane circumstances of Leopold Bloom's life can be found the deeper contours of a great mythic tale transposed onto modern-day Dublin. How does this pertain to the Aquarian Age? I would suggest two different interpretations.

On the one hand, it may be saying that the "mythic" is being collapsed down or flattened to the level of the mundane now; our connection to the archetypal is gradually being erased, and we are left with a world that, in Carl Jung's words, is "nothing but . . ." Yet another, more mystical way to interpret this symbolism might be this: In keeping with the root chakra emphasis of the Aquarian Age, Joyce's book may herald the way that the eternal truths are beginning to manifest *through* the everyday now, and *within* the secular. In other words, if we are to find a spiritual or "mythic" life in the times ahead, it may have to take place within the here-and-now, within the marketplace and the alleyways, rather than in the monasteries or on the mountaintops. This may be the key spiritual message of the Aquarian Age.

"This Doubtless Is the Right Way to Live"

The importance of chakra symbolism for the coming era might be summarized like this: The Aquarian Age will probably sweep away many of the emotional and religious trappings that characterized Piscean-Age consciousness and replace them with a more sober and clear-eyed approach to reality. At times, this could produce an *overly* unemotional or "bottom line" approach to life, as represented by the materialistic businessman or scientist. Yet as the more creative examples reviewed in this chapter show, this trend toward realism could be opening us to a new way of thinking about our world, one that has its own integrity and mystical quality.

Rather than coloring the facts of our world with fantasy or romanticized emotions, the realism of the Aquarian Age may be teaching us how to open up to reality more on its own terms, to find the unique beauty within mundane realities, whether they are the noise and grime of the big city, the plaintive wail of a jazz musician, or a newspaper blowing down the street. Henry James gave eloquent expression to the Aquarian realization when he wrote: "To take what there *is*, and use it, without waiting forever in vain for the preconceived—to dig deep into the actual and get something out of *that*—this doubtless is the right way to live" (James 1947).

7

Revisioning the Cosmos:
The Spirit of Aquarian Science

A young man is struck by lightning while walking through an open field—and lives to tell of it. In ancient times, an event like this would have been viewed as an unmistakable "sign" of great import. For some, it would have been read as an expression of heavenly wrath directed toward this person or his family, while for others it might have been seen as indicating he had been "chosen" for a grand destiny in life, perhaps as a healer or shaman. Whatever the spin, the event would have been seen as a deeply *meaningful* one with implications beyond its surfaces.

We see the world differently now than did our ancestors. Forces in our environment once viewed as instruments of divine intent are now viewed as the reflection of mechanical laws, devoid of higher intelligence or design. We no longer see the lightning bolt striking a human as an expression of supernatural forces, but as the result of discharged electrons flowing between sky and ground. Likewise, the movement of the planets through space is not due to angels pushing them in their courses, but to the effects of impersonal laws like gravity and momentum.

In recent centuries we have stepped from a world characterized by a sense of *mystery* into one ruled by *reason*. Just as each new era introduces a new way of perceiving the world, so the movement toward Aquarius has already begun ushering in an air-based temperament that places far greater emphasis on rationality and a mechanical interpretation of phenomena. Rather than surrender ourselves in a spirit of faith to higher religious authorities or spiritual powers, we are now engaged in an inquiry into truth that utilizes such tools as logic, concrete evidence, and replicability—in a word, *science*. There is little sense in judging this trend as either wholly good or bad, for like all archetypal developments, it has its share of both. Rather, let us take a moment to understand both sides of this story, to better appreciate the opportunities *and* pitfalls afforded us by this development.

At its best, science has been an enormous catalyst in our collective evolution, helping to sweep away millennia of superstitious, uncritical beliefs, and replacing them with a more objective, analytical approach toward phenomena. A perfect example of this catalyst effect is modern medicine. It can be a sobering experience to examine the state of medicine in many prescientific societies, when everyday illnesses were commonly viewed as the result of "evil spirits" or curses hurled by unseen enemies—rather than germs. It was not too long ago (as the red and white stripes on barbershop poles still attest) when bodily complaints were commonly treated by extended bleedings. It is all too easy taking for granted the simple yet extraordinary ways in which our life has benefited from the gifts of the rationalistic worldview.

In theoretical ways, too, science has expanded and enriched our minds through the breadth and strangeness of its findings, from the knowledge of distant galaxies to the submicroscopic world of atoms and molecules. For example, consider the fact that in prescientific times most men and women in the West believed the world to be only 6000 years old, and that our cosmos was limited to the 3000 stars visible on the clearest of nights. Now we know that the universe is billions of years older, with trillions more stars and galaxies than can be seen with the unaided eye. Ask yourself—which cosmos do *you* prefer living in?

What science has revealed about our inner, biological world has been no less astonishing or awe-inspiring. Consider the magnificent complexity of our bodily functions, and the intricate way they work together in harmony. The brain alone offers a lifetime subject for study: for instance, consider that there are as many connections linking the neurons within our brain as there are stars in the known universe. Findings like these only enhance our appreciation of the vastness and majesty of the world, rather than diminish it.

Ultimately, the most important legacy of science has been the intellectual *process* it gives us—the dispassionate inquiry into truth that attempts to pierce beyond personal or collective biases. When Galileo looked through his telescope to see the moons of Jupiter, what was most significant about this act was less the data he uncovered than the act of investigation itself. During his time, most educated people firmly believed that other planets could not possess moons of their own, and that was never to be questioned. By his willingness to question the conventional wisdom and simply see for himself, Galileo exemplified an independence of spirit and openness of mind that would change our way of thinking about the world.[1]

If there have been shortcomings to this conceptual transformation, they have centered chiefly on its relatively narrow focus. The rational-experimental approach can be applied on many levels of experience—physical, psychological, or spiritual. For instance, the greatest mystics of India and China historically employed a genuinely scientific approach when investigating consciousness, setting aside preconceptions to empirically examine the contents of their minds. What distinguishes modern science is the way it applies this rational-experimental approach exclusively toward *physical-plane* phenomena. Here we see yet another aspect of the Aquarian air principle as transposed onto root chakra concerns, touched upon in our last chapter: in other words, rationality is applied toward the understanding and mastering the material plane.

At its extreme, this has sometimes led to an understanding of the world that can be "a mile wide and an inch deep." We have indeed experienced a profound expansion of our knowledge of the universe, but in largely "horizontal" ways. As our understanding of physical phenomena has grown by leaps and bounds, we've seen a general collapse of our knowledge in "vertical" ways, with less credence given to metaphysical and spiritual realities. Perhaps more than any other, this has been science's flaw—the danger of reductionism, the tendency to reduce all phenomena to the level of measurable standards. At its worst, this has given rise to a knee-jerk skepticism that automatically discounts all phenomena or experiences that don't lend themselves to concrete measurement, an approach which places little value on metaphor, beauty, or spirituality.

So while science has rid us of many outworn superstitions about our world, it has also eliminated virtually all considerations of meaning from the cosmos. We no longer see the solar eclipse as a dragon devouring the sun; yet now we have veered to the other extreme by seeing such phenomena as having no significance whatsoever. Now the eclipse is nothing more than the interplay of dead bodies in space, devoid of symbolism or value. Likewise, we no longer see the lightning striking the young man as an indication of God's wrath; for this we must be grateful. But to see such things as *completely* accidental, with no archetypal resonance and no place in the scheme of destiny, seems an equally unsavory option for those seeking a deeper vision. All this has given rise to a mood in which many view the universe as a dynamic yet essentially dead realm, devoid of spirit or intelligent design.

The shift from Pisces to Aquarius has produced more than a few powerful clashes of world views as the emotional and interior values of a water-based age come up against the intellectual and exterior values of the air-based one. This conflict of paradigms was succinctly dramatized in a memorable scene in the 1998 film *Contact*. At a climactic moment, an adventurous scientist undergoes a transformative journey apparently beyond our solar system. Yet because she has no hard proof of her remarkable experience, her story is doubted. "Where is the *evidence?*" a character skeptically questions her in a hearing before Congress. This scene shows the clash between the values of Pisces and Aquarius, between belief and evidence.

During the inwardly oriented Piscean era, enormous value was accorded to interior experiences and values, to the extent that faith in something was sufficient to establish its validity or value. By contrast, the outwardly oriented Aquarian Age could prove to be a time when purely subjective claims are measured against the yardstick of objective evidence and rational analysis. The result is that subjective insights and experiences like those described by the scientist in *Contact* could be in for a rough ride, if the data isn't there to support it.

If emotions were overvalued during the Piscean era, they could be *under*valued in the next one. This means that the Aquarian Age could be just as authoritarian in its own way as the Piscean was, though less in religious ways than in intellectual, secular ways. Now the pressure to conform might stem not from priests in holy robes but from scientific, governmental, or corporate authorities. The spirit of rational individualism pioneered by figures like Galileo or Isaac Newton could give way to a new "consensus reality" that rejects the obvious dogmas of earlier times, yet still harbors its own set of implicit assumptions and biases. But don't forget—the Aquarian Age is still young. There is no reason to believe that the more extreme tendencies of the Aquarian consciousness won't eventually be balanced out with a more moderate approach that attempts to reconcile emotional and rational dimensions.

That said, let us turn now to the scientific discoveries themselves. For the symbolist, all major discoveries or shifts in worldview possess a synchronistic dimension in the way they link to broader trends throughout the culture. For the rest of this chapter we will explore several key discoveries or breakthroughs from the last century that strongly suggest a link with emerging Aquarian trends. Just as a symphony will often announce its principal themes in its opening bars, so the longer-range contours of Aquarian science may be present in findings already familiar to us.

Opening Up the Subatomic World

Prior to the twentieth century, the atom had been seen as the essential building block of matter. But with the discovery in 1897 of the first subatomic particle—the electron—scientists found that another strata of matter existed inside the atom. It was as if a vast new dimension of reality opened up for examination, one greater in scope than the ordinary one of visible appearances.

If scientific discoveries indeed hold meaning as symbols of inner shifts in consciousness, what did this one mean? One interpretation is that by crossing the threshold into subatomic matter, humanity was also crossing over an *inner* threshold of consciousness. This view is supported by a synchronicity in Western culture which took place at nearly the same time: toward the end of 1899, two years after the discovery of the electron, Sigmund Freud published his famous book *The Interpretation of Dreams*, a work credited with introducing the concept of the subconscious to the public. So, precisely as humans were discovering a new realm in the outer world, they were discovering a new realm in the inner world.

What does this have to do with trends of the Aquarian Age? Notice how the characteristics associated with these two realms—the atom and the subconscious—were bizarre by conventional standards. For example, whereas Newton's universe had been one of orderly phenomena and logical processes, this new subatomic realm seemed to obey a different and seemingly illogical set of laws. Particles could be in two places at once, or travel forward and backward through time. There were particles and there were antiparticles, and they could behave like waves or solid objects, depending on one's mode of investigation. Our cherished sense of certainty about the world was cast into doubt at the subatomic level of matter as scientists learned that one could measure either the location of a particle or its speed, but not both simultaneously.

Curiouser and curiouser, as Alice said, and indeed, the paradoxical world portrayed by Lewis Carroll seemed increasingly apt for describing the strange realm of subatomic matter, in all its absurd logic and distortions of convention. In our investigation of the psyche, we were likewise encountering a similar quality of strangeness, the "laws" of this realm seeming more akin to dream logic than waking rationality. Phenomena seemed to defy time and space, and could express the wildest flights of imagination, qualities that inspired surrealist artists such as Salvador Dali and Rene Magritte.

In both cases, physics and psychology, these unusual features had much in common with the kind of rationality associated with Aquarius. At its most complex, the Aquarian mind is unique in its capacity for paradox, multitrack thinking, acausal connections, multiple viewpoints, forward and backward logic. It's a kind of thinking that may superficially appear irrational, yet reflects a different kind of rationality than we are accustomed to. The emerging Aquarian Age is awakening us to a type of thinking that is in many ways more complex than anything before. Projected outward onto the universe, it results in a view of nature that is reminiscent of Lewis Carroll and James Joyce (both of whose horoscopes featured dramatically Aquarian patterns).

The Quantum Leap

Central to the development of subatomic physics was a model known as the quanta. First proposed by Max Planck in 1900, this theory postulated that energy and matter existed in discrete bundles or packets, each of which comprised a single quanta (etymologically related to the word "quantity"). Previously, scientists assumed the world was relatively even or smooth, that energy flowed in continuous streams. But the quantum model suggested this wasn't the case at the level of the extremely small. If you throw logs into a bonfire, the fire will get hotter, but at the subatomic level, the world responds similarly to when you change channels on a TV set: instead of an even, smooth slide, you get a series of dramatic *jumps*. Phenomena at this level display a similar sense of suddenness and discontinuity.

For culture, the concept of the quantum leap soon became a powerful metaphor for describing many of the broader transformations taking place. It was that sense of sudden change that captured the public's imagination. Here, too, we find a quality consonant with the archetypal energies of Aquarius. In contrast with the comparatively fluid qualities of a sign like Pisces, Aquarius is more abrupt and unpredictable in character. Even the glyph used to designate Aquarius resembles the jagged edges of parallel lightning bolts zigzagging through the sky (see figure 7-1).

Figure 7-1. The Glyph for Aquarius

In a way, this zigzagging might describe life in our age. Just as electrons can jump suddenly from one energy level to the next, so many aspects of our lives seem to express this quality. Look at how we travel or change residence state to state, country to country, making quantum leaps of lifestyle, so to speak. This energy is mirrored in digital clocks. In the old days, hands on a clock moved gradually, but with digital clocks time changes abruptly. This Aquarian feature may continue manifesting in our life in ways difficult to envision now. If science fiction is any indication, perhaps we will learn how to teleport instantaneously from point to point in space, or time travel from period to period like the characters on TV shows like *Quantum Leap* or *Doctor Who*. Perhaps the quantum leaps may be in *consciousness* instead, resulting from our ability to augment human evolution through genetic or neurological sciences.

The Starry Sciences

Scientists have always been fascinated by the sky. Thanks to scientists like Copernicus, Galileo, and Stephen Hawking, human knowledge has continually been changed by new discoveries concerning the nature and movements of the celestial bodies. The Aquarian Age will no doubt continue to witness further developments in our understanding of the cosmos.

As we've already seen, the symbolism of stars is closely linked to Aquarius. For instance, Uranus, the governing planet for this sign, derived its name from the Greek mythological figure of the titan Ouranos, the sky-god. Suggestive, too, is the fact that the same year he discovered Uranus, astronomer and musician William Herschel (along with his sister Caroline) inaugurated a new era in modern stellar astronomy by developing a telescope powerful enough to chart 4,200 new star clusters, nebulae, and galaxies.

Since the 1980s, we have seen major expansions of our scientific knowledge as a result of innovations like the Hubble telescope and the *Voyager II* spacecraft. We have gained important insights into phenomena such as black holes, pulsars, the birth and death of galaxies, comets, and the inner workings of our sun. In the millennia ahead, we can expect even more surprising discoveries in astronomy and astrophysics that could radically shift the way we see the universe, including the possibility that our universe may be one of many.

Will the Aquarian Age be a time when astrology also experiences a renaissance, as many now believe? It is unlikely that astrology will ever be fully embraced by the mainstream scientific community, for the reason that it represents a more esoteric and metaphoric understanding of the cosmos than most scientists subscribe to. Yet there are good reasons to believe this field could experience important developments over the next two thousand years. I say this partly because this is *already* beginning to occur.

Over the last 100 years, astrology has developed enormously in practical and theoretical ways, fueled by the introduction of improved research methods and an easier exchange of ideas among practitioners due to improved telecommunications and publishing outlets. One of the seminal developments in modern astrology was the merger of astrology with psychology, thanks to pioneers like Dane Rudhyar. We might take as another clue the curious fact that our last two Aquarian presidents (Franklin Roosevelt and Ronald Reagan) were avid followers of astrology.

Astrology offers a valuable key for the coming age because of its wide-ranging implications for many different fields. In the study of human nature, for example, it provides a way of seeing how psychological experience can be understood partly as an interplay of certain archetypal principles, while also providing a way of charting the cycles of our shifting inner states. In more philosophical ways, it offers the possibility of a restored sense of meaning to our lives, and a reestablished connection to the cosmos. Astrology shows us we are not separate from the world, but mysteriously bound up in its processes in ways that challenge the existential assumptions of much twentieth century thought.

For esotericists, astrology offers a golden key by which we might establish a table of correspondences by which to categorize and cross-correlate phenomena in our lives and the world. Astrology can even contribute to modern science in several respects, for example, through its unique understanding of time. As we saw in the last chapter, we have devised ways of measuring time in extraordinary ways, and have learned about time's elastic nature through Einstein's theory of relativity. Yet despite such advances we still have little understanding of the specific *qualities* that characterize different moments in time. For example, certain periods may reflect qualities of obstruction or heaviness while others express qualities of expansion or ease. In the same way that geography allows us to map out a physical terrain, so astrology provides a tool for systematically studying and mapping out the textures and meanings of time itself.

Systems Thinking in the Aquarian Age

Among the most Aquarian of scientific developments in recent times has been the emergence of systems theory. When studying any phenomenon, we can approach it in different ways. One way is to examine it in isolation, as an independent phenomenon, or to break it down to its essential parts. This is the reductionist approach. The systems approach attempts to understand phenomena in terms of larger wholes by studying their interacting elements, seeing how each fits into the patterns surrounding it. A good example of this approach is ecology. Whereas the reductionist approach examines each creature or plant on its own, the systems viewpoint examines how such things interact within the ecosystem, seeks to understand their part in a greater network of interlocking cycles and feedback loops. Rather than examine things and parts, the systems approach looks at patterns and processes.[2]

As a historical movement, the origins of systems thinking extends back many centuries, though it was during the twentieth century that modern systems theory became an articulated discipline. During this time, applications for the systems approach were extended to different areas and phenomena, from thermodynamics and biology to quantum physics and sociology. For instance, scientists studying subatomic phenomena realized that a particle was less of an isolated "thing" than a complex web of relationships. As physicist Henry Stapp wrote in 1971, ". . . an elementary particle is not an independently existing, unanalyzable entity. It is, in essence, a set of relationships that reach outward to other things" (Stapp 1971).

If you wished to analyze one of two electrons contained in an atom, you couldn't do it without seeing them *in relation* to each other. The systems approach is a useful tool for mapping the behavior of subatomic particles because subatomic particles are so unpredictable that pinpointing how any

one might behave seems impossible. Yet by analyzing large groups of particles over time, one can establish certain trends. This insight has a parallel
in sociology or group psychology; while one can't predict what any one person would do in a given situation, it is far easier to determine what large
numbers of people might do in similar circumstances.

By carefully studying different types of systems, researchers found they
could distill certain features common to all systems, extrapolating from this a
general theory of systems. For example, most systems have an "ingestor" function to do with consuming fuel or energy; they also have a function for dis-
pelling waste or by-products; and all systems exhibit certain boundaries that
allow them to maintain their identity. In this way, working parallels can be
drawn between the way a society works and the operations of a cell or a planet.

Systems thinking also opened the door for the important new science of
chaos theory. By contrast, seventeenth- and eighteenth-century scientists
found it easy to develop theories which explained how rudimentary systems
in nature operate, such as the way one planet orbits around another or how a
projectile moves through space. Yet these simple theories did little to help
explain more complex and seemingly chaotic phenomena like the behavior of
gas molecules in a room, or the interaction of many planets in a solar system.

As a result of developments in advanced mathematics and thermodynamics (and, more recently, the introduction of computers), scientists began
to see how they could map complex systems like these to a degree of accuracy that would have shocked earlier generations of scientists. This research
showed that many phenomena previously seen as random in nature, actually had an order and patterning, one that revealed itself only through a systems style approach.

Take the flow of water molecules arising out of a large fountain. There
are so many of them cascading through the air at any given time, and their
motions are so apparently random, that it's virtually impossible to predict
where any given molecule might wind up at a given point in time. The
motion of the molecules throughout the stream could be described as
"chaotic" in that any given arrangement of them will never repeat itself the
same way twice. Yet if one analyzes those molecules as part of the larger
system, one sees a distinct pattern underlying it all, allowing one to make
certain general predictions about the water molecules *as a whole*. Though
the individual components of the system may seem unpredictable, they
reflect a deeper order that cannot be perceived through the standard "atomistic" methods.

The same is true for many patterns in our world, from the formation and structure of clouds in the sky to the movements of motorists along an expressway. Things which seem to be random may follow orderly laws and mathematical lines of probability. Researchers refined their understanding of such phenomena by grouping them into several basic categories, such as "point attractors," "strange attractors," or "chaotic attractors." For instance, water going down the drain expresses the dynamics of a point attractor, while the movement of air molecules in a room express the dynamics of a chaotic attractor, and so forth.

A key feature of systems thinking and chaos theory is a branch of research called dynamical systems theory, the study of how systems evolve over time. This arises from the realization that many systems in our world are not unchanging but in a state of flux, frequently transforming themselves through time. In some cases, systems even exhibit the ability to reorganize themselves into higher and more structured versions of themselves—the proverbial "order out of chaos." One example of this would be classic evolutionary theory, which holds that simple creatures can give rise to more complicated biological forms over time, through a combination of genetic mutation and adaptive influences.

Another example is the way a society can adapt to an influx of new immigrants; initially there may be disorder as the system struggles to deal with the new components, yet if the new components are effectively assimilated, a new and more complex society results. Even nonliving systems can sometimes be propelled toward higher levels of order, as exemplified by water spiraling down a kitchen sink, or the evolution of complex stars out of interstellar matter.

Viewed broadly, systems theory offers us an Aquarian way of understanding our world with an emphasis on patterns and relationships rather than isolated things. As we will see in the next chapter, the systems view reflects the more decentralized way of thinking which underlies Aquarian consciousness. When physicist Steven Weinberg remarked that the "essential nature of reality is a set of fields," he was inadvertently stating the motto for the Aquarian approach to life.

Systems Theory—A "Spiritual" Scientific Model?

In recent decades, some contemporary thinkers, such as physicist Fritjof Capra, have proposed that systems-style thinking represents a holistic shift in modern thought that is richer and more complete—perhaps even more "spiritual"—in its way of seeing the world. Roughly since the seventeenth century, the argument goes, mechanistic science has engaged in a more atomistic and analytic approach toward phenomena, one which tended to dissect and fragment whatever it studied. By contrast, systems thinking encourages a perspective that is more oriented toward perceiving wholes and relationships among phenomena, and which is therefore closer in spirit to the mystical teachings of the world's spiritual traditions (Capra 1982).

This is not the view I am proposing here. From an archetypal standpoint, the atomistic and systems views are two different and complementary ways of perceiving reality, but neither one is inherently more spiritual than the other. Each represents a perfectly valid way of understanding our world, with its own unique insights and applications. But it's good to keep in mind that there are many phenomena and circumstances in life which don't lend themselves to the systems approach; there may even be times when this approach is the least appropriate one for dealing with situations.

By way of example, take the way the systems approach is employed by insurance companies. Patients are regarded as statistics, grouped according to actuary tables devised by number crunchers. This is systems thinking with a vengeance, and ironically it would be better replaced by a more atomistic model where individuals are treated one person at a time.

For another example, imagine a young girl coming to her father in tears over a bruised knee. What is the most appropriate way for the father to respond to her in that moment? Should he take a systems approach and cite the vast number of injuries that occur to children each year, put her injury in context and show it isn't worth getting upset about? Rather, a better approach is to treat her as an individual, not part of a collective. By the same token, what we value in any healthy democracy is the very fact that it doesn't overemphasize the system at the expense of the individual, as totalitarian governments do.

There are many different ways of understanding our world, none of which, in itself, offers a complete understanding of the "Ultimate Truth." The systems approach we've been looking at will undoubtedly permit us to uncover many important insights about the world in the coming centuries. But it isn't more innately "spiritual" than the atomistic approach.[3] Indeed, in the Aquarian Age we will need to be careful that the systems approach doesn't raise as many new problems as it solves.

8

Drawing Down the Fire of the Gods

Imagine that someone from a far-off land came to America, where they stumbled upon a photo of comedian Stan Laurel, from the famed comedy team Laurel and Hardy. Presuming they had little or no previous exposure to Western culture, suppose they asked you to explain who this funny-looking person was. Could you do so without referring to Laurel's partner, Oliver Hardy? Try as you might, it would be difficult, since these two figures are entwined in our minds as complementary parts of a greater whole: the thin, sour-faced Laurel and the portly, prissy Hardy. Seeing either in isolation gives one no sense of the dynamism that characterizes their synergy as a team.

The same principle can be applied to zodiacal signs. Each of the twelve signs is half of a polarity, and can be understood only in connection with its opposite sign. For instance, the assertive sign Aries is complemented by Libra, the diplomatic, rational sign that opposes it. Each is a graphic contrast to the extremes of the other. Domestically minded Cancer complements opposing sign Capricorn, which tends to be ambitious and career-oriented. One can continue in this way through the zodiac, which, we find, is comprised of six archetypal pairs of opposites.

The polarity principle offers a key insight into history's Great Ages as well, in that every zodiacal era is part of a twofold dynamic. Consequently, when a new era emerges into consciousness, we find not only the themes of that sign but those of the sign *opposite* it. During the age of Taurus, timeless stone monuments were erected in areas like Egypt, yet these were often dedicated to the themes of death and transformation—principles associated with the sign Scorpio, which is opposite Taurus. During the Age of Pisces, a world religion based on principles of sacrifice and martyrdom came into prominence, yet it was coupled with the imagery of a Virgin, a symbol associated with the opposite sign, Virgo[1] (see figure 8-1).

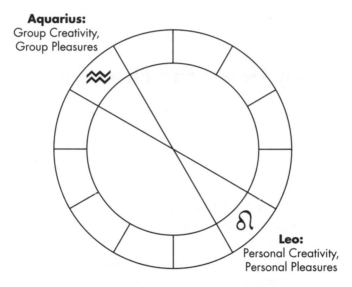

Aquarius:
Group Creativity,
Group Pleasures

Leo:
Personal Creativity,
Personal Pleasures

Figure 8-1. The Leo/Aquarius Polarity
Each sign of the zodiac represents one-half of a polarity and includes the sign opposite it. The Age of Aquarius will therefore bring about a joint emphasis upon the signs Aquarius and Leo. As a whole, this axis governs such areas as creativity and pleasure, though from distinctly different vantage points. For instance, while Leo rules all forms of personal creativity, Aquarius governs all forms of group creativity.

In so far as each sign of the zodiac is part of a polarity that includes the sign opposite it, the coming age will witness a joint emphasis on the signs Aquarius and Leo. In the case of Aquarius, the opposite zodiacal sign is that of Leo, the lion. That is to say, we are not simply entering the Aquarian Age, but what might be called the Aquarius-Leo Age. This axis governs such principles as pleasure and creativity, though from two different vantage points. For instance, while Leo rules all forms of personal creativity, Aquarius governs all forms of group creativity.

At the start of this book I suggested there were three skeleton keys that could help us unlock the meaning of the historical transformations before us. The first is the elemental significance of Aquarius, and the second is the chakra symbolism associated with this sign. Understanding the Aquarius-Leo polarity represents the third of our keys for grasping the trends and symbols of the millennia ahead. For the remainder of this chapter, we will look at how this polarity illuminates a broad array of themes associated with the Aquarian Age. In subsequent chapters we will explore further implications of this polarity for our future.

The Dance of Fire and Air: Where do we begin in uncovering the meanings of this zodiacal dynamic? Let's start with a simple image that captures the essence of this archetypal dance between signs: Two or three children are frolicking on a playground, laughing and singing in blissful abandon. Around them stand a dozen scientists in white lab coats, observing and recording every move for a research study on the nature of play.

As with all images, there are multiple levels of meaning to be extracted from this scene. Let's consider the elemental symbolism first. On the one hand, the fiery energies of Leo can be likened to the children on the playground, expressing the quality of experientiality, or being in the moment. At its most spiritual, Leo exemplifies such ideals as courage, enthusiasm, and enlightened awareness. Of all four elements, fire is the light-bearing one, and thus relates to consciousness in a fundamental way. Buddhism has a saying, "Spontaneity is the mark of the Buddha," and Leo embodies that spontaneous, playful awareness at its best. In its negative form, however, this same principle can lead to excessive self-centeredness and the inability to stand outside one's perspective and see problems objectively.

As the principle opposite Leo, Aquarius represents the element of air, the principle of rational mind. Like those scientists on the fringes of the playground, rationality stands outside the field of activity to best observe and conceptualize what it sees, systematically relating those ideas with other ideas and frameworks of meaning. At its most abstract, air is concerned with understanding and delineating the theoretical relationships among the parts of a system. In contrast with the fiery principle of dynamic being, Aquarian air represents the principle of detached understanding. At its most extreme, this trait can make one detached even to the point of coldness, standing so far outside experience that one loses touch with the emotional realities of life. The noted detachment of former President Ronald Reagan illustrates this trait. Or think of a corporate researcher who tests out cosmetic products on laboratory animals with little thought for the suffering of those creatures.

But in its highest form, that same rational detachment makes possible the objectivity and discernment necessary for profound thinking, long-range planning, and clear communication of any sort. Precisely because it has the ability to stand back and conceptualize, air makes possible *all* forms of meaning—including the words you are reading at this moment. On a creative level, in the coming era this elemental principle will hold the potential of ushering in a new stage in humanity's intellectual development, as well as an understanding of personal freedom unprecedented in history.

But aside from their meanings individually, how do these the opposing elements of fire and air interact with each other? Astrology informs us that they are complementary, feeding off each other.

The Individual/Group Dynamic: The relationship of the individual to the collective is one of the chief concerns of the Leo/Aquarius axis. Yet each sign approaches this dynamic from opposite directions. Leo may be likened to the reigning individual, the proverbial King or Queen ruling from atop the throne, while Aquarius is the average man or woman and the principle of the masses. For this reason, Leo governs the institution of royalty, while Aquarius governs democracy and all forms of self-rule, or what might be called government "from the bottom up." If Leo relates to the will of a single powerful individual, Aquarius might be described as the will of the people.

With the dawning of the Aquarian Age, we are already seeing the erosion of long-standing monarchies around the world and their replacement by democratic forms of government. Indeed, most of the popular revolutions of recent centuries have occurred in connection with planetary patterns occurring between Leo and Aquarius. For example, all the major developments of the French Revolution occurred under aspects between Pluto and Uranus in Aquarius and Leo, while Russia's Bolshevik revolution of 1917 took place during an opposition between Leo and Aquarius involving Uranus, Saturn, and Neptune. The worldwide surge toward "people's power" during the 1960s may be directly tied to the aftereffects of the powerful Leo/Aquarius configuration that occurred in February 1962.

When overemphasized, either end of this polarity poses its own problems. When Leo becomes too dominant, we often see dictatorial tendencies arising, but when Aquarius is overly dominant, there is a trend toward subversion and the need to undermine existing power structures. On the collective level, this is precisely why Aquarius is said to govern the principle of mob rule—the tyranny of the majority—recalling Nietzsche's sentiment that representative government is the means that allows cattle to become masters.

In any healthy democracy, there needs to be a careful balancing of these two extremes, between the needs of individuals and those of the collective. Here again, let us recall the example of the jazz band for the way it beautifully expresses that sense of balance between individuals and the group. It was to this kind of balance that America's founding fathers aspired when forging the nation. The rights of the people are important, yet not if it means negating the rights of individuals. Hence, the need for a Bill of Rights that *protects* the individual from possible abuses by the majority.

In contrast with this measured approach, the French Revolution extolled the ideal of the people to so great an extent that specific individuals meant nothing; they were expendable on the altar of the "common good." In rebelling against the tyrannies of monarchy, the French carried matters to the opposite extreme, thereby giving birth to a tyranny of the mass mind. The result? A vacuum of Leonine individualism into which would step an even worse tyrant, that charismatic Leo, Napoleon Bonaparte.

Creativity: Our image of the children on the playground highlights another key aspect of the Leo/Aquarius dynamic: creativity. Leo governs all forms of personal creativity (exemplified by the lone artist working in her loft), but Aquarius governs *group* creativity, where many people come together to pool their energies toward a common project. At its most negative, of course, the notion of group creativity conjures up images of a corporate art-by-committee approach toward creativity, one that easily stifles personal self-expression. A more harmonious expression of the group creativity concept is the jazz band.

In contrast to Piscean-Age art forms like the Gregorian choir, where individual creativity tends to be sacrificed toward a higher ideal, the jazz band *encourages* personal expression within the context of the group. Yes, there is a governing structure or musical theme holding it all together, yet it is loose enough to allow for individual creativity. This is why a musical group like the Beatles illustrates the emerging Aquarian sensibility so well, in demonstrating how distinctive personalities could form a cohesive group without sacrificing their individualism. The result was a whole synergistically greater than the sum of its parts.

Still another example of group creativity in modern times is an average film or television crew, in which there may be hundreds of men and women working side by side to create a single work of art or entertainment. In some cases, films have been made under the supervision of multiple directors (*Gone with the Wind* or *The Wizard of Oz*). While this group-oriented approach toward film admittedly has been responsible for producing commercialized garbage of the worst sort, it has also given us such brilliant ensemble pieces like *Citizen Kane* and the *Godfather* series. Though the directors of these films were true individualists, their genius lay in an ability to draw together many of the finest talents from the field and coordinate them into a working collective.

This jazz-style approach to creativity can be glimpsed in other contexts. In areas of technology, Thomas Edison's workshop operated along essentially jazzlike lines, bringing together different creative minds in a single environment to solve problems. We see the same spirit underlying the modern day "think tank," where ideas are bandied about like riffs among players in a musical group. In the world at large, this trend may lead to ordinary people becoming more involved with developing their creativity. This move is already noticeable in the proliferation of creativity workshops and "do-it-yourself" books on art which have saturated the market in recent years. In a slightly different way, we see the influence of the Leo/Aquarius axis manifesting in the rise of interactive video games and virtual reality technologies, which allow participants to participate in creating imaginary environments. We see the influence of the Leo/Aquarius axis in modern-day theoretical physics, in science's ongoing efforts to unlock the secrets of creativity on the cosmic scale through attempts to probe ever closer to the origins of our universe and the mysteries of the "Big Bang."

Pleasure: The Leo/Aquarius polarity is also associated with the experience of pleasure in our lives. With Leo, that concerns *personal* pleasure, as in an ordinary love affair, or as exemplified by our children frolicking on the playground. With Aquarius, it concerns the experience of group pleasure, especially of a more cerebral or technological sort.

One might think here of physicists swapping jokes over the Internet about the Grand Unified Theory, or even our hypothetical scientists on the fringes of the playground, for whom such meticulous research might be excitement enough. For ordinary men and women, an example would be a high-tech "pleasure palace" like Disneyland or Universal Studios, where the passion for *fun* can be pursued in ways that allow hundreds (or even thousands) of people to partake of the same experience.

For similar reasons, the emerging Leo/Aquarius axis is directly responsible for that unique sociological phenomenon we call mass entertainment, such as television, radio, and cinema. It's possible now for millions of people watching a TV show to enjoy the same program at the same moment. Under the influence of Aquarius, we will continue to find ways of using technology to enhance our pleasures in increasingly powerful ways, perhaps to the extent of devising machines that act directly on pleasure centers in the brain itself. (Could Woody Allen's "Orgasmatron" device, pictured in his 1973 film *Sleeper* be that far off?)

Note the tremendous impersonality and detachment involved with such forms as these. In watching TV, the action is experienced indirectly and vicariously, in a way that echoes our scientists standing outside the children's playground. In the coming centuries, Aquarius could cause us to become passive witnesses of reality, divorced from the flesh-and-blood gusto of everyday experience, making us *spectators* rather than *players*. Inventions like the telephone and the Internet have already begun making it possible for us to relate to our friends and family in a dissociated way. One is reminded here of the couch potato who lives passively and indirectly through the TV, or the Cyberspace fanatic who prefers to experience life second-hand through virtual simulations of the real thing.

Over the last two millennia, the Piscean Age has fostered a climate that has been largely pleasure-denying in its character, even to the extent of fostering guilt over all experiences of pleasure. Yet over the last two centuries, the emerging Leo/Aquarius axis has begun a sea-change in our attitudes, what might be called a democratization of pleasure. Each person now is awakening to their rightful experiences of joy and happiness, seeing these as vital and meaningful parts of life.

This is something America's founding fathers acknowledged when they declared our right to "life, liberty, and the pursuit of happiness"—perhaps the first time such words had ever been inscribed in a national charter. (Astrologers might see this as related to the placement of America's North Node—in the horoscope, it signifies spiritual destiny—positioned in Leo at the time of its birth, July 4, 1776. Among other things, this could indicate our national interest in the quest for happiness and joy.) Self-realization, happiness, freedom, and democracy—all are intertwined in subtle but important ways in the Leo/Aquarius axis.

This shifting of archetypal values between the Piscean and the Aquarian Ages is portrayed in Lasse Halstrom's film *Chocolat* (2000). Set in the 1950s, the movie centers on a conservative Christian town in Europe, where all forms of personal pleasure or even happiness are avidly discouraged by the local civic and religious authorities. Their worldview is challenged when a free-thinking woman comes to town and opens a gourmet chocolate shop, the offerings of which awaken all citizens' long-repressed desires.

Even more upsetting to some in the community is her blithe refusal to join the church; instead, she prefers to pursue an independent lifestyle. The problems reach their climax when she begins fraternizing with a group of long-haired vagabonds who have arrived by barge on the nearby river; their liberal ways are even more threatening to local sensibilities. When the two worldviews finally clash, tragedy results—though not without the community being transformed and awakened to a new world of personal pleasures.

The rigidly dogmatic and self-denying qualities of *Chocolat*'s community show the negative values of the Piscean Age, while the woman and her vagabond friends express the life-affirming and liberal qualities of the Leo/Aquarius axis. The clash between these two demonstrates what has been happening in civilization over the last few centuries, through figures like the poet Lord Byron and our modern-day hippies, all pointing the way to a more pleasure-seeking, life-affirming approach to life.

What effect does this emphasis on pleasure ultimately have on the soul? Will the pursuit of fun enhance our spiritual lives? Or will it become an end in itself, a hedonistic drive divorced of moral and spiritual considerations? In that case, it could impede our spiritual development and perhaps distance us further from the *true* source of joy within. Recall how the underlying motif in *Citizen Kane* is "Rosebud." As we learn at film's end, this isn't a book, a piece of clothing, or the memory of a mother's cooking, but a child's sled. As a symbol of pure childhood joy, this is what astrologers would call a "fifth house" symbol—a concern of Leo.

The irony here is that the film's lead character is shown as devoting his life to the pursuit of pleasures, to the extent of creating his own "pleasure palace," which he calls Xanadu, yet the one thing that continually eludes him is joy.

If Charles Foster Kane symbolizes the darker potentials of our collective future, then this drama may serve as a cautionary tale for us in the coming era. In all of our pleasure-seeking, through a million types of stimulation, let us be careful that we don't forget that *true* pleasure derives not from things, but from the mastery of our own nature. In a lecture given in 1943, the Indian-born guru Paramahansa Yogananda commented on the pleasure-seeking tendencies of the Western psyche, in words that might be a cautionary note for future times:

> Most people of the West think only of comfort. [My guru] never bothered about where I slept; and if I tried to be more comfortable

in the human way, he criticized me. By such constructive criticism and training I found complete freedom from food consciousness, dress and social consciousness, and body consciousness. I was so happy, free from the prison of my own making. [My guru] gave me that freedom by his guidance—freedom from habits and moods and limiting thoughts (Yogananda 1997).

Chance: A frequently overlooked aspect of the Leo/Aquarius polarity concerns its connection with all spontaneous or chance-based activities. For example, in astrology activities like gambling and speculation are associated with the segment of the horoscope related to Leo, the "Fifth House." This holds an important esoteric truth. In addition to constituting a form of play, gambling involves a certain element of chance and randomness. This can be said of many areas, such as romance, creativity, conception, or childbirth. We are in every case witnessing something essentially spontaneous or unpredictable in nature. Conceiving or giving birth to a child is one of life's greatest crapshoots, not only in terms of whether pregnancy will occur, but in terms of what *kind* of child one will bring into the world. Saint? Sinner? Businessman? All bets are off!

This element of chance hints at a deeper truth in Leo and the Fifth House; namely, the spontaneity expressed in these areas mirrors the free-flowing qualities of spirit itself, that source of consciousness inside where energy unfolds freely and intuitively, unfettered by logic or calculation. When we engage in play or creativity, we tap into this creative source. Our use of the term "recreation" to describe ordinary pastimes recognizes this. Even an activity like gambling stems from this same divine impulse, though in a more distorted form.

So what does it mean when this spontaneous energy is channeled through the opposite sign of Aquarius? At a superficial level, it produces *mass* gambling or *institutionalized* games of chance. In contrast with the image of a few individuals throwing dice, the emerging Great Age has bustling "palaces" that house thousands playing electronic slot machines side-by-side. Today, many flock not to their local church but to modern-day shrines of chance like the casinos of Las Vegas or Atlantic City, in the hope that a new set of gods may be invoked for altering fate.

We also see the Aquarian approach toward chance in places like Disneyland and Las Vegas in their shared concern with controlling the unpredictable. At an amusement park like Disneyland, activities that traditionally have involved risk are brought under tight supervision to provide us with all the thrills of chance-laden experiences without all the messy randomness and unpredictability. Rather than actually risk one's life by setting out on a big-game safari, one can now experience a simulated version of the same thing from the safety of an electronically guided vehicle.

Just as childbirth has always been one of life's more unpredictable activities, modern science is showing us how to reduce the element of chance here as well, with new advances in fertilization and genetic engineering. The striking film *Gattaca* features a scene that illustrates a possible dilemma: set at some unspecified point in our future, a married couple comes to a fertility clinic to consult with a corporate counselor on the planning of their next child. The counselor tries to convince them to take this process all the way, by picking out every characteristic of their future child in advance. But the couple is resistant, wondering if it wouldn't be better to leave just a *little* bit to chance, to the gods of randomness, as it were.

The counselor persists, perplexed that anyone would even *want* to leave some part of the conception process to chance. In much the same way, the Aquarian society of our future may be one where we will attempt to control as many elements of randomness and unpredictability in our world as possible. In short, the Aquarian Age will seek to harness chance.

This aspect of the Leo/Aquarius dynamic sheds light on the efforts by modern scientists to unlock the so-called laws of chance in all aspects of our world. Over the last century or so, disciplines have sprung up devoted to uncovering the hidden order that resides in apparent randomness; new fields have resulted, such as systems theory, statistical research, quantum physics (with probability theory), chaos science, and synchronicity studies. With chaos theory, complex phenomena long believed to be random in nature (such as the movements of motorists on a freeway) often belie deeper laws or statistical patterns, hidden from casual view. Here is yet another aspect of our image of scientists standing outside the playground, charting out the behaviors of children at play in hope of drawing meaning from otherwise spontaneous phenomena.

Within personal horoscopes, planetary patterns between Leo and Aquarius can sometimes indicate a struggle to balance personal spontaneity (Leo) with the restrictions of convention (Aquarius). In their constructive form, our social behavioral codes channel the fiery impulses of our natures into what we call civilization. Yet those same codes can become straight-jackets that suffocate spontaneity and vitality.

Warren Beatty's audacious film *Bulworth* provides an insight on the dichotomy between spontaneous action (fire) and the rigidities of convention

(Aquarius, in its more Saturnine aspect). The story centers on a disillusioned senator who had been a progressive figure on the national scene at one time, but who gradually became little more than a cog in the political machine. Due to an unlikely chain of circumstances, he suddenly breaks free of his socially prescribed role and begins living in a spontaneous manner, communicating to others mainly through rap songs. Beatty (himself a fire sign) underscores the deeper message of this seemingly comedic premise with the recurring line—a call to the slumbering fire principle in all of us—"You gotta be a *spirit*, you can't be no ghost!"

The One and the Many

Another way to approach an understanding of this zodiacal axis is by reflecting on some of the traditional symbols associated with these two signs. Within the body, for example, classical astrology associates Leo with the heart and Aquarius rules the arterial distribution of blood through the body. This fact alone holds clues for us into the workings of these two signs: Leo governs the principle of *centralization*, while Aquarius rules *decentralization*, the movement away from singularity toward complexity. For the same reason, Leo is associated symbolically with white light, while Aquarius is associated with the splintering of light into a spectrum, or a rainbow.

This emphasis on decentralization sheds light on many dynamics of the Aquarian Age. In political terms, for example, monarchy centralizes power in a reigning king just as the heart centralizes blood through a single point in the body. On the other hand, Aquarian democracy decentralizes power to all the citizens of a nation, like arteries carrying blood to a body's extremities. This correspondence is one of the reasons why Aquarius is so closely linked to the study of systems, networks, and associations of all kinds. As if commenting on the emerging trends of our time, the Irish poet W. B. Yeats once wrote, "the center cannot hold." In the coming age, we will continue to witness a growing decentralization in *every* area of society, from economics to spirituality (a point to be taken up in chapters 16 and 17), and the surfacing of complex alliances and networks of many different kinds—systems within systems within systems. The Internet is an example of this trend. If one asks where the Internet exists, one couldn't come up with a single address because it is a decentralized technology with as many centers around the world as there are users of computers.

In personal horoscopes, the linkage of Leo and Aquarius often indicates a penchant for drawing together diverse ideas or people into unifying frameworks, like a circus ringmaster. Some examples include esotericist H. P. Blavatsky (b. Aug. 12, 1831, a Leo), psychologist Carl Jung (b. July 26, 1875, a Leo), media host Oprah Winfrey (b. Jan. 29, 1954, an Aquarian), and philosopher/psychologist Ken Wilber (b. Jan. 31, 1949, an Aquarian). Fittingly, Wilber's first published book was *Spectrum of Consciousness*.

The Promethean Axis

Deeper insights into the meaning of this polarity may be unlocked by examining its placement in the chakra system as discussed in chapter 5 (see figure 8-2).

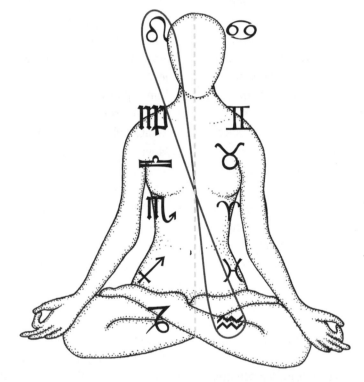

Figure 8-2. The Promethean Axis

Inwardly, the Leo/Aquarius polarity represents a bridge between the chakras associated with these signs—Aquarius with the root chakra at the bottom of the spine (the Saturn level), and Leo with the brow chakra in the forehead (the Sun level). The combination of these two centers, and this polarity's proximity to the central spine, makes this zodiacal polarity an especially powerful one in either constructive or destructive ways.

According to this arrangement, Leo is related to the "third eye" (or *Ajna* chakra), a point commonly associated with the seat of consciousness. In part, this helps explain why Leo is related to creativity, pleasure, and spontaneity, since these qualities are linked to the spiritual center within the forehead, our seat of creativity and higher visionary thought. Here, the energies of our subtle nature are centralized into a single point, a kind of "sun" to our own "solar system."

On the other hand, the sense of scientific detachment associated with Aquarius takes on new meaning when viewed in relation to its placement in the root (Saturn) chakra. This is the level of the chakra ladder farthest away from the "third eye." Like our scientists on the outside of the playground, consciousness at this level is similarly outside looking in, relative to the playground of pure awareness in the Ajna.

But only by looking at this dynamic as a whole can we begin to see the importance of this correspondence for our lives. For instance, note how closely the polarity between Leo and Aquarius is aligned to the central spinal column, which in yoga is described as the location of *sushumna*—the pathway of *kundalini*. This is a form of spiritual energy that lies dormant in most people, but which holds the key to our spiritual awakening.

While it wouldn't be accurate to say that the Leo/Aquarius polarity is *identical* to the kundalini current (Leo/Aquarius being more "masculine" and forceful in nature, more akin to what the yogis call the right-hand channel *pingala*), it arguably comes closer to it than any other polarity in the zodiac. The Leo/Aquarius axis taps into something powerful in our nature linked with consciousness at its most concentrated and luminous. (Perhaps this explains why images of laser beams and "light sabers" hold such appeal for moviegoers.)

What does this mean for our future? To answer that, we need to keep in mind that during the Aquarian Age the lower end of this polarity will be emphasized. This may lead to a growing trend to take "higher" energies from above and bring them down into everyday reality, in physical, intellectual, and spiritual ways. To use an analogy, a technology often associated with the Leo/Aquarius polarity is that of solar power, which beautifully illustrates the dynamics of this chakra polarity. Just as solar power technology draws down energy from the sun for everyday use, so Aquarius draws down energies from the Ajna into everyday experience, the realm of root chakra experience. I refer to the Leo/Aquarius polarity as the Promethean axis, in reference to the Greek mythic figure who carried fire from Mt. Olympus down to humanity.[2]

We see many ways in which fire is already being "drawn down" into daily life in the world. In politics, democracy offers the promise of placing power in the hands of ordinary men and women. In the workplace, unionization transfers power from the top to the bottom of the labor ladder. In the economic sphere, capitalism shifts wealth from kings and landholders into the hands of entrepreneurs. On a technological level, atomic power replicates the processes of the sun for human use, while the mastery of electricity makes the once-awesome powers of lightning available to people through outlets in the walls of their homes. The image of Ben Franklin with his kite attempting to conduct lightning takes on an iconic power in light of the "Promethean" aspects of the new Aquarian Age.

In psychological terms, the Promethean impulse is seen in the widespread drive towards personal empowerment in modern culture, which allows average people to realize their potentials. Its effects are visible in the worldwide democratization of knowledge as a result of publishing and the Internet. In a spiritual context, this Promethean shift could point to a day when people will have greater access to the energies of the Ajna chakra. In recent times, we've seen a renewed interest in the Prometheus myth itself through the writings of Percy Shelley *(Prometheus Unbound)* or his wife's novel, *Frankenstein* (originally subtitled *The Modern Prometheus*).

Playing with Fire

But as Mary Shelley's story of Dr. Frankenstein demonstrates, great power is accompanied by great responsibility. For this reason, the Leo/Aquarius axis might be called the "third rail" of the zodiac, since tapping into its energies can be an electrifying experience. Classical mythology provides us with numerous warnings of the dangers of powers acquired prematurely. In modern times, it is a message also familiar to us through Disney's rendition of the "Sorcerer's Apprentice" in *Fantasia.* (And what about all that water-bearer imagery throughout this animated tale?)

Over the last century alone, we've seen many examples of what can happen when power is wielded without the counterbalancing force of compassion and reflectivity. The ability of a commoner like Hitler to rise from the lowest ranks of society into a position of global power is but one testament to the perils of playing with fire, on both political and psychological levels. Hiroshima and Nagasaki are also dramatic examples of this danger in technological and scientific ways. It doesn't seem entirely accidental that the closest we have come in modern times to global Armageddon was an event (the Cuban missile crisis of 1962) that happened soon after a powerful activation of this zodiacal polarity, when seven planets in Aquarius (including a solar eclipse) combined to oppose Uranus in Leo during February of 1962.

In this chapter we've seen a number of the ways that the Leo/Aquarius polarity could manifest in society, on cultural, political, and technological levels. The transformation of consciousness being ushered in will grant us access to powers that can lift us to great new heights, or plunge us to the depths of destruction. Yet there are other implications which could prove no less momentous in their impact on our day-to-day lives. In the next few chapters we will continue to explore these, and conclude with a look at the spiritual implications of this polarity.

9

The New Aquarian Hero

As Joseph Campbell shows in his classic work *The Hero with a Thousand Faces,* the theme of the hero is a recurring one in the myths and folktales of cultures around the world. In one instance after another, we find variations on the timeless motif of some larger-than-life figure who undertakes a great quest to achieve a goal or obtain a treasure. So studying how a culture portrays its heroes tells us much about that culture's values and the archetypal forces underlying its unfoldment.

During the next Age, the heroic quest will undoubtedly find itself clothed in the symbols and concerns of the Leo/Aquarius polarity, the dual signs at opposite ends of the zodiac that will be shaping our perspectives and lifestyles. To begin with, Leo is itself the sign most associated with heroism. Whenever we see Leo strongly emphasized in a person's horoscope, we often find a capacity for surmounting great challenges toward attaining a personal dream. The careers of Arnold Schwarzenegger and Madonna are two instances of this. Beyond their flair for showmanship, Leos draw on powerful reserves of willpower and stamina, expressing the desire to transcend the limits of ordinary human possibility, whether for worldly or spiritual ends.

During the coming Age, however, Leo will be the *counterbalancing* sign at work, rather than the dominant one which is Aquarius. As Aquarius is the sign of the common man, this suggests we will see a certain democratization of heroism. Rather than centering on just one or two figures within society, the Aquarian Age ushers in a time when the heroic mantle could fall upon common men or women, making them ordinary heroes, as it were. "I sing the divine average," wrote Walt Whitman, who championed the importance of common men and women in his time. As one biographer put it, "In Whitman we have a democrat who set out to imagine the life of the average man in average circumstances changed into something grand and heroic" (Callow 1992).

Just such a theme has already begun to shape our thinking in many ways. In the iconography of pop culture, we see this theme in the American comic book figure, Superman. Here is a man who possesses enormous powers and integrity but who masquerades as someone very ordinary: Clark Kent. As Superman's alter ego, Kent is a mild-mannered citizen who sheds his ordinary clothing to become a superhuman champion when required.

In a more modest form, the same Aquarian heroic impulse can be seen in Charlie Chaplin, the little tramp, a lowly figure who toils against overwhelming odds. The "everyday hero" motif gives new meaning to Joyce's masterpiece *Ulysses*. As we noted earlier, Joyce borrowed his thematic outline from one of antiquity's great heroic tales, Homer's *Odyssey*. By grafting this onto the life of an average man in then contemporary Dublin, Joyce's Leopold Bloom symbolized the modern counterpart of the mythic hero.

There are other implications to be drawn from this notion of the ordinary hero, some sublime, some ridiculous. For the remainder of this chapter, then, let us examine a number of these.

The Culture of Celebrity

At its most worldly, the heroic impulse of the Leo/Aquarius axis has already become visible in that modern phenomenon we call celebrity. Symbolically, Leo is the sign most commonly associated with society's "stars"—and fittingly, too, since this is the only zodiacal sign actually governed by a star rather than a planet (namely, the sun). In more traditional times, society's luminaries almost exclusively hailed from its political or religious quarters, but with the rise of pop culture during the last century, ordinary people rose up and became "stars" in their own right. As Andy Warhol (Leo) put it, *everyone* can find their fifteen minutes of fame, and become an object of worship. In a sense, ours has become a culture of disposable deities.

The modern phenomenon of celebrity is tied to the emergence of mass media since 1900, surfacing with particular force during the historical "windows" discussed earlier in this book. During the 1920s, for example, the world saw such figures as Rudolph Valentino, Mary Pickford, Douglas Fairbanks, Charlie Chaplin, and Charles Lindbergh achieve near-divine status as pop heroes. While jazz was a largely group-oriented art form, one of its virtues was a flexibility in accommodating the geniuses of individuals in ways that earlier musical forms like the Gregorian choir or European symphony could not. This was demonstrated in the 1920s by the rise of Louis Armstrong (a Leo), who became jazz's first great soloist. The 1960s were another turning point in the emergence of the celebrity phenomenon, as the burgeoning media technologies made it possible for unprecedented numbers of ordinary people to rise out of obscurity and become pop stars. Hero worship became a cottage industry during this tumultuous decade, as hordes of adoring fans paid homage to larger-than-life figures like Mohammed Ali, John F. Kennedy, astronauts John Glenn and Neil Armstrong, and the Beatles and Rolling Stones.

Because 1962 hosted a powerful activation of Aquarius and Leo in early February, this year holds valuable clues for the Aquarian mythos. In my research, I turned my attention to the films of that period to see whether they offered synchronistic clues as to the influence of that zodiacal polarity, and in turn to the values of the coming age. What first struck me was how many notable films were released in 1962. One prominent critic, Michael Wilmington (1999) of *The Chicago Tribune,* called it the most important year in the history of filmmaking, topping such commonly cited years as 1939 and 1941.[1] The year 1962 saw the release of *The Manchurian Candidate, To Kill a Mockingbird, The Man Who Shot Liberty Valence, Lolita, The Miracle Worker, The Trial, Days of Wine and Roses,* and the first of the highly successful James Bond franchise, *Dr. No.*

Many of these works bore directly on Aquarian Age-related themes in symbolic or literal ways. For example, *The Manchurian Candidate* tells the story of individuals attempting to break free from the effects of mind control, foreshadowing *The Matrix* and *Dark City.*[2] Orson Welles' *The Trial* depicts a Kafkaesque world of bureaucracy taken to nightmarish extremes (echoing the publication of Joseph Heller's *Catch-22* the year before). *Liberty Valence* touches on the role of media in shaping our view of the world ("When the fact becomes legend, print the legend."); *Days of Wine and Roses* is about individuals struggling to escape the grip of alcoholism (i.e.,

Pisces domination); and the first of the James Bond series, *Dr. No*, centered on spies and espionage, a growing concern in an era of covert intelligence organizations and high-tech surveillance.

In the end, David Lean's masterpiece, *Lawrence of Arabia,* seemed the most logical place to search for clues about the coming age, or for that matter the rest of the 1960s (since the planetary configuration of 1962 would exert most of its effects in the years directly following 1962). I found that this film touched on several key themes related to the Leo/Aquarius axis.

To begin with, the film features distinct and overlapping story lines, one with a social emphasis, the other focusing on Lawrence's personal struggle. Regarding the first, the film describes the birth of modern Saudi Arabia as a nation and its struggle to take a decentralized (Aquarius) group of warring tribes and unite them under the leadership of a centralized ruling King (Leo). This in itself held obvious relevance for the coming age, in prefiguring the challenge that global culture is facing as it tries to harmonize a world of disparate voices into a global community. America confronted a similar challenge when it set out to forge a unified identity that didn't compromise the identity of its respective members—an intent still visible in the Latin phrase inscribed on this country's Great Seal: *E Pluribus Unum* ("Out of many, one").

The personal aspect of Lean's film was most fascinating to me in its relevance to the Aquarian Age. The movie describes the real-life story of T. E. Lawrence, the famed British writer (Leo) who became politically involved with the cause of the Arab tribes. The film charts his unexpected ascent through the ranks of the British army to become a hero-figure for these disunited peoples, and it follows his subsequent fall from grace. In this respect, Lawrence's story offers several clear links to the archetypal concerns of the Leo/Aquarius axis, particularly the phenomenon of celebrity.

Lawrence was one of the twentieth century's first media "stars," having been propelled into worldwide fame by the media (personified in the film by a photojournalist modeled after the real-life Lowell Thomas). With his white robes, blond hair, and exhibitionist tendencies, Lawrence becomes the embodiment of the Leonine hero, down to narcissism and delusions of grandeur.[3] The film seems to foreshadow not only how the phenomenon of celebrity would become a dominant force during the 1960s, but in the Age of Aquarius as a whole.

Lean's film prefigured the emerging trends of the times in another key respect—its overriding concern with the struggle for freedom. On the political level, the Arabs were shown banding together specifically to gain liberation from the Turks and the heavy-handed British presence in the Middle East. But in terms of his personal struggle, Lawrence's life is depicted as moving toward a greater freedom of expression. He starts out as a regimented "company man," working a desk job in the uniform of the British Army, yet eventually he puts this aside to assume the flowing white robes of the wandering Bedouin. This image was a harbinger of the shattering of social codes and fashions that characterized the 1960s, as echoed in the flowing clothes of the hippies.

One sees a parallel here in the evolution of the Beatles during this decade; they also evolved from quasi-corporate uniforms into the freer, personalized dress of their later years. To the extent that the 1960s prefigured the Aquarian Age, there may be clues in these trends: the phenomenon of celebrity, the power of the media, the struggle for freedom, and the potential for hubris and narcissism that often taints the heroic impulse.

The Social Activist As Hero

The Aquarian heroic trend can take other forms as well, such as what I call the social activist as hero. During the Piscean Age, the hero archetype assumed a more feminine quality, with images like the crucifixion of Jesus embodying a message not of conquest but surrender. Were one to pick a single figure to symbolize the introverted tendencies of Pisces, it might well be the monk. Rather than charge headlong into the world to change conditions, the monk withdraws from worldly affairs to contemplate an interior universe of feelings and devotional impulses. But in the Aquarian Age, the heroic principle once again resumes a masculine, extroverted cast, turning its attention to society. The archetypal figure shifts from monk to social activist—the man or woman who leaves the cave or monastery behind to change the world through social reform and brotherhood.

Under the high-tech influence of Aquarius, this sometimes may mean the Aquarian hero expresses that social activism through media. The lead character in *Citizen Kane* is originally depicted as an aspiring social reformer who uses the media to champion the interests of the ordinary person. In the story of Superman, our hero's day-job is not fisherman, doctor, or truck driver, but newspaper reporter, and he undergoes his transformation into Superman in a telephone booth, obviously a symbol of telecommunications. Real-life illustrations of this principle are Ted Turner, who has often used his media connections to champion environmental causes, or Oprah Winfrey, who has used television and print media for social and spiritual causes.

Another way in which the Aquarian hero will no doubt express herself is through business. It is tempting to think that corporate interests could be a force for evil in the coming world; yet these can be applied in constructive ways, too, as any number of modern philanthropists have shown. One notable example is actor Paul Newman, whose line of food products funnels its profits to charities. Instances like this show that business can serve humanitarian interests. In a similar vein, the economic boom of the 1990s generated a new crop of millionaire philanthropists who sought ways of channeling their earnings in charitable directions. In a possible synchronistic echo of this trend, Steven Spielberg's 1993 classic *Schindler's List* told the true-life story of a non-Jewish German citizen during World War II who used his business savvy to save the lives of many Jews.[4]

The Shadow Side of Aquarian Heroism

For some, this emerging heroic impulse brought a desire for becoming *more* than human somehow, perhaps even *superhuman*. Friedrich Nietzsche put his finger on this sensibility when he wrote of *der übermensch*—the "superman" (or overman)—in the opening to his *Also Sprach Zarathustra*. In *The Passion of the Western Mind*, Richard Tarnas eloquently summarizes Nietzsche's ideas on this subject, in a passage that could be read as a commentary on the dawning Aquarian consciousness:

> The highest truth, Nietzsche prophesied, was being born within man through the self-creating power of the will. All of man's striving for knowledge and power would fulfill itself in a new being who would incarnate the living meaning of the universe. But to achieve this birth, man would have to grow beyond himself so fundamentally that his present limited self would be destroyed: "What is great in man is that he is a bridge and not a goal. Man is something that must be overcome." For man was a way to new dawns and new horizons far beyond the compass of the present age. And the birth of this new being was not a life-impoverishing otherworldly fantasy to be believed by ecclesiastical decree, but was a vivid, tangible reality to be created, here and now, through the heroic self-overcoming of the great individual. Such an individual had to transform life into a work of art, within which he could forge his character, embrace his fate, and recreate himself as heroic protagonist of the world epic. . . . Then

the God who had long been projected to the beyond could be born within the human soul. Then man could dance godlike in the eternal flux, free of all foundations and all bounds, beyond every metaphysical constraint (Tarnas 1991).

What happens when this heroic impulse is perverted toward less than idealistic ends? We've touched on a few of the dangers associated with this energy in our discussion of celebrity and fame. As *Lawrence of Arabia* shows, getting in touch with one's "inner hero" carries the risk of what Jung calls inflation. Rather than realize one's potential, one becomes intoxicated by the glorification of the ego. At times, this can lead to deadly consequences, as with Napoleon Bonaparte. His astonishing rise to power, and the millions of deaths that resulted from it, offers a sobering reminder of the dangers of the Leo/Aquarius axis when it is allowed to unfold in self-aggrandizing ways.

David Lean's depiction of Lawrence offers another synchronistic clue about the problematic side of the Leo/Aquarius axis. With his blue eyes and leonine golden hair, Peter O'Toole's Lawrence could serve as a poster boy for the Aryan ideal of the "superman" as championed by Nazi sympathizers since the rise of Hitler in the 1920s. In any number of ways, the Nazis exhibited an uncanny genius for tapping into the darker underside of the emerging Aquarian consciousness, as demonstrated not only by their advanced technology and faceless totalitarianism, but in their quest to create a new race of supermen and superwomen. Influenced by Nordic mythology and a misreading of Nietzsche's superman concept, this aspect of Nazi ideology was a distorted take on the Leo/Aquarius polarity. In some ways, the title of Leni Riefenstahl's film of the 1936 Berlin Olympics said it all: *The Triumph of the Will.*

We have begun to taste that potential for personal empowerment which seeks to propel us toward ever new heights, based on a realization of our awakening inner wills (Leo). Yet it is one thing to dream of lifting humanity by spiritual or psychological means, and another to engineer this through racist science and by eliminating "inferior" types from the population. In their own way, the Nazis demonstrate a bit of democratized heroism, yet they expressed it in the least spiritual manner possible, concocting a vision of society comprised not of God-inspired men and women, but of *physically* enhanced humans who harbored a blind allegiance to a totalitarian state.

Both the constructive and destructive streams of this heroic trend are subtly interwoven in Stanley Kubrick's 1969 epic *2001: A Space Odyssey.*

This film follows a hero's trajectory, with the tale of a great journey that climaxes with a transformation of the central character. In its closing moments, we watch as the astronaut is reborn from an aged man to a star-child of sorts. Kubrick's choice of music for these key moments in the film is crucial: those booming strains of Richard Strauss's *Also Sprach Zarathustra*. Strauss had been inspired by Nietzsche's writings on the superman when composing this piece, and Kubrick cleverly uses it during his film to herald the evolutionary jumps experienced by humanity at select moments. By employing it in the final scene of the reborn star-child, Kubrick hinted at the possibility of another step forward in our evolution to the possible level of the "superhuman."

But in light of Hitler's distortion of Nietzsche's concept, it is not easy to dissociate the negative connotations evoked by this music as it thunders forth during this scene. It leaves us with several possibilities to ponder. Kubrick created a visionary work that points to the uplifting of humanity to new heights in the times ahead, but it also hints at the possible dangers of humanity falling prey to hubris and inflation, as a result of the effects of sciences and technology. (This is a point I will take up in the next chapter.)

The Empowered Child

The closing image of the star-child in *2001* suggests another variation on our contemplations of the hero for the coming age. I call it the empowered child. Traditionally, Leo is symbolically associated with adolescence, that stage of life where one has not yet reached adulthood, but is starting to feel one's powers and identity. Combine that youthful vitality with the rational potentials of its opposing sign, Aquarius, and you arrive at the symbol of a youth endowed with extraordinary powers, technologically, mentally, or paranormally.[5]

One finds many striking examples of this principle from Western culture, both fictional and real-life. For instance, consider such popular icons as Harry Potter, Lewis Carroll's Alice, and Dorothy from L. Frank Baum's *The Wizard of Oz*. As one scholar of the *Oz* stories expressed it, "Grimm and Andersen stories are really morality tales, written to set parameters for young people, illustrating what happens if you don't behave. But Oz speaks to children in a kinder and gentler way, and it's the child who overcomes the greatest evil of all, which is the wicked witch. In the end, *it's the child who triumphs*" [emphasis mine] (Scarfone and Stillman 1999). One might see this archetype in terms of the Greek tale most often associated with Aquarius the constellation, namely, Ganymede, a beautiful young boy who was made immortal by Zeus.

Interestingly, the year 1999 hosted one of the most powerful activations of the Leo/Aquarius axis in recent history. As a result of that August's "eclipse of the century" (which centered on planets aligned between these two signs), throughout that year the empowered child archetype emerged as a prominent one in popular culture. For example, the two biggest box office hits of that summer featured stories about adolescent boys with extraordinary powers, boys who even looked strikingly similar. *Star Wars: The Phantom Menace* told the saga of the young Darth Vader, a golden-haired child who displayed an abundance of "the Force" as well as an aptitude for high-tech gadgetry. *The Sixth Sense* featured a young boy with an ability to "see dead people."

In another repetition of this trend, that same year witnessed a real-life prodigy emerging into public awareness, Gregory Smith who bore a resemblance to the young actors in both films. Born on June 8, 1989, this boy gained attention on TV shows like David Letterman's *Late Show* and *Oprah* for his preternatural poise and intelligence and his humanitarian concern for helping needy children around the world.

But as the tale of the young Darth Vader suggests, there are more destructive potentials inherent in the empowered child archetype, what the French call the *enfant terrible* syndrome. The precocious boy or girl deploys their talents for selfish or destructive ends. In contemporary culture, this image has many variants, including the golden-haired Dennis the Menace (acted on TV originally by Jay North, a sun-sign Leo); the paranormally gifted children of the 1960 British thriller *Village of the Damned;* or the Nazis' "Hitler Youth."

The image of the destructive child prodigy has been a recurring one in the books of Stephen King, and was the core idea of 1974's horror blockbuster *The Exorcist.* In the 1983 film *War Games,* it manifests as an adolescent boy who has advanced computer skills, but who unwittingly pushes civilization to the brink of catastrophe. In various ways, these recall Disney's "Sorcerer's Apprentice" in the 1940 film *Fantasia:* a youth adorns himself in the Aquarian imagery of stars and planets and nearly brings destruction upon himself and his world through an unwise use of power. Looking to the events of 1999 (the year of the eclipse in Leo and Lucas's *Star Wars: The Phantom Menace*), we find a real-life synchronicity of this trend in the unprecedented rash of high-school shootings and bombings across America. In the high school shootings in Columbine, Colorado, teenage boys vented their rage on fellow classmates and teachers using guns and bombs.

What does all this mean? My suspicion is that we could read these images in literal or metaphorical ways. For instance, the symbol of the Aquarian child prodigy may herald the rise of gifted children throughout the world in the years ahead, perhaps in the manner of earlier child prodigies like Mozart and Welles. In the New Age community especially, there has been much talk in recent years about the growing numbers of children spiritually and/or creatively talented beyond their years.

If instead we read images in a symbolic vein, they might point to a general awakening of creativity that will continue into the next Great Age. Baudelaire once wrote that "Genius is childhood recaptured at will." Possibly the coming age will witness a major breakthrough in our ability to recapture our own creative genius, at whatever age.

The correspondence between Leo and the creative energies of conception might portend something about our attempts to unlock the secrets of life in DNA research. Either way, the more destructive versions of the empowered child archetype could sound a cautionary note for us as we plunge headlong into unmapped realms.

10

The Genetics Revolution: Mysteries of the Double Helix

During an interview conducted during early 1998, a little-known research scientist from the suburbs of Chicago, Dr. Richard Seed, remarked to a reporter from National Public Radio that he hoped to someday become the first scientist in history to clone a human being. The casualness of his remark gave little indication of the firestorm of controversy that was about to ensue.

Over the next few days, media outlets across the world carried the story of this figure and his remarkable comments, with even late-night comedians joining in on the act by poking fun at his unlikely name (*"Dick Seed!"* TV personality Jay Leno exclaimed in feigned disbelief.) By the time the dust settled several weeks later, the impact was apparent: In direct response to Seed's remarks, nineteen European nations and eighteen states in the U.S. had rushed through legislation that permanently banned human cloning research.

What was it about this man's statements that provoked such outrage? Scientists had spoken of cloning before; indeed, just one year earlier Scottish scientists successfully cloned an adult mammal for the first time.[1] What was different was Seed's willingness to speak openly—and favorably—about using this technology on ourselves. He crossed an intangible yet decisive line. Consider Seed's comments from his original interview with National Public Radio:

God made man in his own image. God intended for man to become one with God. We are going to become one with God. We are going to have almost as much knowledge and almost as much power as God. *Cloning, and the reprogramming of DNA, is the first serious step in becoming one with God"* [emphasis added] (Byrne 1998).

To become one with God, to step into the realm of genetic science, is to enter a realm as steeped in myth and archetype as fact. In this chapter we will look at some of these archetypal resonances and consider how they might shed further light on the "heroic" impulse. Let's first review some aspects of DNA research relevant to this consideration.

The Code of Life

For thousands of years, philosophers pondered how creatures acquired their distinct forms. Why did the giraffe have a long neck, the turtle a shell? What accounts for the diversity of characteristics within a species?

Prior to the 1950s, humans had little understanding of the physical mechanism involved in such processes. But in late February of 1953, Francis Crick and James Watson announced to the world they had discovered the *code* which explained it all. Called DNA, it consists of two intertwining strands of long molecules which serve as information, and is found in each cell of our body. The "information" is written in the language of four chemical "letters"—adenine, thymine, cytosine, guanine. Whether a person is white, black, red, short, or tall, all differences arise out of a varying arrangement of these molecular building blocks, from a difference in coding.

Try as we might, it is impossible to grasp the complexity and vastness of this code as each genetic strand in a human cell contains roughly three billion bits of information. Take all the genetic strands in a body and stretch them out end-to-end, and they will extend from here to the sun many times over. Each of us contains an encyclopedia of data in our cells, encoding information about ourselves and the entire human species over time.

Crick and Watson's discovery of this code solved certain long-standing problems, but it raised new and equally troubling ones. For instance, how did this code arise in the first place, let alone develop to the complexity found in higher animals? Darwin suggested that evolution proceeded essentially through a series of chance mutations, blindly, as it were; yet as some pointed out, that would be like believing that a room full of monkeys pounding on typewriters could eventually produce Shakespeare's *Hamlet.*

Look at the propulsion system in a simple bacterium. You'll see it consists of a complex set of interlocking parts, all necessary to the workings of that system. How could such an interlocking arrangement arise solely through "chance" mutations, when anything less than a fully functioning system would never have sustained itself for any time?

As some scientists have expressed it, the leap from inorganic chemicals to even the simplest cell is far greater than the leap from a cell to a human being. So how do we explain the origin of DNA itself and its subsequent transition through the higher life forms? One possible solution is that evolution took a far greater amount of time than scientists currently suspect. A more controversial answer would be that DNA was developed under the auspices of a guiding intelligence, either divine or extraterrestrial. In any event, this riddle poses a vexing challenge to existing theories of evolution.

Another vexing problem is how DNA actually *works.* By way of analogy, it is one thing to identify all the parts of a TV set, but another to determine how those parts interact to produce an image. The discovery of DNA provided scientists a look at the basic genetic "parts" that underlie our forms; but how do the parts interact to guide growth? Might there be complex patterns involving the DNA components which aren't easily discernible? By tinkering with one component of DNA, we might set off a chain of effects with an impact on many aspects of personality or biology.

Finally, is it possible (as scientists like Rupert Sheldrake have suggested) that DNA isn't the source of our physical form but only its *conduit,* much in the same way a TV set *receives* programs but doesn't *generate* them?[2] Such are a few of the many questions that remain unanswered as we step into the world of genetic manipulation of life.

The significance of genetic research in the unfolding Aquarian era is related to several thematic streams. Let us take these one at a time.

Theme 1: Playing God

The most obvious of these themes centers around what Dr. Seed hinted at: the conceit of "playing God." In contrast with other kinds of science and technology, genetic research doesn't simply involve inert matter or impersonal laws, but introduces the all-important element of life into its equation. It carries the scientist across a crucial line into a domain of creativity that recapitulates the divine source itself. To that extent, it also echoes, astrologically, the energies of the Leo/Aquarius axis. Earlier, I used the metaphor of solar power to describe the relationship between Aquarius and Leo, suggesting that Aquarian rationality and technology "draw down" the higher energies of Leo into practical manifestation. Similarly, genetic technology taps into the higher creative energies of life and draws them down into everyday life at a cellular level.

In contrast with directly accessing the divine creative energies, as might be experienced by the mystic, genetic creativity is like a lower level mimicking the divine source. Capturing the energies of the sun by means of a solar power generator is not the same as sitting in meditation and tapping into the "inner sun" of the third eye. Remember that Aquarius lies at the bottom of the chakra system, Leo at the top. Why is this important? Because when someone says that genetic manipulation is "the first serious step in becoming one with God," as Dr. Seed did, this may confuse the map for the territory.

But whether one is accessing the creative energies from the upper or lower ends of the chakra system, through mysticism or technology, there is the still the possibility of abusing those energies. As the Sorcerer's Apprentice tale reminds us, there are always risks to evolutionary growth. This is an acutely relevant point to keep in mind as we enter the Aquarian Age. Perhaps this knowledge of the risks helps explain some of the appeal now for tales of Atlantis, accounts of the disasters which befell its inhabitants through the abuse of the "third eye" energies (according to one story). It is a theme stressed in *Dark City*, a film that portrays a city lorded over by a race of "watchers" who misuse the creative powers of their third eyes.

How best to deal with this problem? Since the genie is already out of the bottle (or just about fully out), there is only one answer, and it is obvious. We must make sure we develop a strong moral compass for framing decisions about cloning or medical experimentation. Ask questions like the following: Will this experiment cause suffering to any person or creature? What will be the long-term consequences, either direct or indirect, of a given action? Without these concerns at the forefront, we may find ourselves becoming "god-like" in the centuries to come, though in ways considerably less than divine in either motive or outcome—like gods, but not God.

Theme 2: Cloning and the Assembly Line Society

The second thematic stream with genetics is cloning. There is a difference between cloning and genetic reprogramming. The first case involves a simple replication of life forms, like taking a frog and creating multiple "carbon copies" of that original. Genetic reprogramming actively alters DNA to transform or create new life forms. A basic example of this would be genetically reprogramming a human to live 300 years. Since cloning and reprogramming are two genetic technologies considerably different in symbolism, we'll consider cloning in this segment, and genetic reprogramming in the next.

Cloning hearkens to the most impersonal aspects of the emerging mythos, expressed by the factory assembly line or the chain fast food restaurant. This is the Aquarian principle at its most faceless and homogenized; the opposing Leo principle has been squelched and the "system" reigns supreme. With the assembly line, personal creativity is eliminated in favor of a mass-produced, uniform line of identical items. With cloning, we have much the same idea: cookie-cutter duplications of the same thing. The fear this strikes in many is the same fear which causes us to abhor totalitarian systems of government: the denial of individuality.

Other synchronistic links to other areas and expressions of modern culture can be seen. In the pivotal scene of *Fantasia*'s "Sorcerer's Apprentice," Mickey Mouse brings a broom to life, then destroys it; but then he finds it unexpectedly splitting into many brooms, like clones, and these nearly overpower him. One is also reminded here of that haunting scene at the end of *Citizen Kane* where the central character walks through a hall of mirrors, his image reflected endlessly and exactly replicated—a symbol, perhaps, for the Aquarian identity at its most exhausted and anonymous.

If there is one creature that embodies the clonelike, "assembly-line" idea, it is the insect. So it is interesting to see how the symbolism of insects and bugs have figured prominently in contemporary society. One of the most popular automobile lines in the world is the Volkswagen "Beetle"—a creation of Hitler's Nazis. When Hollywood produced its first computer-generated feature films, two of those three—*Antz* and *A Bug's Life*—focused on insect societies, and treated the theme of the individual versus group. Consider that most popular musical group in history, the *Beatles;* a lighthearted pun on the insect order (perhaps actually a subtle homage to the group's musical heroes, Buddy Holly and his "Crickets"). Finally, there are "aliens"—whether we regard them as faithful descriptions of real events or hallucinations on a mass scale, many people around the world have described encounters with UFO occupants who are insectlike in appearance or personality, as if members of a "hive-mind."

If there is significance to these images, it may be that they tell us something about the collective identity crisis we will grapple with during the Aquarian Age as we come face-to-face with the consequences of a mass society.

Theme 3: Bioengineering the New "Superman"

On its surface, this next stream deals with the technology of genetic reprogramming, but in relation to the "heroic" theme underlying the Leo/Aquarius axis.

This involves the awakening urge of men and women to become superhuman. We previously noted that Kubrick's *2001:A Space Odyssey* ends with a large-headed star-child floating above the Earth, as if to herald the advent of a new human. Indeed, there are many indications that the Aquarian Age will be a time when we are lifted up to a higher level of growth. Though there are likely to be several factors involved in this development, one certainly will involve our genetic sciences. Specifically, by learning how to adjust our genes, we may find ways to enhance our capabilities and possibly create a race of superhumans. Astrophysicist Stephen Hawking has remarked:

> There haven't been any significant changes in human DNA in the past 10,000 years. But soon we will be able to increase the complexity of our internal record, our DNA, without having to wait for the slow process of biological evolution. It is likely that we will be able to redesign it completely in the next 1000 years—by increasing our brain size, for example (Hawking 2000).

It is tempting to speculate just how far this redesign might go in the directing of human growth. Imagine a child given the strength of an ape, the eyesight of a hawk, the brain of the smartest person, some dolphin cognitive skills thrown in for good measure, and the ability to regenerate limbs. What kind of person would this be, physically and psychologically? Would it even be a "person" as we normally think of it? Here we see the relevance of the metaphor of the "quantum leap" to human physiology and personality, as humanity hoists its way up the evolutionary ladder to new levels. We are entering an age when personal empowerment will be a key concern, but genetic technology amplifies this process exponentially.

This insight sheds light on another meaning of the Greek tale of Ganymede, the story most associated in Western culture with Aquarius. A youth was lifted up into heaven to join the fraternity of the gods. In a way, genetic technology may do this "lifting" of humans to a seemingly godlike level. In joining the gods, Ganymede was made immortal. Here may be another parallel with genetic science. (As servant to the gods, Ganymede is believed to have held a cup containing *ambrosia*, the drink of immortality.) Perhaps the most discussed aspect of modern genetic research concerns life-extension, and the possibility that scientists may learn how to give humans hundreds of years of life, possibly the ability to live forever.

It was not only Greek culture that associated immortality with this constellation. As Kenneth Johnson notes in *Mythic Astrology*, the Babylonians associated this essential idea with Aquarius, too. In the *Epic of Gilgamesh*, for example, the four fixed signs of the zodiac are symbolically represented through the four creatures encountered by Gilgamesh in his quest for the herb of immortality: bull (Taurus), lion (Leo), scorpion (Scorpio), and human, Utnapishtim (Aquarius). Of them all, Utnapishtim is the great immortal, and holds the secret of eternal life (Guttman and Johnson 1998). Mythologically, the Age of Aquarius is linked to the theme of eternal life.

There are disturbing aspects to the work of genetic science, as demonstrated by the Nazi ideal of *der übermensch*. Who will decide what kind of human is made, which traits will be enhanced? Will only the wealthy or politically connected be able to have "designer" children? If so, will this lead to a genetic rift in society, a new definition of haves and have-nots?

What presumptions necessarily underlie any talk of "perfecting" the human race, of creating *superior* beings? To say someone is "superior" implies others are "inferior." In their hopes of forging a race of blond-haired, blue-eyed Aryans, the Nazis believed that anyone not fitting this racial stereotype was inadequate. There is something deeply troubling about discussions of genetically "improving the human lot," with its implicit elitism. It's little wonder, synchronistically, that the Nazis were the first to institute nationwide eugenics-based (a pseudoscientific precursor to modern genetics) breeding programs.

In some ways, this reminds us of the Greek myth of Ouranos, the tyrannical sky god who disdained his less-than-perfect children, consequently imprisoning them in the nether regions. From one perspective, Ouranos embodies the totalitarian type of Aquarian rationality that likes everything neat, systematized, and orderly, and brooks no imperfections. This rationality has little patience for the feminine dimension of life generally, and the emotions in particular, which are never as neat and orderly as the rational mind prefers. Not unlike the mentality of the Nazis, the Ouranian mind sees an impaired or disfigured child as "inferior" or "imperfect"; contrast this with the attitude of that child's parents, who love it unconditionally, for *all* its qualities. At its worst, the Aquarian Age may be a time when all the sleek, shiny surfaces of society leave little or no room for "imperfections" of any kind, human or technological.

In practical terms, who's to say that a society of genetically "perfected" humans is desirable? What would be the consequences of weeding out traits considered inferior? Imagine if Beethoven's deafness had been detected early on and the gene that caused it eliminated. Would he have still written his *Moonlight Sonata* or his *Ninth Symphony?* If singer Ray Charles had been cured of his blindness early on would we still have his body of work? Similar questions present themselves when we turn to the subject of spiritual talents. Look at all the cases through history where great insight or spiritual strength was obtained as a result of bodily or emotional hardship. Would those individuals still exist in a society where all such challenges had been removed through genetic planning? If we were to homogenize society in terms of smoothing out the rough spots associated with disability, would that affect the spiritual tenor of society, diminish the range of spiritual opportunities and lessons available?

Theme 4: When the Created Overtakes the Creator

This line of questioning brings us directly to the last of our themes underling the genetic sciences. What happens when things don't go as planned? One of the concerns of the Leo/Aquarius axis is controlling the unpredictable, harnessing chance.

The totalitarian side of Aquarian rationality seeks to control nature in as many ways as possible, and extend itself in its efforts to control human conception. Based on current developments, we may become a society that *chooses* its children's traits and characteristics, perhaps down to the tiniest detail. But if there is anything we should have learned by now, it's that nature doesn't easily subject itself to the strict controls of humankind. As the poet Robert Burns wrote, "The best laid schemes o' mice and men gang aft a-gley [i.e., 'often go awry']." Try as we might to take all possible contingencies into account, there is often some loose thread that unravels the fabric, confounding our "surest" expectations. As Jeff Goldblum's character in *Jurassic Park* said concerning the indomitableness of life under trying circumstances, "Life will find a way."

Of the common themes in science fiction over the last two hundred years, from *Frankenstein* to *The Terminator,* one has been the creation overtaking the creator. If Aquarius does not find the balance in its creativity and controls those spontaneous Leo energies too firmly, there could be hell to pay! It may portend a time when we have to face the challenge of being overtaken by our creations, be they mechanical or biological. Read symbolically, this could point to the potential dangers of becoming too engrossed in the wondrous world we have created for ourselves. Like Narcissus lost in his own reflection, let us be careful that we are not drawn so completely out of ourselves by externals that we forget who we are.

And who might that be? Even *that* may be about to change.

The Whole World Is Watching: The Individual in a Mass Society

Each Great Age introduces its own set of pressing concerns, and during the Aquarian Age a dominant one will surely be this: What is the proper balance between the individual and the collective?

As the world's population grows exponentially with each century, we find ourselves dealing with challenges never confronted by earlier generations. How do my purchases at the department store affect workers in third-world countries? By voting for a candidate, how will the economies of distant regions be affected? How are *my* values and thoughts influenced by global society through the media? Can any of us retain our unique vision in a mass society that numbers in the billions? The lives of the masses and those of individuals are intertwined to such an extent now that we are being forced to reexamine who we really are.

This chapter looks at events from the 1990s relevant to this dynamic between individual and collective, and the connection to factors like the media and celebrity.

Saddam Hussein vs. the United Nations

In late 1990, Iraq's Saddam Hussein sent his military forces across the border into Kuwait and claimed authority over a region which had been a source of territorial dispute for years. In response, American president George Bush convened with his allies to form an international coalition of nations to rebuke Iraq's advances, and in mid-January of 1991 the Gulf War began.

All wars occurring near the cusp of a new Great Age tend to reflect the thematic dynamics of that shift, through the symbols and issues involved in the conflict. In the Gulf War, several factors relate it to the Aquarian Age and the individual/collective dynamic.

The most significant outer-planet configuration taking place at the time was a major configuration between the signs Aquarius (the group) and Leo (the individual), involving Saturn and Jupiter. (These planets stood in direct opposition to each other on March 15, 1991, just as Bush and his allies were "mopping up" in the wake of their victory.) The actions of the parties on both sides of the war perfectly mirrored the qualities of the astrological principles. Aquarius rules groups and alliances of all types, so with constrictive Saturn situated there, it's expected we'd see a multinational group assuming a disciplinary role to enforce "law and order" on the world stage. Jupiter in royal Leo was reflected in the expansionist intentions of Hussein—the man who would be king. In the interaction of these two forces—global alliance versus Hussein—the Gulf War acted out the themes of the Leo/Aquarius opposition, showing how the power of the collective checks the actions of an individual leader.

Apart from the controversial politics of this war (watch *Three Kings* to get a quick introduction to that), we can draw some lessons from the symbols thrown up around this conflict. During the Aquarian Age, we will surely see many examples of how the individual and the group can affect each other, in constructive or destructive ways. The individual can support or heal the larger collective, or it can disrupt it. The collective may support the individual, or it can actively oppress it. The important point is: the group isn't a necessarily bad thing. After all, we approve of society containing or reprimanding its criminals, who would otherwise run free without those collectively imposed limits. The problem is, in the Aquarian Age the group could become so powerful it could prove difficult for *any* individual—law-abiding or otherwise—to go about his business without the mass mind checking up on him. The collective may set limits on our "negative heroes" like gangsters Al Capone or John Gotti, but it can just as easily set limits on an emerging Buddha or Jesus as well. The dynamics of the Gulf War are an expression of how the group can effectively limit an individual or nation single-mindedly pursuing its own interests, for better or worse.

What is striking about the Gulf War is how closely it was paralleled by another development: the notorious Rodney King incident of March 1991. A black motorist outran the Los Angeles police one night after a routine traffic stop; on being caught, he was beaten into submission with clubs by the police. As with the Gulf War, the event was caught on videotape and broadcast around the world, making it the other leading news story of the period. We saw how a group of disciplinary figures (the police) could check the actions of a lone "expansionist" figure. The Rodney King incident illustrated how the principle of Aquarian collectivity can be a limiting force on Leo individuality. Nor should we overlook the irony of the last name of this hapless motorist: *King*. And speaking of royalty . . .

The Mythic Life and Death of Princess Diana

On the surface, you can hardly imagine two more different individuals than Saddam Hussein and the late Princess Diana. Yet in her way, she was also an example of the struggle between the individual and the collective.

A key expression of the Aquarian Age is the rise of "people power," and the importance of the collective as a force in the world. One result of this has been the corresponding decline in the influence of monarchies (Leo), as kings, queens, and royal figures of all types come under attack from society. While we may not decapitate our crowned heads anymore, we still "persecute" them in other ways through our invasive attacks on their privacy through the global media (an Aquarius initiative). Celebrities these days are a moving target for people-watchers everywhere; add the element of royalty to the mix, and the result is explosive.

The life of Princess Di was a prime example of this development. Not only was she a celebrity and a royal, but she was blond and glamorous. Jackpot. Her every comment and action became the subject of intense scrutiny (and often criticism) by the world's press. With the Leo/Aquarius axis underscored in her horoscope (b. July 1, 1961), her adult life was entwined with the individual/group dynamic, as she found herself arguably the most sought-after personality on Earth. This symbolism was woven into the circumstances surrounding her death, as she fled photographers down the city streets of Paris. Later, Parisian officials attributed the crash to intoxication on the part of the driver, though few believe that the driver would have been speeding in the first place had there not been paparazzi in pursuit.

We are left with this image: A royal "star" dies while fleeing members of the international media. It is surely one of the archetypal images of recent times, yet another example of the Leo principle brought to bay by the collective energies of Aquarius. Upon hearing of her death, I wondered whether there might be any configurations between these two zodiacal signs at the moment of the crash. In fact, I thought, it would be especially fitting if it turned out that part of this configuration involved the moon in Leo. That's because the moon is a symbol for femininity, Leo a symbol for royalty, and Princess Di a symbol of female royalty. The horoscope for August 31, 1997 (12:25 A.M. CED; Paris, France), showed that was the case: the moon was positioned in Leo during that fatal moment, forming a polarity with planets in Aquarius. This seemed to confirm the fact that this event held implications for the culture at large, in terms of the growing tension between personal interests (represented by Diana) and those of the masses (represented by the world's media).

In a related vein, shortly after her death several other developments took place almost as dramatic in their implications. The British royal family was brought to its knees by popular criticism in the wake of their cool reaction to Diana's death. The public felt the royals were a bit *too* removed from the public outpouring of grief following her death; consequently, the royal family felt compelled to make unprecedented public statements on television, even to mingle with the "commoners" who had come to offer their condolences. As some television commentators said at the time, it was all a remarkable display of "royalty bowing to people power."

The final *coup de grâce* was delivered by singer Elton John, who sang his tribute to Di in Westminster Abbey during the memorial service. To conservative sensibilities, this pop star's performance in these otherwise hallowed halls nearly bordered on sacrilege; yet like Di's death, it further highlighted the broader democratization taking place in our culture, as the distinction between "high" and "low" culture becomes increasingly indistinguishable.

There is another lesson to be drawn from the life and death of Princess Di vis-à-vis the Aquarian Age, relating to the uneasy tension and ironic relation that has begun to develop between the phenomena of *stardom* and *personal privacy*. In the last chapter we touched on the phenomenon of celebrity, and the modern tendency of unknowns to become stars. "We can be heroes," David Bowie once sang, "if just for one day." Yes, we *can* find fame and fortune nowadays, but there is a price; for while modern telecommunications afford us greater access now to the eyes and ears of the world, so *the eyes and ears of the world have greater access to our own private lives.* The same media revolution that is making it possible for one's personal star to shine before the entire world has a more invasive side, in the way it invites the entire world into that star's private life. Moreover, the process is proportional, in that the more famous one is, the more likely one's personal space will be violated.

Few people dramatized this as vividly as Princess Di. She was a premiere graduate of our star-making academy, thrust out of obscurity to become a worldwide pop legend. The flip side was that she spent her adult life in a fishbowl, subject to the scrutiny of the global press. With every word and deed recorded for posterity, she found her life had become an open book for the world to see.

The problem is one that's beginning to affect us all: In the Aquarian Age, each of us will find the line increasingly blurred between public and private life, as the issue of personal privacy moves to the forefront of our concerns. As the world becomes increasingly interconnected through technology, information about our personal habits is becoming available to all, not only through the media but through databanks on our spending habits and communications (e.g., phone records and e-mail), and surveillance cameras and spy satellites recording our public activities. As a further illustration of this trend, let us turn now to another incident from the late 1990s, the strange case of Monica Lewinsky.

The Clinton/Lewinsky Scandal

A powerful older man falls for a flirtatious younger woman—it's a tale as old as time itself, and certainly nothing unusual in the backroom dealings of Washington politics. So what caused this dalliance of a president with an intern to become the global scandal that it did? World leaders had engaged in many such trysts before, including American presidents, but generally with impunity. There were many real-world factors that contributed to the formation of this scandal, among them partisan politics and the mounting evidence of indiscretions by a world leader. But as with the death of Princess Di, there were deep archetypal currents at work here, too.

It is well-known among astrologers that Clinton and Lewinsky are Leos, and share surprisingly similar horoscopes. What is less widely known is how closely this scandal played itself out in relation to planetary energies in

Aquarius throughout its duration. The scandal first erupted into public attention on the very day a planetary lineup in Aquarius kicked into high gear on January 20, 1998.[1] The Aquarian symbolism underlying this configuration foreshadowed the heavy media attention that would eventually surround this event. The scandal played itself out over the following months, and like clockwork came to its welcome conclusion one year later as another Aquarian configuration peaked in intensity, in the form of a solar eclipse in Aquarius during February 1999. Traditionally, eclipses symbolically amplify whatever zodiacal areas they touch, and here that involved Aquarian themes of global media and the mass mind.

The key point here is that these configurations at both ends of the scandal formed powerful relationships with the Leo planets in both Clinton's and Lewinsky's personal horoscopes, thus indicating the importance of the Leo/Aquarius polarity within this scandal.

As in the life and death of Princess Di, the Clinton/Lewinsky scandal illustrates some important aspects of the relation between the individual and the collective. Just as we have seen heightened attacks on royalty by media in recent times, here was an event that involved Leo-figures subject to unprecedented scrutiny by the global media (with help from an enterprising prosecutor and numerous political opponents). It provides another illustration of the stardom/privacy issue, for here were two figures who had come from obscure backgrounds to become preeminent "stars" of our times; one as the direct result of the scandal, the other as a result of a long-standing political career. Yet they found the most intimate details of their lives being dragged out and paraded on public view before a world stage. Bob Dylan once sang that "even the President of the United States sometimes must have to stand naked," and here was an example of that: the world's most powerful leader stripped bare for public scrutiny. Also noteworthy was the way this scandal centered on a matter of personal pleasure, an area specifically associated by astrologers with Leo.

During the peak of the scandal, an editorial appeared in *The New York Times* written by a black professor who suggested that one key reason black Americans sympathized with Clinton in this situation was their appreciation of the right to privacy. While living in slavery, this right had been denied them; as this professor pointed out, it is among the most important of all rights, for when this goes, our democratic system is put in jeopardy. To that extent, the Clinton/Lewinsky scandal, like Princess Di's life and death, touched on a fundamental problem of the Aquarian Age: Our lives are becoming entwined with the life of a global society, but our personal space is being compromised in the process through telecommunications technology. Whether we know it or not, we are *all* surrounded by the eyes of the world now, or as protesters during the 1960s said, "The whole world is watching."

Further Clues from the Cinema

Keeping my eye open for further synchronistic clues in the environment during this period, I was intrigued to see that, as the Clinton/Lewinsky scandal was unfolding, several films appeared that centered on the privacy theme.

For example, in the summer of 1998, Peter Weir's *The Truman Show* detailed the story of a man whose life had been the subject of media coverage since his birth, yet he didn't know it. Every day and night, he was watched avidly by millions of TV viewers who followed his story like a soap opera. As in the case of Clinton and Lewinsky, the eyes of the world were focused on Truman, his most private details dragged into view, no dark corners left, no hidden facts, as everything was laid bare. The film demonstrates the way our lives are becoming increasingly infiltrated by media of all types.

That same year saw the release of another film, the action-thriller *Enemy of the State*. A private citizen suddenly finds himself at the mercy of a high-tech global surveillance system. Suspected of possessing something the government desperately wants (and which has been planted on his body unbeknownst to him), his movements are carefully tracked by an elaborate array of snooping devices that can observe virtually every action he undertakes. This involves satellites, infrared cameras, public surveillance cameras, and data retrieval systems, all of which provide the governmental officials observing him with volumes of information concerning his lifestyle and personal preferences. The message of the film is that if this could happen to this one individual, it could happen to any or all of us.[2]

It is interesting to see how prominent a role the invasion of privacy theme also played in Welles' *Citizen Kane*. It is underscored by the recurring motif of Kane's tabloid, *The Inquirer*, digging up dirt on various figures to boost its circulation; the theme is alluded to in the media exposé of Kane's extramarital affair (shades of Clinton/Lewinsky), and it's punctuated by the secret newsreel footage of an elderly Kane in his wheelchair. It is also evident in the way the film is presented from the viewpoint of a media reporter whose job is to probe into the private life of the movie's title character. Hoping to uncover the meaning of this dying man's final word, "Rosebud," the reporter travels cross-country for the most intimate details of this figure's life to put on public display.

Examples like these evoke George Orwell's Big Brother concept and Jeremy Bentham's notion of the "panopticon," a circular penitentiary in which every move of its prisoners can be observed. As time goes by, fictional constructs like these seem to turn into reality, as we find ourselves exposed to the intense gaze of electronic eyes on seemingly every front. As their proponents claim, there are probably some benefits to these technologies, in terms of monitoring and apprehending criminals, but what are the risks to our liberties? In a way, we are *all* becoming visible before omnipresent eyes. At the snap of a finger, any of these surveillance cameras might be turned on you or me, and on some occasions, they have—such as in the wake of the Tiananmen Square massacre in China in 1989. There, public video cameras were used by Chinese authorities to track protesters, leading in many cases to imprisonment or execution.

There is a direct link in democracy between personal freedoms and right to privacy, as affirmed by the Fourth Amendment. Tamper with the one, and you affect the other, since no one who is subject to the prying eyes of the community or government can ever consider him or herself completely free. In the Aquarian Age, we will all be interconnected; the question is, can we hang onto our hard-won liberties at the same time?

The Modern Ego under Siege

A deeper message can be drawn from these developments when they're viewed as symbols. Notice how in these cases, Leos or Leo-type figures (dictators, royalty, performers) are under attack from the collective, especially through the media. To say it another way: the Leo principle is under siege by the forces of Aquarius.

But what is the Leo principle? This archetype stands for the personal ego, that kingly consciousness in each of us that strives to shine before all in its glory. The cases here can be interpreted as large-scale reflections of an "attack" waged on the individualized ego; in the Aquarian Age, it is ultimately the system which is king, not the individual. Consequently, the challenge facing each of us will be maintaining our autonomy and integrity as individualized selves. Can we retain a sense of who we really are in the coming age?

As with all of the trends considered in this book, this one can be interpreted in a negative or positive light. As a destructive force, it points to the insidious possibilities that may confront individuals in a mass society, especially in dealing with a mass telecommunications system. Our identity is gradually becoming spread out across the world as volumes of information about our personal lives are distributed through the global information network. Developments like these are making it increasingly hard for any one person to maintain control over her own life.

In a similar way, this trend poses problems in terms of our ability to think for ourselves. When we are barraged by information, how do we know which ideas are ours and which have been implanted through our environment? How does an individual express her creative vision in an increasingly entrenched "system" where personal creativity is so often squelched? In *The Matrix,* humans who attempt to awaken from a technologically imposed slumber are violently repressed by agents of the system. These repressive figures might be seen as personifications of the inertia and constrictiveness of *any* "system," corporate, governmental, or technological. This doesn't necessarily make such forces evil, just problematic for our efforts to break free from their system. For better or worse, Saddam Hussein, Rodney King, Princess Di, and President Clinton illustrate what happens to individuals who attempt to "do their own thing," to express their Leo "star" a bit *too* brightly. Films like *The Truman Show* exemplify the same "heroic" challenge of the coming age, for just as Truman had to break free of his media-saturated world, we may also need to break free of the mass mind to become ourselves and to forge our own creative visions.

A more positive way of reading this situation is from a spiritual standpoint; the seeming "attack" on the ego may be part of a larger transformation needing to occur in our conventional sense of identity.

Perhaps the conventional ego can no longer afford to remain insular, encircled by provincial beliefs and viewpoints. The rise of global culture is forcing us to push beyond our ordinary boundaries and assume a more complex viewpoint, or set of viewpoints. There is no more room for kings or queens in our world, but this change may tell us we cannot enter the coming age with defined personal or tribal boundaries anymore, as was possible in earlier times. Lest we become anachronisms, surviving in the new world will require us to broaden our senses of who we each are, and learn to develop a kaleidoscopic self. This will be the subject of later chapters.

12

The *Challenger* Disaster—
Anatomy of a Modern Omen

No one who was watching that cold morning in January of 1986 will ever forget the sight of the shuttle lifting off its launch pad and moments later exploding into pieces and falling back down to earth. As the first in-air disaster of this magnitude ever to befall the United States space program, it was a jarring moment for those who might have grown complacent about humanity's capacity for technological achievement.

For the symbolist, no event stands completely alone, and that is all the more true in those cases where the event is unique or impacts the culture in deep ways. In the case of the *Challenger* disaster, both of these were true. The symbols constellated around this tragedy encode a wealth of clues about the lessons and challenges of the coming era. Yet to fully understand these we need to see this event in a larger context, within the broader history of aviation.

Uranus and the Birth of Aviation

The period surrounding the discovery of Uranus in 1781 was important as it heralded an awakening of Aquarian themes in our world. When any new planet is discovered, it mirrors an inner awakening in consciousness;

Uranus takes on special significance in that it was the first new planet to be discovered in recorded history.

For thousands of years, humans had believed there was a divine order in the known system of seven visible planets. The discovery of Uranus overturned all that, forcing us to acknowledge a larger cosmic reality. As such, Uranus became the transitional symbol in marking the boundaries between our solar system and the cosmos. The astrologer Dane Rudhyar called Uranus an "ambassador to the galaxy," in terms of bridging the "personal" cosmos with the "collective" cosmos, the local with the universal. The discovery of Uranus represented a momentous crossing of boundaries in our evolution, symbolizing our awakening to a more universal perspective, a more cosmic rationality. That this planet would eventually be associated in meaning with Aquarius further cements its place in the emerging of a new Age.

Hence it is during the late 1700s that we see humanity throwing off the shackles of traditional values and limitations to open itself to new possibilities. It was a time of enormous strides in democracy, the advent of the industrial revolution and capitalism, and a newly awakened faith in the powers of rationality. Many became convinced that *anything* was possible. Freedom—political, financial, material—became a hope for millions. Prometheus is a most fitting mythic figure to illustrate the heroic mood of those times, with its concern for independence and the rebellion against tyrannical structures and traditions.

Were we to pick any one symbol or invention from that time to embody the new spirit of freedom, it would be the birth of aviation. On November 21, 1783, two years after the discovery of Uranus, the Montgolfier brothers undertook their hot-air balloon flight from the Tuileries Gardens in Paris. It was the first time on record that humans had embarked on a lighter-than-air voyage.[1] For millennia, men and women had dreamed of transcending gravity to soar through the air; 1783 saw the first step toward realizing that dream.

As a symbol, that step represented an enormous shift in human consciousness; our ability to defeat gravity and rise off the Earth became the metaphor for humanity's new spirit of independence, its breaking free of limitations associated with the Saturn principle on many levels (materiality, tradition, and boundaries of all types) and graduating into more expansive possibilities of mind.[2] In a way, it seems fitting that just weeks earlier, this same Paris location hosted the signing of the Treaty of Versailles, the document formally conceding victory to America in the War for Independence against England.

1977—Discovering the Rings of Uranus

Let us fast-forward several centuries and look at another shift in our scientific understanding of Uranus through an event in 1977. That year scientists announced they had discovered rings around this far-off planet, a feature previously associated only with Saturn. For esotericists, rings have long been regarded as symbols of limitation and restriction. Rings set boundaries in our life, and help bring things into a tight focus. That isn't necessarily bad; after all, when we want to show our commitment in love we put rings on our fingers, indicating we will channel our devotion to one person. But it was surprising to find a symbolic feature like this associated with a planet normally identified with freedom and transcending limits.

What could this mean? Could it be saying there is more to our old Uranian friend than meets the eye? A possible clue lies within the headlines of the time.

That same week in 1977 there occurred the single worst aviation disaster in history. On March 27th, two 787 Boeing jet airliners collided on a runway in the Canary Islands, leaving 583 people dead and many others injured. From a synchronistic standpoint, the timing of this aviation tragedy in relation to the discovery of Uranian rings suggested there might be a more constrictive side to this planet than previously realized. When Uranus was discovered, technology and rationality were seen as largely positive forces, holding the answers to all our problems. But after several centuries of unchecked growth, the great dream of techno-rationality had gradually revealed a different face. Perhaps it wasn't the key to our ultimate freedom after all.

The Canary Islands disaster dramatized the problems that can arise with the energies of Uranus if we are not careful. This planet brought certain distinct gifts, including technology and scientific rationality, yet even these have limits and boundaries which have to be respected. Failing to recognize this invites disaster. Make no mistake: Uranus is not a planet to be taken lightly, as the collision of the two jets on the runway—the result of human error—made abundantly clear.

It was shortly after investigating this crash that I began turning my attention to another event that was scheduled to occur years later, and which also promised to play an important role in the unfolding drama of this ringed planet: the *Voyager II* mission to Uranus in early 1986.

The *Voyager II* Mission to Uranus

In 1977, NASA launched the *Voyager II* spacecraft to sweep past the outer planets (excepting Pluto) of our solar system to provide close-ups of these planets surpassing any previously attained using Earthbound telescopes. It would pass by Neptune later on in 1989, but in January of 1986, it was timed to rendezvous with Uranus. This was an exciting prospect because it would be our first close-up glimpse of the planet most directly associated with the Age of Aquarius, and thus might provide a "future window" for the coming era. So I decided to pay attention to all events taking place up to and surrounding the fly-by.

But what *sort* of events? Would there be powerful breakthroughs in science and technology? Humanitarian actions and social reforms? Or something like the Canary Islands disaster, highlighting the constrictive side of technology and the Uranian principle? This latter scenario was at least a possibility, since we would be getting a close-up look at not only the planet but its ring system.

As it turned out, the months and weeks leading up to the fly-by were a curious blend of positive and negative possibilities. It was a time of exciting scientific developments and breakthroughs. In astronomy, just weeks before *Voyager II*'s closest approach, astrophysicist Margaret Geller announced her findings about the large-scale structure of the universe. Computerized three-dimensional maps of the galaxies suggested the presence of large bubble-shaped structures strewn throughout the cosmos, something at odds with existing views of how our universe should have formed, since it was long presumed to have been more uniform.

At the same time, an intriguing announcement came out of Purdue University by physics professor Ephraim Fischbach and colleagues on the possible existence of a previously unknown force in the universe they called "hyper-charge," a potential fifth force in the universe. What is intriguing about this theory was the way the "hyper-charge" force seemed to resonate so closely with the qualities of Uranus, which itself represents a kind of counter-principle to gravity, or Saturn. Fischbach's theory of "hyper-charge" likewise seemed akin to anti-gravity, being repulsive rather than attractive in nature. Fischbach's theorized force has never been fully confirmed, even though for our purposes it was a symbolic expression of the time.[3]

Darker clouds loomed on the horizon, too. For example, the period leading up to the fly-by saw an unusual number of aviation disasters around the
world; in fact, 1985 was the worst year for aviation disasters in history. In
mid-December, 1985, one month prior to the fly-by, scientists announced
they had their first sight of the Uranian rings through the *Voyager II* lens as
it made its approach; within twenty-four hours of that announcement, on
December 12, a DC-8 carrying 258 military personnel crashed on take-off in
Gander, Newfoundland, killing all aboard. It was the eighth worst aviation
disaster up to that time.

With developments like these, might the *Voyager II* fly-by synchronistically usher in something comparable in terms of an aviation disaster? As a
way to put the symbolist perspective to the test, and see whether its general
principles could be used to make predictions rather than just applied in
hindsight, I wrote letters to several colleagues expressing my concerns over
the possibility of a major aviation disaster in the days surrounding the
Voyager II fly-by on January 26, 1986. To a friend of mine at the University
of Chicago, I went further still and predicted that this could involve the
space shuttle, since I knew there would be a launch about that time.[4]

The *Voyager II* spacecraft was scheduled to make its closest approach to
Uranus on Friday, January 24, 1986; meanwhile, NASA announced that the
photos from this rendezvous would not be computer processed and released
to the public until the Monday following the fly-by. Nothing particularly dramatic occurred that Friday, so I waited to see what unfolded in the days
ahead. A curious thing happened late that weekend. Prior to take-off, the
Challenger's seven crew members posed for a photo staged by Cape
Canaveral: they sat around a table spread with food, just like DaVinci's *Last
Supper*. Perhaps this sort of thing had been done prior to shuttle take-offs
before, but I had never seen it, at least not on newscasts.

The morning of the launch arrived, Monday, January 28. The crew
members filed down the gangway onto the spacecraft, and a flight techni-
cian handed civilian astronaut Christa McAuliffe an apple. Late that same
morning (following a full moon between the signs Leo and Aquarius), the
Challenger roared off its launch pad and exploded seventy-three seconds
later at an altitude of 46,000 feet. The tragedy occurred within hours of
researchers obtaining their first look at the close-up photos of Uranus and
its ring system. Several synchronicities occurred in the wake of this event:
for example, the next day a rare earthquake shook New England in the
region astronaut Christa McAuliffe hailed from. Even more intriguing,

investigations later revealed that the cause of the shuttle disaster involved defective "O-rings"—a suggestive link with the ringed symbolism of Uranus itself.

Anatomy of a Tragedy

How do we begin to make sense of this event? The significance here is complex and multilayered, and once again requires that we step back and see the historical context.

I have suggested that aviation represents one of the great symbols of the Aquarian spirit, with its optimism and Promethean belief that there is nothing we cannot accomplish, given time and resources. Early on, this trend took the form of hot-air balloons, then later the airplane and the jet, and finally rocket technology. With its unprecedented capacity for transcending gravity and rising off the Earth, the rocket has become a premiere symbol for the Aquarian spirit of freedom and the desire to overcome limitations.

As with the Canary Islands disaster of 1977, the destruction of a great rocket that came just as we were obtaining our first close-up look at Uranus in 1986 says something about the limits of that original heroic dream. We were realizing some of the problems and dangers of the powerful forces we had awakened, even though they once seemed an unqualified source of boundless freedom. In a way, it was as if something were coming full circle from that first point in 1781. If you look at the events surrounding the shuttle disaster, you find problems arising in all the areas mentioned earlier in connection with the late eighteenth century: people power, capitalism, and technology. Since these are areas connected to the Aquarian Age, by carefully examining them in relation to the shuttle disaster, we can gain insight into key emerging trends.

People Power: The latter half of the eighteenth century was a time when Europeans and Americans were feeling emboldened by the possibilities of people power, as evidenced in the rise of modern democracy. But another long-term result of this shift was the eventual development of unions which provided workers with a voice in management. Over time, this would prove to have constructive and destructive effects. Fittingly, in the weeks surrounding the *Voyager II* fly-by, a rash of union-related problems occurred, the most dramatic example of which was the protracted strike at the Hormel meat-packing plant in Minnesota; it lasted several years. On the night preceding the fly-by, *Nightline* devoted its half-hour to examining unions and their problems. With the discovery of Uranus in the eighteenth century, ordinary individuals had awakened to the enormous power they wielded en masse; yet during the period accompanying our closest view of this planet, TV showed us the problems that can arise from "people power," and which may continue to pose challenges in various ways during the age ahead.

Capitalism: Another area where developments appeared to have come "full-circle" was capitalism, which assumed its modern form during the period coinciding with the discovery of Uranus. More than ever before, individuals during the late eighteenth century found they had the option of creating their own wealth, equipped with nothing more than ingenuity and effort. One can readily see the important role the entrepreneurial spirit played in the forging of early America, providing an incentive for ordinary people who dreamed of success and economic freedom. It was the Horatio Alger ideal.

Yet over time, ironically, that same trend made possible the rise of corporations and bureaucracies whose spirit at times ran counter to that original impulse, stifling competition and individual entrepreneurs. In this respect, the period of the shuttle disaster is significant, as it occurred during the reign of Ronald Reagan whose administration was widely viewed as among the most sympathetic in recent history to corporate interests. It was a time of massive deregulation, when large businesses were given free reign to pursue their economic goals in whatever ways they saw fit. Indeed, the 1980s would be called the "decade of greed," a sentiment summarized in Oliver Stone's 1987 film, *Wall Street*, in which the main character chants, "Greed is good!" The American dream certainly didn't die during the 1980s, but it did seem at times as though it were being auctioned off to the highest bidder. The shuttle disaster mirrored the sense of disillusionment many felt about these corrupted ideals. The fact that it involved the first civilian to enter space further underscored how the "average" person was being caught up in these processes.

Another capitalistic issue was highlighted by the accident. Though the precipitating cause of the shuttle's failure was faulty O-rings, the broader issue cited by some critics was a failure of bureaucracy. Not only because of cost-cutting measures in the shuttle's construction, but the tangled web of interdepartmental communications that surrounded the entire mission from start to finish was a classic case of one hand not knowing what the other was doing. So the shuttle disaster may hold clues about the potential challenges we face in the Aquarian era, with respect to ever-larger bureaucracies.

Technology: The shuttle disaster brought things full circle from the late 1700s in terms of technology. The Industrial Revolution ushered in a spirit of great possibility; gave us greater control over nature; provided us with innumerable conveniences; gave us a new mobility through new ways of travel; and enhanced communications and forms of media. The rocket is the crowning achievement of this. I once watched a night launch of a space shuttle near Cape Canaveral, and what struck me most as this machine careened into the night sky was what a marvel of group effort and ingenuity it was: millions of interlocking parts, put together by thousands of skilled workers. If the construction of a Gothic cathedral represented the pooling of hearts toward a single goal, the rocket represents a pooling of minds in a single effort. This invention brings together all the key threads of modern technology.

So the destruction of the shuttle in tandem with our first close-up view of Uranus was a deflation of those technological dreams.[5] There was something synchronistic in the fact that shortly after the shuttle tragedy we saw another technological disaster: the Chernobyl near-meltdown of April 26, 1986. As a result, thousands died or were permanently disabled, and nearly a million more faced an uncertain future. If the modern environmentalist movement began with Rachel Carson's *Silent Spring* in 1962, it came to a head with Chernobyl in 1986. Both the Chernobyl and *Challenger* tragedies revealed how, for all its potential, technology is a volatile force to be handled with great caution.

Stepping Out of the Garden

Does all this mean the shuttle disaster was in some sense a bad omen for the coming age? Not necessarily. Like many of history's great events, the message here is subtle and might hold constructive aspects when seen in an evolutionary context.

With every major step in evolution, the door is opened to greater possibilities and achievements and greater risks and problems. When a child first learns to ride a bike, her horizon of consciousness is opened to new sights and possibilities; yet the child also runs the risk of falling and hurting herself. Each new advance comes with a price, and it seems to grow in proportion to the benefits acquired. But this cost isn't a punishment for that advance or a sign of failure. By way of analogy, when seen in isolation, the bruise on the child's knee after her first fall could be construed by other children as proving the child's foolishness, perhaps even the "evils" of bicycles! Viewed in a larger context, the injury is an inevitable result of the evolutionary process, the kinds of mistakes that accompany any learning curve. So while the other children may not have blemishes on their knees, neither are they growing in their skills.

The message here is that what seems superficially to be a "fall" can sometimes be a step *forward* in evolution. It's a tale as old as the Garden of Eden itself; for while humanity's step out of the Garden made us more vulnerable to suffering and the problems of mortal existence, it also signaled, from an esoteric standpoint, humanity's awakening into consciousness, and the possibility of becoming "like unto the gods." (Or, in the words of Saint Augustine, *O felix culpa!*—"O happy fault!") To a certain extent, this double-edged quality applies to *every* major advance in consciousness; each time we move to another level of growth there is a certain "loss of innocence" as old illusions are stripped away, and in their place new horizons and possibilities arise.

This was a point made brilliantly in the 1998 film *Pleasantville*, which centered on the often-heard belief that "things used to be so much better back in the old days than they are now." In the movie, that viewpoint is exemplified by black-and-white television shows of the 1950s, which portrayed our world in morally black or white ways. Weaving an ingenious fantasy to make its point, the film shows two teenagers getting mysteriously sucked into this 1950s-style television world. What they eventually discover is that, yes, things were "simpler" back then, but also less evolved and less conscious. By comparison, the film argues, the complexity of our time makes our society that much richer than past times. True, there has been a loss of innocence, yet in some ways, that is the hallmark of growth in consciousness.

For most critics, this film was seen as drawing a contrast between the simplistic 1950s and the complex 1990s. Yet for me the genius of its script was the subtle way it used this concept to make a point about *any and all* of life's transitions, from our entrance into puberty to our awakening into moral complexity. The film draws upon a web of metaphors that allude to many types of "threshold crossings" in our life, and it throws in a few references to the Garden of Eden story. The message is this: All growth experiences involve a movement from simplicity to complexity, and with that movement comes greater possibilities *and* greater problems, because it's inherent to the growth process.[6]

This same message holds an important lesson for the Aquarian Age as well. Starting around the time of Uranus's discovery in 1781, humanity symbolically crossed over an important threshold in its development, as we opened up to a new type of cosmic rationality with all it entails. The result is that we now have greater knowledge about the forces of the universe, but also a greater capacity to destroy ourselves in the process.

This message was reinforced when *Voyager II* crossed the orbital path of Uranus in early 1986, and the space shuttle self-destructed before millions of horrified viewers. Like the Chernobyl disaster shortly thereafter, the symbols centering around this event illustrated the magnitude of the problems we're exposed to now, not just with technology but big business, "people power," and scientific rationality in general. We are acting out the tale of the Sorcerer's Apprentice, but on a grand scale now, as we learn to deal with the promises and perils the energies Uranus has opened us to. It's probable we will make further mistakes as we continue grappling with these forces; yet it would be premature to automatically interpret these as signs of *failure*.

So returning to our question: was the *Challenger* explosion a "bad omen" for the coming age? We may as well ask whether the bruise on the child's knee after she's fallen down spells disaster for her future in riding bicycles.

13

Ganymede and the Cosmic Brotherhood

One day, I had lunch with some friends at a restaurant. I found myself drawn into a heated conversation about intelligent life elsewhere in the universe and whether humanity had already been in contact with them. One friend was open to the possibility, while the other was skeptical; not only was it highly improbable, he said, but it was all fundamentally irrelevant. "Even if there *are* other races out there," he explained, "I frankly don't see the importance of it all for us. There are just so many other pressing problems in our world right now."

An understandable reaction, and one I've grappled with for years. But playing Devil's advocate for a moment, I posed this question to my friend: "If you were a journalist and could be transported back in time to Europe in 1492, what single news story would you most want to cover?" After all, there were many pressing social issues during that time, and some fairly convoluted court politics. But in terms of stories with the longest-range impact on the world, is there any doubt which was the most important of the time, the one most of us would choose to cover?

The same thing might apply to our time on the question of extraterrestrial intelligence. Yes, there are many pressing issues demanding our attention now; but if it *does* turn out that humanity has had (or is about to have) contact with extraterrestrial intelligences, it would certainly rank as among the most important developments of our time. Like Columbus's arrival in America, it would open our minds to new worlds and new ways of thinking, with repercussions on our technologies, arts, religion, and politics.

If the symbolism of the Aquarian Age is an indicator, it's a safe bet that such contact will indeed be a key factor in humanity's future. More than any other, Aquarius is the zodiacal sign most associated by astrologers with the stars and space travel. With Aquarius's cosmic focus, the prospect of extraterrestrial contact seems natural.

The presumed element of anti-gravity associated with UFOs similarly holds a resonance with Aquarius. In our last chapter, we saw the close link between Aquarius and aviation through the air symbolism underlying both, and noted that aviation counters gravity, the "Saturn" principle. Anti-gravity takes this concept a step further, with its suggestion of a full-blown defeat of gravity. The disclosure of anti-gravity technologies by the government would certainly be an important milestone in the ushering in of Aquarian sensibilities.

The Once—or Future?—Contact

The big question is: Have they already been here?

If one accepts as valid even a fraction of the stories that have come to light over the years, one has to conclude that *something* peculiar is going on in our skies. Having looked at both sides of this question for years, I strongly believe that the UFO phenomenon represents a mystery that could involve nonhuman intelligences, though whether those prove to be terrestrial, extraterrestrial, or extra-dimensional is still to be determined.[1] It is worth taking a few moments to address some of the pointed objections to the UFO matter:

The distances separating solar systems in space are too vast to make interstellar travel practical.

This oft-heard argument rests on the assumption that our level of technology represents the zenith of all possible knowledge everywhere. Yet look at how far we have come in just the last century, from the Wright Brothers to men on the moon. Considering the antiquity of the universe, it isn't hard to imagine that civilizations thousands of years older than ours might have solved certain problems of physics still vexing us, including travel through the universe.

If there are UFOs visiting our world, where is the hard evidence?

Though alien crafts may not have landed on the White House lawn yet, considerable evidence suggests that something unexplained is moving through our skies. As leading UFO researcher Stanton Friedman has sometimes remarked, people have been sentenced to death with less proof than what exists for UFOs. This includes such things as anomalous trace evidence found at UFO sites; thousands of eyewitness accounts from trained observers around the world, sometimes confirmed by radar; and most intriguing of all, the growing testimonies by current or past governmental figures like astronauts Edgar Mitchell, Gordon Cooper, or the late Colonel Philip Corso, who have argued that the UFO phenomenon is genuine.

Large-scale cover-ups on matters like this are unlikely, since the government can't keep a secret even about small things, let alone a historic story.

As history demonstrates, this is untrue. There have been many instances in which governments have successfully kept important secrets from an inquisitive public for decades on end. One example is the news that the U.S. government conducted radioactivity experiments with plutonium on its citizens for many years, a fact divulged only decades later in the early 1990s. As some noted at the time, how many other stories like this are out there waiting to be uncovered?

But another fact to consider is this: Major secrets *can* be successfully kept—providing they are so outrageous no one would believe them even if they *were* leaked. Rumors of FBI director J. Edgar Hoover's homosexuality and his propensity for dressing in drag floated around for years. Assume these stories are true: What would have happened if someone close to Hoover had gone to the press with this news in the late 1950s? Not a major newspaper or magazine would have touched it; not only would it have seemed unbelievable, it would have been *explosive.*

This same point can be made about stories involving the government's involvement with UFO technology. Until recently, such stories have seemed so outrageous that no respectable news office has dared touch them. In fact, it's only been since former government figures themselves began telling their stories about these developments that mainstream media outlets have begun featuring them, even then, with some skepticism.

It may well be that posterity will look back on the hard-core UFO skeptics in the same way we view the contemporaries of Galileo who refused to look through the telescope, thinking there couldn't *possibly* be moons orbiting Jupiter. Fortunately, for our purposes, it doesn't matter whether these stories are true or not. We can explore them for their symbolism, and the clues they hold for the Aquarian Age.

The Heavenly Abduction of Ganymede

The mythic figure most associated in the Western mind with the constellation of Aquarius is Ganymede. He was said to have been the most beautiful youth alive. While watching over his father's sheep, he was abducted into the heavens by Zeus, where he became immortal and a servant to the gods. How is this relevant today? It is interesting that just as we are entering an age ruled by a tale of heavenly abduction, we see a proliferation of accounts from around the world about people being abducted by celestial beings. There have been stories of abductions throughout history, such as the fairy legends of Celtic lore or the Biblical ascension of Enoch, yet there is no question this phenomenon has accelerated in recent decades since the Betty and Barney Hill case of 1961, which seemed to start it all off.

The abduction motif figures prominently in many of our notable science fiction films, such as *Close Encounters of the Third Kind,* in which a beautiful young boy was abducted into the heavens. The 1998 film *Dark City* describes an entire city abducted by aliens; the closing portion of Kubrick's *2001: A Space Odyssey* has the lead character drawn, presumably by alien intelligences, through a dimensional "stargate" into another realm. We might also mention the Christian doctrine of the coming rapture which has been gaining attention in recent decades; it holds that people across the planet will be called up into Heaven at some moment in the future. So in a number of ways, the Ganymede abduction is a theme permeating our collective imagination.

What does "abduction" mean? While abduction stories may prefigure actual relations between humans and extraterrestrials in our future, they may also be symbolic in their implications, telling us about an *inner* shift we are experiencing as we segue into the next Age. From this standpoint, the theme of "abduction" refers to the process of being caught up in a powerful state of consciousness beyond the control of one's conscious ego, so that the psyche is overtaken.

But there is a distinct difference between *upward* abduction and *downward* abduction. For instance, Persephone being abducted into the Underworld by Hades suggests a process of getting sucked down into an emotional, subterranean level of psychic energy. In a sense, whenever we're overwhelmed by anger, depression, or fear, we're "abducted" into our own "underworld." However, the myth of Ganymede features someone being abducted *upward* into the heavenly realms, a different connotation indeed! This suggests a shift in consciousness that is predominantly *mental* in character. (Some would see the direction of "up" has a more spiritual connotation; yet spirituality is related to the balance-point of the horizon, the proverbial crack between worlds.)

The myth of Ganymede could portend the ways in which humanity will find itself swept up into an increasingly cerebral mode of experience during the coming millennia—a likely probability when one considers the meaning of air associated with Aquarius. This may point to a genuine awakening of humanity's higher mind, but practically speaking, it probably points to a more prosaic possibility, such as our lives becoming dominated by TVs and computers and the dissociated lifestyle that accompanies this domination.

Joining the Cosmic Fraternity

There are other possible implications to the myth of Ganymede. Notice how this tale describes a mortal becoming part of the Olympian fraternity, evoking the Aquarian associations of groups and brotherhood, but raised to a cosmic level. Perhaps humans will be invited to "join the club," as it were, to link up with other races and civilizations across space. This would give us another interpretation of the design of the United States flag with its network of stars. If the U.S. is indicative of the age to come, then its democratic alliance of states could prefigure a vaster space federation in our future, similar to that depicted in *Star Trek*.

It is provocative to consider the real-world implications here. Imagine turning on your TV or going online to view events or news transmitted from a distant solar system. Here the Aquarian notion of network takes on cosmic implications. Picture transport technology that allows individuals to travel from solar system to solar system, possibly between dimensions with the same ease that we now change channels on our TVs. Such things may be feasible in an age that experiences contact with intelligent beings from other worlds. This is one way to approach the symbolism of Ganymede.

We might point out that in being abducted, Ganymede became a servant to the gods. Over the years, there has been a school of thought which contends that contact with extraterrestrials would be a largely negative event, with humans being conquered or enslaved by these beings. Obviously, this theme has been a staple of science fiction films and novels since day one. This possibility would take the Orwellian scenario of "Big Brother" to a new level, a *cosmic* "Big Brotherhood" with humans kept under the thumbs of nonhuman races. Anything is possible, I suppose; but if alien races are planning to take over the planet, they sure seem to be taking their time about it.

Ganymede's "subservience" may be more symbolic than literal, referring perhaps to some intellectual or sociological gulf that might exist between us and other races not unlike that which now exists between us and the animal kingdom. In the face of vastly advanced cultures, it's possible that a formidable gulf could arise between "us" and "them" in terms of conflicting worldviews and ideologies. It might not be anything particularly *oppressive*, but it could pose new problems in our world, like a kindergarten pupil suddenly finding himself thrust into the midst of a United Nations' meeting. Perhaps we would be expected to fall into line and abide by certain "house rules," forcing us to reexamine our attitudes toward such things as nuclear weapons, space exploration, and environmental exploitation. For example, that child at the U.N. couldn't simply throw its toys across the room anymore, as it had done for so many years, and might find itself having to behave in new ways.

Another possibility is that extraterrestrials encountered may partake in a more "hive mind" mentality than we do, like *Star Trek's* Borg. Some have theorized that humans may be a more individualistic lot compared to other species, and thus less disposed toward heeding the constraints of a galactic bureaucracy. If so, this would pose challenges in terms of our ability to integrate with the rest of the club. On all these fronts, the negative possibilities of contact might center on the difficulty of balancing our needs and values with those of the galaxy.

This survey wouldn't be complete without mentioning yet another view of the brotherhood symbolism in the Ganymede story. Admittedly far-fetched, it has garnered support from some unexpected sources. This scenario suggests that any "oppression" or "mind control" related to the UFO phenomenon might stem less from aliens than from Earthbound agencies that have appropriated alien technologies. Suppose that extraterrestrial intelligences possessed advanced technology for influencing human minds on a mass scale; what would happen if those technologies fell into the hands of someone like Hitler or Saddam Hussein? Suppose an industrial firm desired to influence a population to enhance its profits. Far-fetched? Of course—but it's a theory proposed seriously by none other than former astronaut Edgar Mitchell as seen in the following transcript from a 1997 interview.

> Edgar Mitchell: I was very hands off, very skeptical of this whole area, for many, many years. But during the past five years I have been looking at this business seriously, and I am looking at it with very serious people. And I find that there is strong evidence to suggest that a covert effort by governments at back-engineering has found its way into quasi-private circumstances; that is, it is no longer directly under government, or military, control, though it is using government money. . . . I'm speaking of flight technology development and development in the area of mind control. Efforts during the Cold War on the part of both our intelligence community and the Soviet intelligence community may have been integrated with these areas of mind control technology.
>
> Question: How is this mind control being used?
>
> Edgar Mitchell: I don't know for certain. I can only speculate. *But there is strong circumstantial evidence to suggest that this technology is being used to disseminate disinformation.* . . . [italics added]
>
> Question: What is the purpose of this heinous disinformation campaign?
>
> Edgar Mitchell: To take people's attention away from the gravely serious matter that there is back-engineering and, perhaps, adaptation of ET technology with our own technology, by a group of people, out of control, no longer under government supervision, but spending billions of dollars of taxpayers' money (Chambers 1997).

Dr. Mitchell suggests that while the *source* of this technology may be extraterrestrial, it has been appropriated by earthbound agencies for their own ends, in ways beyond governmental or public oversight. If nothing else, models like this draw together many of the themes we've been exploring in this book: governments, corporations, aliens, high-technologies, media, the principles of "brotherhood," all recombined to form a new mix. Whether one reads them as truth or symbolism, they underscore a concern in connection with the Aquarian Age, namely, the looming specter of "mind control" and the importance of guarding our intellectual independence in the face of technology.

2001: A Space Odyssey and the Coming Evolutionary Jump

In the earlier discussion of genetic science, I suggested that Ganymede's transformation into an immortal may prefigure the way we will discover how to extend our life span to unimagined lengths. But in the context of extraterrestrial contact, this same image may instead suggest that humanity will find itself being "lifted up" to higher levels of evolution by the intervention of advanced beings. Read in this way, the "abduction" theme might signal an upraising of our species in intellectual, physical, or spiritual ways through their influence.

There are various ways this could come about. One would be that non-human races take on a role as teachers to humanity, by instructing us or exposing us to new forms of knowledge or ways of thinking. Another scenario would be that humanity finds itself prodded in its biological evolution through genetic manipulation by higher intelligences. The most lurid of our modern abduction accounts describe a hybrid race of human/aliens that incorporates the best characteristics of each species—intellect from the extraterrestrials, emotions from the humans.

Whether fact or fantasy, some abduction stories tell of newly pregnant women seeing their fetuses removed from their bodies; at some later date, they are abducted and shown those babies now older, but a cross between human and alien. Though this idea is often associated with supermarket tabloids, remember it factors prominently in some of our greatest science fiction, including arguably the great science fiction movie of our time— Kubrick's *2001: A Space Odyssey.* In the closing sequence, the astronaut is drawn up into the hyperdimensional "stargate" and transformed into a cosmic star child, in advance of a new race of human beings. Indeed, that image from 1968 was seemingly prophetic of later descriptions of alien/human hybrids by purported abductees.

Again, we don't have to pass judgment on the legitimacy of these tales to ponder their significance as Aquarian myths. Taken literally, they point to the possibility that extraterrestrials could figure prominently in evolution.

Read symbolically, they suggest the possibility of a massive jump set to occur in our evolution, whether it's instigated by ourselves through intellectual or scientific means, or by outside agencies.

The point here is that open contact between humans and alien races would represent a turning point in the commencement of the Aquarian Age, as would our entrance into the galactic community. Is there any way to tell when this is likely to happen? I'm dubious whether astrology can pinpoint a date for an event like this, since something of this magnitude would probably unfold only over many years, if not decades, to soften the impact it would have on our culture. Yet I *do* believe there are certain general time frames that could play an important role in this long-term process of disclosure. With that in mind, here are three time frames I propose:

2001–2005: In the first few years of the 21st century, roughly 2001 to 2005, Neptune and Uranus complete their passage through Aquarius, and the effects of the major planetary alignment of May 2000 continue to ripple through society. Though full-blown disclosure is unlikely to occur this early on, it is nevertheless a probable time when major revelations in this field will come to light.

2010–2012: For years now, many different figures have pointed to the period from 2010 to 2012 as a potentially important window for open contact with nonhuman races. (One of my teachers, Goswami Kriyananda, suggested this to me in 1977.) In terms of the clues offered by science fiction, this is the period Arthur C. Clarke suggested as a time of possible contact in his *2010*. It is also worth noting that astrologers like John Major Jenkins have called attention to the fact that December 21, 2012, is not only the end-date for the Mayan calendar, but represents an important astronomical period in terms of Earth's relationship with the larger galaxy. This relates to the fact that, due to the phenomenon of precession, the winter solstice is shifting in place against the stars in a manner similar to the spring equinox. Around 2012, this will place it into alignment with the plane of the Milky Way itself (Jenkins 1998). Viewed symbolically, this could indicate that humanity's interests will be tangibly intersecting at this time with those of the cosmos, perhaps in a way that involves contact with nonhuman intelligences.

2025–2033: One other possible "window" for contact hinges around the orbital cycles of Uranus. As we have seen, the discovery of Uranus in the eighteenth century synchronistically accompanied the birth of modern aviation and the launching of the first hot-air balloon in France. Some 84 years later, when Uranus returned to the same sign of the zodiac, hot-air balloon technology was being put to ever wider practical applications and Jules Verne published his best-seller *Five Weeks in a Balloon* (1863). Even the concept of space travel was emerging in the popular imagination at this time through Verne's *From the Earth to the Moon* (1865).

At the next full revolution of Uranus to this point 84 years later (the 1940s), not only was rocket technology undergoing a major surge in its development, but this period hosted the century's most famous UFO event, the "Roswell Incident." (The Roswell event took place in early July 1947, precisely as Uranus was returning to its 1781 discovery point.)

There seems to be a clear thread connecting *all* of these periods in a way which concerns aviation advances and our progressive defeat of gravity. Extrapolating forward, it's logical to believe that the next swing of Uranus to this same zodiacal point will see further progressions in aviation technology, perhaps even open contact with nonhuman intelligences in the cosmos.

Uranus will pass through Gemini from 2025 to 2033, making this a time to watch for significant developments in this field.

Through the Looking Glass

Examining the more reliable UFO accounts compiled over the last century, one easily gets the impression that something odd lurks behind the surface. I am referring to those cases of "high strangeness" that defy any simple explanation of the entire UFO phenomenon. I'm referring to those sightings which display a more anomalous flavor, such as sightings of UFOs that appear in conjunction with bizarre animals, or close encounters exhibiting a mythic dimension.

Sometimes, occupants associated with these craft are described as behaving strangely, like characters out of a Marx Brothers' film rather than interplanetary travelers. Sometimes, the UFOs display peculiar characteristics, such as blinking out like an image on a TV set being turned off, or changing shapes in ways that challenge reason. Consider the strange role that time seems to play in some of the more spectacular accounts: a witness claims to have been abducted for what seemed to him several days; yet witnesses report he was missing for only an hour. However, the person's wristwatch (and the stubble on his face) testifies to his having been absent for more than a day.

How do we begin to understand the strange recurrence of certain *days* in many sightings—in particular the pivotal date of June 24? After an intensive study of this subject, one author concluded:

> It is obvious that the phenomenon is controlled by hidden laws and cycles. Psychic and occult events seem to follow the same cycles as the UFO phenomenon. The Wednesday-Saturday phenomenon exists in all the frames of reference. For some reason, the twenty-fourth days of April, June, September, November, and December seem to produce exceptional activity year after year. . . . These events are staged year after year, century after century, in the same exact areas and often on the same exact calendar dates. Only the witnesses and the frames of reference used are different (Coleman 1985).

Observations like this strongly suggest that the UFO mystery may be a multiheaded hydra involving various explanations and causes. Perhaps this phenomenon offers us a glimpse into a multidimensional view of reality, compared to the one we normally entertain. In our discussion of science in chapter 6, I mentioned Edwin Babbitt's book *Flatland,* about beings from a three-dimensional world interacting with those from a two-dimensional one, and of the resulting confusion for those in the Flatland world. Could the UFO phenomenon be playing a similar role in our own world? Could what we think of as "ordinary reality" be part of a multidimensional one, where phenomena slip in and out of our perception on a regular basis?

As such, the UFO enigma may be prying open our minds to an understanding of a universe that is not only more complex, but—well, far *stranger.* Astronomer J. Allen Hynek once wrote: "When the long awaited solution to the UFO problem comes, I believe that it will prove to be not merely the next small step in the march of science, but a mighty and totally unexpected quantum leap" (Hynek 1972). Or did anomalist Charles Fort (Keel 1975) come closer to the mark when he posed this great question: "If there is a universal mind, *must it be sane?*"

14

Egypt, Atlantis, and the Coming Archeological Revolution

The sun had been blazing down onto the sands and monuments of the Giza plateau for several hours already. It was February 18, 1997. Since the day before, the film crew had been setting up their equipment in a cavern beneath the sands as other team members ran preliminary tests. At the center of all the attention was a mysterious chamber, roughly 100 feet underground, at the bottom of a shaft located midway between the Sphinx and the second of the three pyramids.

Over the centuries, this room had remained largely unexplored due to high water levels underground; but with the receding of the water table in recent years, researchers decided to investigate. The team I was monitoring had been financed and promoted by a long-time student of antiquities in the area, Dr. Joseph Schor, founder of the Schor Foundation and alumnus of Florida State University. The team's mission involved other figures like James Hurtak *(The Keys of Enoch)*, Boris Said *(Mystery of the Sphinx)*, and Joe Jahoda (of the Edgar Cayce Foundation). Other participants, such as myself, had come along for the ride. Several months earlier, I had been asked by a team member if I'd like to come and I jumped at the chance to witness what could be history in the making, or uncovering, to be precise.

Most of us had spent the better part of that morning waiting patiently above ground on the plateau, trying to find shade. Eventually, someone ambled up from the mouth of the shaft and said something curious had been found. No one was sure what it was. Apparently, while kicking away some dirt to position the movie camera, the team's cinematographer noticed a flat stone protruding from the dirt floor. The best guess anyone had was that it was the surface of an ancient submerged sarcophagus. A few hoped it might prove to be a doorway to an adjoining chamber. I made my way down the ladder to look and take some photos, and was as mystified as everyone else as to what it might be.

But whatever this stony slab was, it wasn't long before the Egyptians on hand realized this could be an important find, something that became apparent from their body language and hushed comments. Since this team only had a filming permit and not an archeological one, the Egyptians forbade any further disturbance of the site, and we found ourselves heading home with no answers as to the secrets of chamber.

Several months later, rumors circulated about excavations undertaken in this chamber; and a year later, the formal news announcement was made: Egyptian archeologists had found a large sarcophagus in the area of the protruding slab. According to Zahi Hawass, the director of the Giza plateau, it was a historic find, possibly the legendary Tomb of Osiris spoken of by Herodotus in ancient times (Hawass 2001). The Schor team received no credit for their work in uncovering this find, but that was less important to those of us who had felt privileged to simply witness an archeological development like this.

There was just one problem. Important as this find was, it wasn't what the team had come there looking for.

Egypt—Gateway to the Past?

So what had lured the members of the expedition to this spot in the Egyptian desert? It was the possibility of locating what Edgar Cayce had called the Hall of Records, a purported room of tablets or scrolls containing the records of humanity's lost past. Though a popular topic among contemporary students of "alternative archeology," this speculation has been around for thousands of years.

The Egyptian Westcar Papyrus (dated back to roughly 2400 B.C., but regarded as a copy of a much older original) has a mysterious reference to a secret "chamber of Thoth" in a building called the "Inventory" (Bauval and Gilbert 1994). Writing in the ninth century A.D., the Byzantine historian George Syncellus makes reference to a lost Egyptian text called *The Book of Sothis*, said to contain records brought to Egypt shortly "after the Flood." Similarly, the fourth-century Roman historian Ammianus Marcellinus speaks of documents hidden before the Flood to preserve ancient knowledge (Flem-Ath and Wilson 2000). In *Secret Chamber* (1999), Robert Bauval points to references in the Hermetic texts (attributed to Thoth) about a secret body of knowledge engraved on stone and stored away "near the secrets of Osiris."

To some, references such as these suggest a lost chamber of records is a tangible reality that could hold valuable insights into our past.

The question is, where would these records be now? Theories have ranged from inside the Great Pyramid to near or underneath the Sphinx, perhaps even in the desert region around the Giza plateau. There is only one way to know for sure: extensive excavations of the Giza plateau region. As a result, researchers have competed over the years for rights to explore this region, using the latest technology. The group I accompanied enlisted the services of geophysicist and seismologist Thomas Dobecki, best known for his work on earlier Giza digs and the popular "Mystery of the Sphinx" TV show. He used ground-penetrating radar to see whether this underground room might have a concealed passageway or hidden chamber. The only results he got were in the region of the protruding slab.

It is ironic that the further we plunge into a high-tech future, the more we are drawn to tales of lost civilizations, ancient artifacts, and the unsolved mysteries of our distant past. On the surface, this might be explained as a romanticized longing for an exotic time in the face of an increasingly technological world. That may partly be true, but it is just one piece of the puzzle. Our fascination with these mysteries might also stem from an intuition of the role these things might play in the change of thought about to occur in the world. Could it be that we are drawn to these locations because of the key they may hold for the unfolding mystery of our time?

As an example, consider Egypt, the one area that has been the source of more attention in recent times than any other. It is curious how this ancient culture has held so "futuristic" an appeal for so many in our time. When the founders of the French and American revolutions searched for images to embody the spirit of their new nations, they turned to Egypt, and its legacy is still reflected in our currency and national monuments. Though some of that interest stemmed from the founding fathers' Masonic affiliations, that doesn't explain its appeal today. Science fiction writers and filmmakers continue to draw upon Egypt's mystique in films like *Stargate,* no doubt because there is something strangely modern about the streamlined design and "space age" sleekness which characterizes much Egyptian art and architecture. A vague hint of high technology swirls indefinably around many of these monuments, and this further stimulates the Aquarian imagination.

How did a people supposedly just out of the Stone Age routinely move 200-ton blocks with a precision we can barely reproduce today? How did they carve the sarcophagus in the King's Chamber of the Great Pyramid without the aid of power tools?

If Egypt has served as center stage for much of our fascination with ancient mysteries, the key player upon that stage has undoubtedly been the Sphinx. A good deal of the importance of this image in our time probably lies in its symbolism. As a fusion of human (Aquarius) and lion (Leo) features, it is the perfect embodiment of the Leo/Aquarius axis. Our collective fascination with this symbol may arise from its power as a symbol for the coming shift of consciousness. The added fact that so many now believe that the secrets to our hidden past lie directly underneath (or near) this monument may further testify to the important role these discoveries could play in the unfolding Aquarian Age. Symbolically understood, our search for lost records around this monument may relate to our longing for *transformational knowledge*—the higher potentials of Aquarian rationality.

The most important impact of the Sphinx may lie in a more tangible direction: its antiquity. According to mainstream Egyptologists, the Sphinx was carved out of bedrock during the reign of the pharaoh Chephren, somewhere around 2500 B.C. But according to independent Egyptologist John Anthony West and Boston University geologist Robert Schoch, there are strong indications the Sphinx may have already existed for thousands of years prior to that time frame. West and Schoch point out how the erosion patterns on the Sphinx and the surrounding enclosure strongly suggest the influence of rainfall over extended periods of time; yet geology suggests that the only time that rainfalls of this amount could have occurred were far earlier in history, long before Egyptian civilization is *supposed* to have developed in this region. Schoch presented the findings to scientists at the American Association for the Advancement of Science (AAAS) conference in Chicago in 1992 and as part of the Emmy-award winning show "Mystery of the Sphinx" on NBC in 1993.

What is so controversial about this theory? Not only does it suggest that Egyptian history might be older than conventionally thought, it pushes back the date on human civilization generally. Why? Because the construction of the Sphinx and its surrounding monuments would have required highly organized social groups and advanced engineering skills at a time when humans supposedly lacked such sophistication. For instance, Schoch and West point to the gigantic stone blocks carved out of the enclosure surrounding the Sphinx (some weighing 200 tons) that were somehow moved into place to form the adjoining temple complex. How could a primitive, tribal people have done this? Ironically, sphinx images were employed in ancient times as "guardians" over important thresholds, as hybrid sentries over the great secrets of life and death. In a way, the Sphinx has come to assume a similar function in our world now, but in terms of its archaeological implications. Today, it stands guard before a new era in our knowledge of the world, and our understanding of who we are.

On this level, the Great Sphinx shares much in common with the mystery of Egyptian culture itself. Simply put, early Egyptian civilization seems a lot less like a *development* than a *legacy*. As John Anthony West eloquently expressed it:

> . . . every aspect of Egyptian knowledge seems to have been complete at the very beginning. The sciences, artistic and architectural techniques and the hieroglyphic system show virtually no sign of a period of "development"; indeed, many of the achievements of the earlier dynasties were never surpassed or even equaled later on. Unlike most other great civilizations of the past, so many of Egypt's major innovations seemed to have been there from the very start, from its hieroglyphics and mythology to its architectural and engineering skills (West 1993).

Did Egypt draw its inspiration from some older culture now lost to memory? Questions like these place us at the threshold of a broader mystery that has gripped the human imagination for millennia: the riddle of Atlantis.

The Search for Atlantis

As it has come down to us from the ancient Greeks, the story of Atlantis describes a high civilization existing thousands of years before our time that met its end in the throes of a great disaster. For some, of course, this tale is nothing more than a fable concocted by Plato to make certain philosophical or political points; but for others, it is a factual account of an actual civilization. Importantly, while Plato's account is unique in its details, stories of great floods in remote history are found in cultural traditions the world over.

Rather than enter into the debate of *where* this lost civilization might have existed, I prefer to take John Anthony West's cue of using "Atlantis" as a term to describe the possibility of lost high civilizations generally. In other words, whether or not there was a continent named "Atlantis" in our past, we can still discuss the possibility of ancient high civilizations in Earth's forgotten past.

What hard evidence exists for this possibility? Some have pointed to the presence of anomalous artifacts found throughout the world that hint at the presence of advanced societies before our time. These include handcrafted items, embedded in rocks, that date back thousands, sometimes millions, of years before the present. In 1852, for example, *Scientific American* carried a story about an ornately designed metal cup blasted out of solid rock in Massachusetts, rock which geologists dated to 500 million years ago. Who could have created such an object?[1] Equally mysterious are monumental structures around the world, such as the temple ruins of Ba'albek, Lebanon, which seem to hint at an unknown technological skill in ancient times that defies modern understanding. Some of the stone blocks comprising the platform of this ancient temple are more than eighty feet long and estimated to weigh over 1,200 tons.

One especially intriguing piece of evidence that points to the possibility of lost high civilizations is a document called the Piri Reis map. One of several mysterious maps handed down over the centuries, this is a parchment document discovered in Istanbul, Turkey, in 1929 but dating to 1513. Signed by the Turkish captain Piri Reis, this map apparently drew on information from at least twenty older maps, including some purportedly from the time of Alexander the Great. There are several surprising features about this document.

For one, it depicts coastlines throughout the Western world at a time when Europeans hadn't yet explored some of these areas. It also seems to depict the continent of Antarctica at a time when Europeans didn't yet know of its existence. More provocative still, it portrays this frozen continent as it would have appeared if devoid of ice. Since that is a condition which hasn't existed in that region for thousands, perhaps millions of years, this suggests that the Piri Reis map must have drawn on information that originated during an exceedingly ancient point in history.

So, does this map point to the existence of a sophisticated culture on the Earth thousands of years before ours, one that possessed a geographical knowledge of the entire world? Over the years skeptics have raised various objections about this map and what it does or doesn't show,[2] but none have successfully addressed what may be its most mysterious feature: an accurate use of longitude. For example, the relationship of South America to Africa is accurately depicted on this map. What makes this astonishing is that coordinate systems using longitude were only developed by modern Europeans during the late seventeenth and eighteenth centuries, with the invention of accurate timepieces and spherical trigonometry. This alone strongly suggests that whatever culture compiled the original source materials from which Piri Reis drew were probably at a level of development comparable to seventeenth-century Europe.

Echoes from the Age of Leo

If there were high civilizations in Earth's prehistoric past, what relevance does this have for the impending Aquarian Age? I suggest several possibilities. The first concerns dating.

There are countless theories as to when "Atlantis" may have thrived or met its decline; some theorists have even suggested that Earth has probably played host to a *series* of high civilizations over time, rather than just one. However, one general time frame keeps cropping in these theories as a significant period to examine: 10,500 to 9000 B.C.

Again, there may be clues in the symbolism of the Sphinx. Earlier we saw how the significance of this monument for our time rests partly within its human/lion form, a combination that perfectly expresses the symbolism of the Leo/Aquarius axis. But some have proposed that its symbolism may also hold a key to the time of its creation, with its leonine imagery referring to the zodiacal Age of Leo (circa 8,800 to 10,800 B.C.). This may be when the Sphinx was actually constructed; or perhaps the Sphinx was built during some later period, but was designed to memorialize that earlier time. To use a modern analogy, any modern-day Christian church would be a recent construction, yet would commemorate events that took place two thousand years ago in the Middle East: the life and death of Jesus. In the same way, the symbolism of the Sphinx may simply be commemorating the ancient period associated with the Age of Leo.[3]

More than one writer has emphasized this Leo period as being a significant one in humanity's past. In *The Timaeus*, for example, Plato cites 9,600

B.C. as the period when Atlantis underwent the greatest of its several catastrophes. In his trance readings, Edgar Cayce said 10,450 B.C. was the turning point in the decline of Atlantis. In recent years, others have reiterated this general time frame as well, including Rand Flem-Ath, Zecharia Sitchin, Robert Bauval, Adrian Gilbert, and Graham Hancock. In terms of Egyptian culture, some suggest there is strong evidence besides the Sphinx to indicate that the Egyptians believed the period around 10,500 B.C. was a significant one in humanity's history.[4]

What is the significance of this ancient period for us now? One thing to consider is that during the impending era governed by the Leo/Aquarius axis, a subtle resonance is set up with that earlier Leo era 12,000 years ago. If every zodiacal sign is indeed part of a twofold dynamic with the sign directly opposite it, then perhaps this holds true for the Great Ages as well, giving us a link between historical periods associated with opposing signs 12,000 years apart from each other. In this way, the growing appeal of the Atlantis legend may stem partly from a growing archetypal resonance between the emerging era and the era of 12,000 years ago (see figure 14-1).

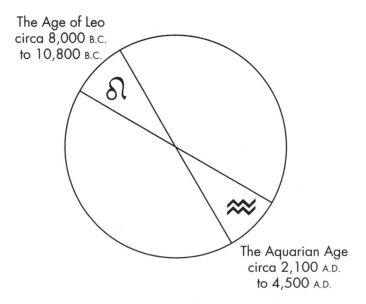

The Age of Leo
circa 8,000 B.C.
to 10,800 B.C.

The Aquarian Age
circa 2,100 A.D.
to 4,500 A.D.

Figure 14-1. The Leo/Aquarius Polarity across the Ages
With the advent of the Aquarian Age, a sympathetic "resonance" could arise between our own time and the Great Age directly opposite it in history—the Age of Leo, 10,000 to 12,000 years ago.

How would such a resonance manifest itself? At its simplest, it might inspire a growing fascination with this ancient period in history reinforced by actual discoveries related to that era. Or it may indicate there will be some deep similarity, culturally or spiritually, between these two periods. For example, Atlantis is often described as having been an advanced society that suffered from an abuse of its powers—a description that might be applied to our civilization.

Perhaps the connection between these opposing eras is a karmic one, in terms of developments or states of consciousness set into motion during the Leo era coming to fruition during this next age, for better or worse. In this respect, some would point to a link between the culture of ancient Atlantis and that of modern-day America. Indeed, this was an association proposed even during the time of the first European explorers, when some wondered whether Columbus's new continent might be related to the legendary Atlantis (since Plato had spoken not just of a continent in the Atlantic, but of one *beyond* it). In the seventeenth century, this was a connection reinforced by the writings of Francis Bacon (1561-1626), whose book *The New Atlantis* suggested to some that America extended the legacy of the legendary Atlantis in a mysterious way.

Note that these two zodiacal Ages are positioned at opposite ends of the zodiac. Despite their commonalties, the sociocultural trends of the Leonine Age and those of the Aquarian may prove to be inverse images of each other. While modern society is an increasingly democratic one, it's probable that civilizations during this earlier era were more theocratic in nature, led by priestly kings rather than business-suited executives. While both of these eras exhibit a fondness for technology, it is likely that Leonine civilization utilized such innovations as a means to an end, such as service to religious ideas, rather than as an end in itself as we do. In chapter 17, I explore some spiritual implications of this mirror imaging between Ages.

The Atlantis Catastrophe—Environmental Harbinger for Our Time?

The importance of the Atlantis legend for our time may lie in its environmental message. Some variations of this myth suggest that Atlantis's collapse was connected to an environmental disaster, possibly triggered by the actions of humanity. The current popularity of this tale may relate to the problems we are facing today. Perhaps we are drawn to this story for the sobering reminder of how highly advanced civilizations can meet an untimely end through environmental problems.

This isn't to say our fascination with this ancient tale is simply a Rorschach-style projection of our own anxieties onto the blank slate of history. As growing numbers of researchers have pointed out in recent years, there is strong evidence to suggest that some great environmental tragedy actually did occur in the period associated with the Age of Leo, between 9,000 and 12,000 years ago. For example, ice cores extracted from Greenland indicate that temperatures suddenly rose by as much as 14 degrees Fahrenheit around 9,600 B.C., a time frame coinciding with Plato's date for the demise of Atlantis. These and other findings indicate that *something* of environmental importance took place during this period.

Could environmental upheavals of that same magnitude *recur* during our time? There is much talk these days of ocean levels rising (due to global warming) and the melting of the Earth's ice caps, as well as the widespread problems resulting from environmental degradation. But is it possible there could be some *cyclical* mechanism linking the environmental problems of that earlier period with those emerging in ours?

To cite just one line of research, some theorists cite as evidence the fact that the Earth has apparently experienced major catastrophes at roughly 1,000-year intervals, which have resulted in the fall and rise of great civilizations. To help explain such periodic disruptions, Victor Clube and Bill Napier, British astronomers working out of Northern Ireland, have proposed that our solar system may be regularly coming into contact with "swarms" of cometary bodies that have an impact on the Earth's surface. Extrapolating forward from the evidence of prior impacts, this suggests we might be in for another such celestial impact around 2,200 A.D. Coupled with the problems of an already compromised ecosystem, an impact of this sort during our time could have an effect far worse than previous collisions (Schoch 1999).

From a symbolic standpoint, it is possible the clues of a looming environmental crisis may even be encoded in the ancient mythologies of Aquarius. In many cultures, the constellation of Aquarius was associated with water pouring out of a bucket or with the image of a deluge. In Greek tradition, for instance, Aquarius was not only associated with Ganymede, but with Deucalion, king of Phthia and son of Prometheus. Commonly referred to as the "Noah" of Greek mythology, Deucalion built a great chest in which he and his family could survive the rising floodwaters Zeus had sent to destroy humanity. It could be more than accidental that just as we find ourselves on the brink of a zodiacal age associated with images of a great flood, we find ourselves facing the threat of rising sea levels around the world.

Consider the symbols associated with the stories of the ancient figure of Ouranos, the mythic namesake of Uranus the planet. In Greek legend, the sky god Ouranos was a cruel tyrant, particularly abusive toward Gaia, the Earth goddess who was his mother and lover. Viewed archetypally, our burgeoning environmental crisis seems to act out the dynamics of this myth on a global scale: just as Gaia was oppressed by Ouranos, so our own mother, Earth or Gaia, is being trampled underfoot by the fruits of our modern-day Uranian consciousness, in the form of technology and mechanistic rationality. So when someone asks whether the Aquarian Age will be a time when environmentalism and reverence for Mother Earth will be the order of the day, I have to answer yes, though for different reasons than some might suspect. More likely, this trend will continue to gain momentum, more as a *compensation* for the effects of the Aquarian consciousness than as its result.

Another aspect of the Ouranos story is his castration, a symbolic act suggesting a consciousness that is cerebral and dissociated from the vital energies of nature, both inner and outer. As to what this might portend for our future, one possibility is that we could see an increasing trend toward living life more exclusively "in our heads," awash in information and mental pastimes, but cut off from the instinctual aspects of everyday experience. To a great extent, we already see this taking place, not only to the degree that our world has become dominated by computers and the media, but in the way we have become increasingly disconnected from our violent impulses. For instance, think of the modern-day bomber pilot who drops his bombs on humans he never sees, or the consumer who buys prepackaged meats without having to confront the reality of that animal's death. True, our media bombards us with violent images of all types, yet these are invariably presented in the spirit of make-believe or journalistic detachment, and therefore serve to distance us even further from those emotions.[5]

Does all this imply a bleak forecast for our planet and civilization in the millennia ahead? That all depends on how one chooses to read the story. After all, in the conflict between Ouranos and Gaia, Gaia eventually won (see figure 14-2).

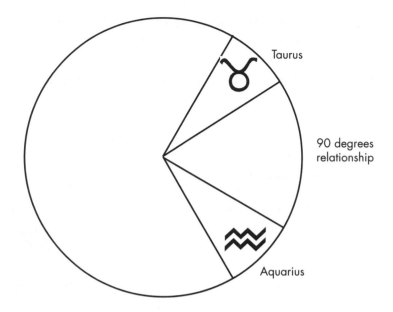

Figure 14-2. The Aquarius/Taurus Relationship in the New Era
With the rise of the Aquarian Age, a dynamic tension will be set up with those zodiacal signs at 90-degree angles to either side of this sign. In the case of the Aquarius/Taurus relationship, this signals a powerful focus on environmental and ecological concerns.

The Extraterrestrial Question

Another way to understand the allure of the "lost civilizations" scenario for Aquarian sensibilities touches on the subject matter of our last chapter: extraterrestrial intelligence. I'm referring here to the possibility that humanity's past may harbor some link to intelligent races from elsewhere in the universe. Did we evolve independently on this planet, all by ourselves? Or were we "seeded" here by beings from elsewhere, as some believe? In support of this hypothesis, some writers point to the extraordinary complexity of our DNA, as well as the lack of any obvious "missing link" in the evolutionary record. In other words, archaeologists are at a loss to explain the steps that led to anatomically modern humans. Did biological complexity evolve by accident, or was it engineered by beings, intergalactic scientists of a sort?

It's a subject that has led to speculation of the most unbridled sort through the years, one that has spawned a cottage industry of "fringe" books and researchers. Yet it has also attracted the attention of serious thinkers and artists, such as that most intelligent of science fiction scripts, *2001: A Space Odyssey*. In Stanley Kubrick and Arthur C. Clarke's script, humans are depicted as having been prodded along at intervals by a higher intelligence, from the dawn of history to beyond the present. Mere fiction or actual fact? If true, it would constitute the quintessential Aquarian intellectual revolution, pointing out our connection to the stars in a literal sense. And in light of our probable exploration of the stars in the centuries ahead, it would further tie together our earliest origins with our destiny in space. How strange that the further we peer into our past, the more we see the face of our future staring back at us.

Revisioning Who We Are

Earlier in this book I touched upon how scientific discoveries often bear symbolic meaning to their timing, that is, in the synchronistic way their occurrence seems connected with shifts occurring in the collective psyche. For example, the emergence of quantum physics during the early twentieth century mirrored a shift in the Western psyche, its strange and seemingly "irrational" qualities paralleling those arising in other areas of human creativity. I have suggested in this chapter that the same principle applies to archeological discoveries. Time after time, breakthroughs concerning our past occur at powerful points in the culture's evolution, as if to mirror revolutions in the collective consciousness. To cite just one example, the uncovering of the so-called "Tomb of Osiris" unfolded within days of a rare planetary lineup in Aquarius during February of 1997.[6]

In a broader fashion, the onset of the Aquarian Age will be accompanied by an archeological revolution the likes of which we have never seen before. It will shatter our long-held conceptions of who we are and where we have come from. Imagine you suddenly learn you aren't related to the family that raised you, that you had been adopted at an early age from a band of gypsies in Eastern Europe. As the icing on the cake, imagine you also learned you were years older than you had thought. Needless to say, you would never see yourself in quite the same way again; and that is because there is a deep and inextricable connection between *identity* and *history*.

Who we are is directly related to *where we have been*. This same principle applies to our collective sense of identity: should we suddenly uncover a vast new chapter in our past, it would have a profound impact on the way we see ourselves as a species. To discover that we were neither the highest nor first civilization on Earth, or that we might have resulted from experiments by spacefaring beings, would not only add to our collective body of knowledge, it would force a radical revision in the way we look at ourselves.

If films like *Star Wars* offer any useful clues concerning the coming age, then it may be significant that the first few installments of that series center on a hero who unexpectedly discovers a long-buried secret about his identity. His biological roots, he discovers, are completely different from what he had thought. As it turns out, his origin stems from an "alien" source: the powerful Darth Vader. Could fictional symbols like this foreshadow an analogous reappraisal *we* will be making in the centuries ahead regarding our stellar ancestry?

In the end, the question of lost civilizations and of our roots, earthbound or extraterrestrial, ultimately comes down to a matter of hard evidence. Though some of the examples touched upon in this chapter are compelling, they do not quite constitute the "smoking gun" needed to trigger the full-blown cultural shift hinted at here. Here are a few suggestions of areas we might watch in the years ahead, any or all of which could open the door to breakthroughs. Each of the following has the virtue of offering a concrete and fully testable case that we can use to actively investigate—and possibly confirm—these hypotheses:

A Hidden City under the Antarctic Ice Shelf? For many years, Rand Flem-Ath has proposed the icy continent of Antarctica as a possible candidate for the location of the legendary Atlantis. Until recently, it has been a difficult thesis to prove. However, recent information could make confirmation of this theory a reality. While reading about the effects of volcanism in Antarctica in a recent scientific paper, Rand's wife, Rose, stumbled upon an intriguing passage in which the author described "surprisingly circular" features underneath the ice sheet in West Antarctica, as recorded by Landsat cameras in space. Just as provocatively, these features were said to possess a "unique magnetic signature" (Flem-Ath 1995).

Flem-Ath found this intriguing, since it happened to be right where he had long believed the ancient capital city of Atlantis resided, a city Plato described as having been encircled by metal walls. Though this might simply be the remains of a dormant volcano, its uncanny location and unusual magnetic properties make this an enticing candidate for further archeological investigation.

Underwater Structures around the World: It's often said that modern scientists know more about the surface of the Moon than they do the bottom of the ocean. What historical wonders remain undiscovered beneath Earth's waters? An especially promising question, since Earth's ocean levels rose by roughly 300 feet at the end of the last ice age. If there had been any advanced civilizations situated along Earth's shorelines in ancient times, the remains would now be submerged at depths that we could now access without great difficulty. Recent explorations have already begun to yield suggestive finds in offshore regions like Okinawa and Cuba. In the coming decades and centuries it will be worth seeing whether further investigations verify such ruins are truly artificial structures from lost civilizations in prehistoric times.

Artificial Structures on Mars: Debate continues to rage over whether unusual features in photos taken of the Martian surface are of intelligent construction or not. While some believe the "Face on Mars" question was put to rest by high-resolution photos released by NASA in 2001, there are many other features on this planet which remain mysterious. As Carl Sagan argued shortly before his death, this is one "fringe" topic that lends itself to conclusive verification or debunking, since we have the technologies necessary to investigate these claims. If confirmed, it would not only indicate the existence of intelligent life beyond Earth, but would throw open our history to mysterious new possibilities. For example, were we related to the creatures who once lived on Mars? Does our culture somehow derive from an earlier one there?

The Hall of Records: Even if the team of researchers mentioned at the beginning of this chapter didn't succeed in locating this legendary room, it doesn't mean that it will not eventually be found *somewhere*. But where? With each passing year, new theories are put forward as to possible locations. Is it under the paws of the Sphinx? In some still-undiscovered chamber inside the Great Pyramid? Buried beneath the sands of Egypt in a spot determined by geometrical or astronomical factors? Or in another part of the world entirely, like the Yucatan? Its discovery could provide the essential key that resolves the mystery of our past, and could help us awaken from the collective amnesia that has clouded our historical vision for too long.

15

The Kaleidoscopic Paradigm: From Schizophrenia to Polyphrenia

Let's begin this with a simple quiz. What do all of the following have in common: Disneyland, Las Vegas, the Frankenstein monster, an average modern-day sports team, the Beatles' "white" album, American society, a contemporary shopping mall, the United Nations, Walt Disney's *Fantasia,* postmodernism, the Unified Field Theory, *Alice in Wonderland,* and Orson Welles' *Citizen Kane?*

They all share a commonality of symbolism, one that could prove crucial in the unfolding Aquarian mythos. Let us recall our association of Aquarius with the principle of decentralization. Leo brings a convergence of energies toward a center, akin to the way blood is drawn to the heart, while Aquarius governs the process whereby unity is split into multiple centers, multiple perspectives, like blood distributed through the arteries. For this and other reasons, Aquarius relates to the concept of holism, the study of systems, be they social, techno-logical, or political in nature. Rather than focus on one central hub, Aquarius emphasizes the complex relationship among all the parts in a system.

Yet as suggested earlier, there are many different types of systems. We have the kinds where the system is more dominant in influence, and the individual comparatively minimized. An example is a totalitarian state, where the citizens are cogs in a vast political machine. At the other end of the spectrum are those systems where the individual parts are in control and the system is relatively weak. An example is anarchy, where all the citizens run riot without checks or balances from a system.

Between the two are those kinds of systems with a *balance* between the system and the parts. Politically, this is exemplified by a democracy, or the jazz model. The individual parts have autonomy, with much interactivity and creative input among them, yet all is held together in a harmonious and balanced fashion, and neither the system nor its parts is overly dominant.

The Web of Incongruities

In this chapter I explore a variation on this idea, what I call the "strong jazz" model, a system in which each part is not only autonomous and individualized, but *wildly* distinctive in character. Imagine a jazz ensemble where the members are not only individuals, but are *dramatically* different in nature: a band consisting of a priest, stockbroker, politician, plumber, and a child prodigy, or: a human, penguin, chimpanzee, an alien from outer space, and a talking sofa! In other words, a system that exhibits radical diversity, radical incongruity, among its parts. Here, multiple perspectives hang together, cohering in a framework, yet without breaking apart into anarchy. (See appendix 2 for a discussion of these systems and their implications.)

I refer to this arrangement as the "kaleidoscopic paradigm," or "kaleidoscopic holism." To use an analogy, were we to pick a creature from the animal kingdom to serve as "totem" animal for this system, it would be the platypus, a creature that is incongruity itself, with the qualities of different species (reptile, mammal, and bird) side-by-side in the same body.

Throughout this chapter, I explore how this paradigm offers a key to understand aspects already surfacing in society, and that can be expected to continue to surface in future times. What makes it important is its flexibility, its ability to accommodate seemingly contradictory elements in a single framework, something which will almost certainly prove valuable in our complex world. Let us begin by looking at some sociological applications of this idea from recent times.

A Profile of a Kaleidoscopic Society

To be sure, all democratic governments tend to encourage a kaleidoscopic spirit of diversity in their populations, by allowing individuals to think for themselves. Yet in contrast to democratic nations like Japan, where we find a relatively homogenous population, America has taken this principle of diversity to its extreme. Regarded as the "melting pot" society *par excellence,* America is a mosaic of individuals from every nation, religion, and racial group on the planet, all gathered in one country. As one immigrant I spoke to once expressed it, "America is the one nation on the planet that is made up of every other nation on the planet!"

This same kaleidoscopic diversity characterizes the United Nations, which houses many countries under the same roof, with no single leader autocratically governing the assembly. A similar thing might be said about the modern civil rights organization, the Rainbow Coalition, a kaleidoscopic ensemble of diverse individuals and races who have come together for humanitarian purposes. Should humanity come to openly establish diplomatic contact with other races in the universe, such models as these might be useful for extending this concept into a galactic sphere, with Earth participating in an alliance of vastly different species from around the galaxy, as in *Star Trek*'s Galactic Federation. Let's review a few categories from our social lives that show this new trend.

Sports: The kaleidoscopic principle is visible in the makeup of nearly any modern professional sports team. In earlier times, sports teams generally consisted of players from a particular region; as such, competition between teams was a competition between regions (or ethnic groups). But today, teams are comprised of players contracted from all over the country, sometimes the world, so they have little uniformity of background or culture. It makes the traditional notion of a "home team" a misnomer now. As comedian Jerry Seinfeld once said, what we're rooting for now is just a set of uniforms.

Music and Literature: A classic example of the kaleidoscopic principle in popular music is the Beatles' untitled "white" album from 1968. This is an eclectic compilation of songs which do not so much feature music in a single style (as with *Rubber Soul*), but in which every song conveys a different feeling or musical style, from the lilting ballad "Blackbird" to the jagged-edged "Helter Skelter." The kaleidoscopic influence is also evident in the emergence of world music, a trend characterized by influences and instruments from diverse cultures incorporated into an ensemble or composition.

In the literary field, there are several examples that illustrate this principle. Lewis Carroll's famed *Alice in Wonderland* expresses a kaleidoscopic touch in the way it juxtaposes radically different perspectives. There is its shifting sense of scale as Alice makes her way not merely through different places but different sizes. The multiple-perspective aspect is also present in this book's "crazy logic."

Consider what we mean when we say something is "crazy." In and of itself, a rabbit isn't crazy; in and of itself, a tea party isn't crazy; and in and of itself, wearing a hat certainly isn't crazy. But a rabbit wearing a hat at a tea party? Now, *that's* crazy! It's the incongruity of Carroll's story that makes his images seem bizarre to us, and perhaps this is why his book continues to hold appeal for our modern sensibilities.

Aquarian rationality can be complex in its capacity for paradox, multiple-track thinking, acausal connections, and forward and backward logic. Carroll's book speaks directly to this state of mind. It seems fitting that many science writers over the years have turned to Carroll's writings to illustrate the paradoxes of quantum physics, such that it is hardly surprising that Carroll's horoscope features a prominent Aquarian influence.

Another literary example is Gustave Flaubert's *Madame Bovary,* one of several nineteenth century works that introduced the public to a storytelling style that eschewed the single viewpoint of one character or author in favor of multiple perspectives or interpretations. To an even more dramatic degree, we see the kaleidoscopic principle in the works of Aquarian James Joyce. In *Portrait of the Artist as a Young Man,* Joyce tells the story of the lead character through a spectrum of different styles that echo the stages of human life; he also utilizes diverse literary styles associated with different historical periods. In *Dubliners,* he presents different tales whose only unifying thread is a common geographical location, Dublin. In *Ulysses,* Joyce decentralized the conventional storyline into multiple centers of meaning, offering no fixed hub of interpretation for the reader.

Cinema: A colorful expression of the kaleidoscopic principle in cinema would be Disney's *Fantasia.* This work features different episodes accompanied by different types of classical music, all held together by the recurring figure of a narrator and the famed conductor Leopold Stokowski. One of this film's acclaimed sequences centers on a musical composition that in itself represents one of history's most kaleidoscopic and multifaceted art works: Tchaikovsky's *Nutcracker Suite* (first premiered in 1892, the year of the Neptune/Pluto conjunction).

The year following *Fantasia's* release (1941), Orson Welles' *Citizen Kane* employed kaleidoscopic influences on several different levels simultaneously. For one, consider the diverse dramatic *styles* utilized in this film, which span serious drama, comedy, the musical, "gothic" horror, avant-garde, documentary, and romance. For another, consider the diverse environments and geographical motifs touched on throughout the film: castle, zoo, wilderness cabin, corporate boardroom, newspaper office, beach, Southwestern desert, opera house, Islamic architecture, political rallies, and Florida swamp.

It was perhaps *Citizen Kane*'s unique approach to storytelling that reflected the kaleidoscopic influence at its most glorious. Rather than tell its story from a single fixed viewpoint, it offers it as a *patchwork* of perspectives dangling in space like pieces on a mobile. The Argentine writer Jorge Luis Borges once described Welles' work as a "centreless labyrinth," and that seems a fitting way to describe its decentralized approach to its story and its central character (who by film's end is even likened to a jigsaw puzzle).

During the film, we are told the tragic story of this figure through the eyes of everyone around him during his life, each one offering a different judgment on who he was. But at no point do we ever really enter into *his* unique perspective and interior world; that is left a mystery for viewers. Welles wasn't the first to use this decentralized approach to cinematic storytelling, but he took this idea and developed it in a way that was unique.[1]

In the 1950s, this multiplistic approach was taken a critical step further with Akira Kurosawa's critically acclaimed *Roshomon*. Whereas *Citizen Kane* had featured different people offering their perspectives on the same incidents, Kurosawa showed the same incident in fundamentally different ways, without ever explaining to the viewer which one was "right." Through the decades, other filmmakers employed the multiple-perspective approach with varying degrees of sophistication.

American director Robert Altman has long featured multiple storylines in films that draw together numerous characters in complex ways; Oliver Stone's 1991 *JFK* featured various perspectives on the same incident; John Ford's 1962 *The Man Who Shot Liberty Valence* shows the same event (a showdown between gunfighters) from two vantage points. Atom Egoyan's 1994 *Exotica* likewise took multiple perspectives and narrative fragments which gradually converged in a final scene that explained everything before it; the 1996 *Courage Under Fire* (directed by Edward Zwick) shows the influence of both *Roshomon* and *Citizen Kane* in its telling the story of a tragic incident during the Gulf War. Directors like Paul Thomas Anderson have used the kaleidoscopic approach with their work, such as his 1999 *Magnolia,* which features multiple converging storylines.

Business: The kaleidoscopic or strong jazz model can help us understand the direction of business, both locally and globally, in our future.

At the level of individual companies, the traditional "top-down" managerial model has made way in some quarters for a more jazzlike approach in which employees have more input into the decision-making or profit-sharing process. On a global scale, the kaleidoscopic model provides a way of understanding how we might balance regional and international economic interests in relation to each other, a growing concern in our era of globalization.

We've seen how multinational companies can insert themselves into regional economies or cultures to a degree that poses serious challenges to those countries. An American chain like McDonald's might come into a region and introduce a menu that is uniform the world over, with the effect of edging the local restaurants out of business. In systems terminology, this is called the dominance of the system over the part. At the other extreme, an individual country can react to this trend by becoming isolationist in its economic policies and ban the introduction of multinational interests; in turn, perhaps they will miss out on the financial and creative opportunities a global market could afford. In systems terminology, this is the dominance of the part over the whole.

A kaleidoscopic, jazzlike approach is to balance out the extremes by allowing for input *and* output, in terms of creating a two-way street in trade and cultural influence. One example of this would be a multinational restaurant chain becoming more responsive to the needs and tastes of its regional customers, perhaps by incorporating local cuisine into an otherwise standardized menu. From the other direction, this might be achieved by finding new ways for local cultures to export their products or cultural creations to the world at large. The key here is flexibility on both sides.

Einstein's Theory of Relativity

It's often pointed out how Einstein's theory of relativity was really an extension of Newtonian physics rather than a break with traditional physics, as quantum mechanics eventually came to be. But there are several ways in which Einstein's work prepared Aquarian sensibilities in a scientific way of thinking, especially his view of the universe.

Prior to Einstein, the world had been viewed as a uniform realm. Phenomena behaved essentially the same wherever you traveled. But

Einstein shattered this uniformity by revealing that the universe consists of a multiplicity of perspectives and experiences. How does a distant star appear to you? It depends on how fast you are moving, or on how strong a gravity field is encompassing you or the star.

Just as importantly, Einstein's breakthrough signaled a decentralization of time. What time is it right now in the universe? During Newton's era, such questions would have made sense, since it was assumed there was some uniform "now" pervading the cosmos. But in the wake of discoveries that light can take millions of years to reach us from distant galaxies and the fact that time can be distorted by the effects of gravity or acceleration, the notion of a uniform time frame takes on far different meaning. Einstein's theory of relativity revealed to us that, in a sense, there were as many universes as there were observers to perceive them.

The theory was a major step in the modern psyche's breaking loose from the moorings of its belief in a singular "truth," and decentralizing it into multiple "truths" (though with the speed of light as a unifying point of reference).

The Holographic Web

Another example of the kaleidoscopic principle in science is a controversial theory sometimes referred to as the "holographic paradigm." This idea stems from a discovery made about 3-D, or holographic photography, which might be expressed as the principle of the "whole within the part." For example, tear up a normal photograph and you are left with fragments of the image. Break up a holographic image and you'll find each piece contains the whole image. For some, this idea soon came to be regarded as a defining icon for holistic thinking, with applications for brain function, computer design, and philosophy. In fact, this idea recalls an older concept from Hindu mythology called Indra's net: a great web of gems in which each point of the web reflects the entire net. As Linda Olds remarks in *Metaphors of Interrelatedness:*

> If any metaphor could replace the Gothic cathedral for our time, I believe it would be the image of Indra's net, the cosmic web of interrelatedness extending infinitely in all directions of the universe. Every intersection of intertwining web is set with a glistening jewel, in which all parts of the whole are reflected, mirroring the intricate intercon-

nectedness of all reality and its intercausality. Indra's net captures the web, network, tapestry, textured imagery of our time, yet perhaps needs to be seen as a more dynamic field of energy, revealing a shimmering and ever-changing holarchy, where each part reflects the whole, and where nothing exists apart from the whole (Olds 1992).

There has been much debate through the years over the merits of this concept, over whether the holographic web represents a spiritual way of understanding our world (see Ken Wilber's *The Holographic Paradigm and Other Paradoxes* for a summary of these viewpoints, both pro and con). For our purposes, such criticisms are beside the point because whether or not the holographic principle represents some kind of "ultimate" spiritual model of reality (it doesn't), it touches on an important Aquarian truth.

That is, it demonstrates a jazzlike balancing of parts and wholes in which each element shares in the larger network while retaining a uniqueness and completeness all its own—in short, *diversity-within-unity.* To *that* degree, it can help us understand a broad range of ideas important to our time. As one example, look at how this image can be related to the global telecommunications grid across the world. With the Internet, we find a similar type of interconnection where each point has access to the information contained in the entire system.

In fact, if one plays with these terms long enough, one even begins to notice interesting linguistic connections here:

Indra's net = Indranet = Indernet = Internet

Frankenstein's Monster and the Fractured Spectrum

In practical reality, the problem that can arise with a kaleidoscopic system is that when radically diverse elements come together within the same framework, the system can collapse under the weight of its contrary tendencies and internal contradictions. Instead of a rainbow, we wind up with a cacophony of colors; instead of a platypus, Frankenstein's monster. Mary Shelley's creature was a patchwork creation comprised of body parts from many different humans of many different temperaments; yet it had no aesthetic unity to bind it. It was a kaleidoscopic entity, but of the most jarring and disjointed sort—decentralization with a vengeance, one might say.

So we might distinguish between integrative and disintegrative forms of kaleidoscopism. At its gaudiest, a city like Las Vegas might be seen as an example of disintegrative kaleidoscopism. Like the Frankenstein monster, it is a patchwork entity harboring different realities butting up against one another. One minute you walk through an ancient castle, then a moment later a futuristic space station, giving you radical juxtapositions and radical incongruities, largely uncoordinated with each other. Theme parks like Disneyland and Universal Studios express the same quality in their congeries of side-by-side multiple realities.

Even the local shopping mall has become kaleidoscopic in its diversity. In the old days, stores were separate entities housed in separate locations, now the sprawling mall brings together entirely different stores under one roof. It recalls the dizzying sense conveyed by Charles Foster Kane's mansion Xanadu in *Citizen Kane*, where motifs and sculptures from every part of the world are thrown together with little regard for aesthetic unity.

The Postmodern Phenomenon

Those familiar with modern philosophy may recognize the positive and negative effects of the kaleidoscopic principle in the important intellectual trends of the last century. One detects early seeds of it in the works of psychologist William James, with his concept of the "multiverse." It is also evident in the writings of philosopher Friedrich Nietzsche, a prophet of Aquarian trends on several fronts. Consider Nietzsche's influential idea of "perspectivism," the idea that there is no absolute knowledge which transcends all possible perspectives, and that our world consists of many differing perspectives about reality. In a manner of speaking, Nietzsche's theory was a radical decentralizing of truth. One recent book summarized Nietzsche's views on the matter as follows:

> Perspectivism is the view that every "truth" is an interpretation from some particular perspective. There is no neutral, all-comprehending, "God's-eye" view available (even for God). There are only perspectives. There is no world "in itself," and even if there were such a world, we would not know it or even know *of* it (Solomon and Higgins 2000).

For these reasons, Nietzsche has been called by some a forerunner of the twentieth century phenomenon of postmodernism. A simple explanation of this term goes like this: In most premodern societies, men and women generally enjoyed the luxury of a consistent, singular worldview, due largely to the presence of a dominant religion and a homogeneous society uncomplicated by "foreigners" and their "heresies." Even with the advent of science and its modern worldview, that overriding sense of certainty didn't vanish; it shifted allegiance to a secular and scientific framework.

But over the last century, even that sense of certainty vanished. Due to revolutionary changes in physics, philosophy, and linguistics, we now entertain the possibility that there may not *be* any single or "absolute" truth. The unifying perspective and sense of certainty that characterized both the pre-modern *and* modern stages has dissolved into a multiplicity of perspectives and worldviews, each vying for our attention. This is the postmodern crisis, that philosophically, no one perspective or theory is privileged now, and our world has become a "mix master" of ideas and influences. Our fashions, films, and neighborhoods reflect the influences of many cultures and historical periods brought together.

The postmodern phenomenon is a further reflection of the Aquarian paradigm and of the kaleidoscopic complexification of our world. Properly speaking, it's not the first time this has occurred in history. One immediately thinks of ancient Alexandria, which featured a similar mix of viewpoints and cultural influences including Greek, Egyptian, Mesopotamian, Roman, Celtic, Hebrew, Persian, African, and Indian. But there are significant differences between Alexandria and our present, one of which is the fact that this phenomenon is taking place now on a *global* scale, rather than in one small corner of the planet.

Shall we classify postmodernism as a positive or a negative expression of Aquarian kaleidoscopism? It is a bit of both.

In its negative form, postmodernism has called into question our aesthetic and spiritual values to such an extent that it has led some to question the worth of *any* viewpoints. With no unifying framework by which to categorize or assess value, all perspectives are deemed equally meaningful—or meaningless. So in exchange for the dogmas and narrowness of previous worldviews, we now have the opposite problem of shattered certainties and cultural disorientation, leaving us feeling a bit like drunken sailors in a hall of mirrors. This may be called destructive (or disintegrative) postmodernism, and it expresses the spirit of kaleidoscopic relativism at its most fragmented and regressive.

Yet as some have pointed out, there is an integrative, constructive side to postmodernism, in the way it opens the door to broader possibilities of consciousness and creativity. We've already seen several examples of this earlier in this chapter. Without our newfound cultural complexity, we wouldn't have the literary works of Joyce or the popular music of the Beatles. Nor would there be the cultural stew of modern cities like New York, London, or Hong Kong. By foregoing the simple perspectives of old, a new complexity may prepare new possibilities of consciousness on the global stage. As philosopher Richard Tarnas expressed it in *The Passion of the Western Mind:*

> . . . it is evident that the most significant characteristics of the larger postmodern intellectual situation—its pluralism, complexity, and ambiguity—are precisely the characteristics necessary for the potential emergence of a fundamentally new form of intellectual vision, one that might both preserve and transcend that current state of extraordinary differentiation (Tarnas 1991).

The New Integrative Philosophies

But what "new form" of intellectual vision might this be? One clue might be found in the work of philosopher Jean Gebser, who was among the first to articulate the integrative possibilities of this emerging trend with his theory of "integral-aperspectival thought." While a detailed overview of Gebser's work is beyond the scope of this chapter, here are a few essential elements.

Gebser described the stages of human intellectual evolution from its most primitive up through the present as Archaic, Magical, Mythic, Rational, and Integral-Aperspectival. Since the Renaissance, humanity has been at the Rational stage of consciousness which views the world in terms of orderly, logical frameworks of thought as entertained by an individualized ego. In the arts, this has been paralleled by the development of perspective, a convention that orders everything around the visual framework of a single observer. But around the turn of the twentieth century, our rational way of viewing the world has been undergoing a profound change, with a shift from viewing reality from a single perspective to multiple perspectives.

This is what Gebser refers to as the "aperspectival" stage of culture: there is no single, overriding perspective in place. It was a fundamental shift in our rationality, giving us a new ability to move among competing beliefs, ideas, and systems. In the arts, this shift was reflected in the way

"Renaissance perspective" lost its hold and artists now experimented with depicting their subjects in less ordered ways, such as Cubism.

Gebser proposed a complementary stage of consciousness which he termed Integral-Aperspectival. This is a higher form of rationality that not only allows for diverse perspectives, but which incorporates these into new and more complex syntheses. In his book on Gebser *(Structures of Consciousness)* Georg Feuerstein points to the art form of the collage as an example of integral-aperspectival creativity, in the way it appropriates and reassembles preexisting elements into new and harmonious combinations. Importantly, Gebser didn't view this stage of consciousness so much as an evolutionary certainty as a latent possibility toward which humans could aspire (and which certain individuals in our culture have already attained). Gebser pointed to historian Arnold Toynbee, architect Frank Lloyd Wright, the philosophers Husserl and Heidegger, Albert Einstein, Paul Cezanne, and Arnold Schoenberg as examples. To his list we can add James Joyce and Orson Welles. What distinguished all of these was their ability to draw on older elements and bring them together into new syntheses which were greater than the sum of their parts.[2]

Gebser wasn't the only one to theorize about the integrative possibilities of our higher rationality. Writers like Indian philosopher Sri Aurobindo and contemporary philosopher Ken Wilber have offered their own thoughts on this subject. Indeed, Wilber's work provides an example of this integrative initiative at work, with his varied attempts to synthesize ideas from diverse fields and disciplines into larger theoretical frameworks (e.g., "four-quadrant" theory, "spectrum psychology," the Integral Institute). Curiously, while none of these thinkers apparently based their work on astrological principles, their ideas on the emergent rationality closely match what astrology suggests about the Aquarian mind in its integrative or kaleidoscopic possibilities.[3]

The New Kaleidoscopic Psyche

The human psyche, too, has felt the decentralizing effects of the emerging Aquarian influence. In a certain sense, as a result of our changing world, we are finding ourselves fragmented into a patchwork of perspectives and subpersonalities. The complexities of life have become such that we now find ourselves having to wear many different masks during a lifetime, sometimes during a single day. New media technologies and the Internet also make it possible for us to pass through different worlds and cultures in a short time, even to don new identities at will. The effects of our changing neighborhoods and demography are producing a climate in which someone can grow up without the same rigid sense of cultural or biological identity which characterized many peoples in earlier times.

The result has been a loss of our fixed center, that singular sense of identity that characterized human experience for thousands of years. Postmodern philosophers like Jacques Lacan and Michel Foucault have described the "death of the solid self" and the birth of the "decentered self." While not approaching their subject from an astrological perspective, their ideas mesh with the decentralizing effects of Aquarius we're examining here.

In a way, we are *each* becoming a bit like that modern-day sports team mentioned earlier, incorporating diverse influences and identities into a single entity. In cinema, we find evidence of this trend in 1999's *Being John Malkovich,* with its climactic scene of many different people literally piling into (and inside) the head of the title character, actor John Malkovich (playing himself)—an apt metaphor for the way each of us has to assume multiple identities.

Here, too, there are positive and negative possibilities. In its destructive form, the kaleidoscopic psyche can leave us feeling scattered or uncertain of our roles in the world. Who are we, really? In a way, each of us may feel at times as though we are suffering from multiple personality disorder. In the 1998 film *Dark City,* a city is depicted in which people's identities and memories have been scrambled to such an extent they don't know who they are. In a slightly different way, Paul Veerhoven's 1990 *Total Recall* shows its lead character trying to determine which of the various identities he experiences is truly *him.* In more symbolic form, there is also that famed climactic sequence from Welles' 1948 feature *The Lady from Shanghai,* where the lead characters are shown fragmented into broken images in an amusement park's hall-of-mirrors.

A more constructive way of reading this trend is to imagine its decentralizing effect ushering in a new psychological complexity that holds many creative possibilities. Walt Whitman alluded to this new complexity in *Leaves of Grass:* "Do I contradict myself? Very well then I contradict myself. (I am large, I contain multitudes.)"

Average men and women today may not be as rooted in a single tradition or culture as their medieval counterparts, nor have as fixed a social identity as tribal peoples might have; yet this is also making possible eclectic modes of thinking and self-expression that draw upon many sources rather than just one. The creativity of artists like James Joyce or Pablo Picasso wouldn't have been possible in earlier times, for example, with all their global references. Likewise, the average schoolchild is growing up now with an awareness of other cultures and races that wasn't possible before the rise of media.

As if a reflection of this decentralization trend, modern psychology has given rise to therapies and theoretical models that address our multiplistic natures. Roberto Assagioli's theory of psychosynthesis speaks to the numerous "sub-personalities" within each of us, with an eye toward their integration and transcendence. We also find this kaleidoscopic influence in the work of James Hillman, whose theory of "polytheistic psychology" uses the gods and goddesses of ancient mythology to metaphorically illustrate the complexity of human psychic experience. In recent decades, the growing popularity of astrology, with its inherently "multiplistic" approach to personality (i.e., the various planets operating in concert), is another aspect of this trend. Indeed, some foresee a time when astrology will be openly integrated with psychological theories and techniques.

What can we do to help ensure that we will express the constructive possibilities offered by the kaleidoscopic influence in the coming age, rather than its disintegrative ones? Or, to use terms proposed by Jean Houston, how shall we move from a state of schizophrenia to "polyphrenia"—the orchestration of our multiple selves toward a more expanded sense of psychic health?

In part, this is a problem that can be addressed on the collective level, in terms of offering unifying paradigms, rituals, or institutions that can help guide or heal individuals in this process. On a personal level, the solution to the decentralizing effects of modern life lies in learning how to forge one's own center within. To elaborate on this point, we turn in the final chapters to the spiritual implications of the kaleidoscopic principle in the coming Aquarian Age.

16

The Six Billion Faces of God: Aquarian Concepts of Divinity

"Pay no attention to that man behind the curtain." It has become one of the most quoted lines in all of pop culture, arising at a climactic moment of *The Wizard of Oz*. Dorothy and her companions have finally completed the tasks assigned them by the "great and powerful wizard," and have returned to receive their gifts. Instead, they discover the wizard isn't a wizard at all, that the things they had sought for were *inside* them all along.

An enchanting modern fantasy, most would agree; but who would have guessed that this story also represents an esoteric expression of the tectonic shift I call the Aquarian Age? If one hopes to uncover the "signs of the times," one must sometimes look in seemingly unlikely places; this much-beloved movie is just such a repository of clues about the changing face of society, even our religious beliefs. To explain how, we need to understand something of the implication of Aquarius for modern spirituality.

With each Great Age comes a different way of relating to the divine. In our time, that change might be described as a democratizing of the God-principle. By way of analogy, the decentralizing influence of Aquarius in politics has initiated a shift of power from kingly rulers to ordinary men and women. On a spiritual level, the same thing is beginning to occur in relation to the divine, as attention shifts away from a centralized "God" (or religious authority) back to *ourselves*. As Carl Jung wrote:

> The Gods first lived in superhuman power and beauty, on the top of snowclad mountains or in the darkness of caves, woods, and seas. Later on they drew together into one God, and then that God became man. But in our days even the God-man seems to have descended from his throne and to be dissolving in the common man (Jung 1968).

This trend has seen both exoteric and esoteric implications for modern culture, and not all of them have necessarily been spiritual. So let us begin by looking at some of the exoteric examples.

The "Religion" of Personal Empowerment

For most men and women in our time, the emerging Aquarian emphasis on the individual has brought about a heightened focus on the individual personality. In counterbalance to the more self-denying tendencies of the Piscean era, the Aquarian Age ushers in a more self-affirming philosophy toward experience and a greater emphasis on personal empowerment. Rather than surrender ourselves to some higher cause or principle, we are now becoming more concerned with realizing our own physical and psychological potentials. We see the effects of this emerging spirit in such diverse ways as the early "I can do it!" optimism of a Horatio Alger story, to the "body beautiful" ethos of our local health clubs. At its most superficial, it has led to little more than narcissism and the championing of the personality, something we might call the new religion of Me.

Yet for all its problems, this same emphasis on the individual personality also gave us the best of the "human potential" movement as exemplified by figures like Abraham Maslow and Carl Rogers. Earlier figures like Freud had defined the psyche in largely negative terms, as little more than a garbage heap of repressed emotions, but the later movement of humanistic psychology focused on understanding and enhancing our potentials. To see the traces of this legacy, look at any of those movements today which feature the "self" prefix: self-help, self-actualization, self-empowerment, self-work, self-enhancement, self-responsibility. The title of Jean Houston's book *The Possible Human* captures this spirit. As an example of someone who has promoted this trend in recent years, consider Oprah Winfrey. Her "Change your life!" approach toward programming in the late 1990s sought to inject a more uplifting and empowering content to television shows. In various ways, this trend could play an important role in the spiritual directions of our future by offering an approach to the divine which doesn't deny the everyday personality but incorporates it into the process.

Aquarian Mysticism—Awakening the God Within

At a more mystical level, this Aquarian individualistic trend brings an approach toward spirituality that extends beyond basic concepts of personal empowerment to a realization of our inner divinity. In his *Creative Mythology*, Joseph Campbell wrote:

> Just as in the past each civilization was the vehicle of its own mythology, so in this modern world . . . each individual is the center of a mythology of his own, of which his own intelligible character is the Incarnate God, so to say, whom his empirically questing consciousness is to find. The aphorism of Delphi, "Know thyself," is the motto. And not Rome, not Mecca, not Jerusalem, Sinai, or Benares, but *each and every "thou" on earth is the center of this world.* . . . [emphasis added] (Campbell 1968)

Here we see the meaning of Promethean fire in its esoteric dimension, drawing down *spiritual* consciousness from the realm of the gods to the level of every man and woman, a process Carl Jung referred to as the "Christification of the Many" (Edinger 1992). When the controversial occultist Aleister Crowley proclaimed that each person was a "star," he was expressing a distinctly Aquarian truth, but one that would, understandably, be lost amidst the distraction of his flamboyant lifestyle and statements.

But hasn't the teaching that "the divine lies within us" been part of every great religion through history, at least when understood esoterically? After all, even Christianity informs us that "Heaven lies within," while John 10:34 affirmed that "Ye are Gods!"

Yet there are certain differences between the perennial versions of this truth and the way we see it surfacing in Aquarian contexts. Traditional mysticism tends to extol our inner divinity to the exclusion of our surface personality. However, the emerging Aquarian perspective sees our everyday identity as having value in itself, that our individual embodiment is a unique expression of the divine (Campbell 1968). In this same spirit, Aquarian mysticism places less emphasis on gurus, God-symbols, and organized religious systems of all kinds, though it does this possibly to an extreme.[1] And while the belief that God lies within was present during earlier times, it was rarely the *common* understanding among ordinary men and women.

For example, during the last two thousand years, the average Christian neither grasped the esoteric message of his faith, nor did he dare utter such sentiments publicly, lest he be persecuted or killed.[2] But the Aquarian trend appears to be one in which the mystical perspective of our inner divinity is becoming the conventional belief—even if only dimly understood by most. It is not uncommon today to turn on the TV and hear a celebrity speak about how "God lies within"—comments that would have gotten them burned at the stake a few centuries earlier. Likewise, one often reads of how people are turning away from traditional churches or synagogues to forge their own spiritual paths and connections to God.

To get an idea of how pervasive this notion has become in modern times we need look no farther than *The Wizard of Oz*. The greatest of all modern fairy tales, some would say, this work features a classic heroic quest: Dorothy and her companions set out to find the solutions to their important life-problems. One wants a heart; another a brain; a third hopes for courage; Dorothy simply wants to get back home. They travel together to the fabled land of Oz in the hope that the "great and powerful wizard" might grant them these things. Yet when they finally confront him, they get a great disillusionment, and a great gift.

For although the wizard is an ordinary fellow, the things they sought reside much closer to "home." To paraphrase what Glenda the good witch says to Dorothy: The answer to your journey has always been *within* you! Read as a parable, it tells us that in our spiritual journey, the "wizard" must be put aside that we might become more self-reliant.

Who is the "wizard" anyway? At one level, it is any concept of God we might hold too tightly, or our excessive dependence on external gurus and teachers of *any* kind. With its Aquarian emphasis on personal autonomy and independence, this story reflects a sea-change in the mythic sensibilities of our time. We are entering an era when we learn to live our connection to the divine from *within*. Our relationship to the divine is shifting from a vertical to a horizontal plane as we awaken to our role as cocreators of the cosmic drama.

Did Baum intend this esoteric message to be a part of this children's story, or are we guilty of simply reading such ideas into his work? The evidence strongly suggests he knew what he was doing. As Oz scholar John Algeo has shown, Baum was a one-time member of the Theosophical Society (having joined it in 1892) and was an enthusiastic student of the esoteric teachings of H. P. Blavatsky; he even wrote publicly about Theosophical ideas for a South Dakota newspaper *(The Aberdeen Saturday Pioneer)* during the early 1890s (Algeo 2000). Among the central tenets of Theosophy is the belief that "divinity" resides inside us, rather than in external forms or intermediaries. As Blavatsky once put it, the essence of spiritual esotericism can be summed up as the idea that "the personal God exists within, nowhere outside, the worshipper" (Blavatsky 1985).

Slightly differently, one is reminded of Nietzsche's proclamation about the death of God, a statement never intended to herald the actual death of divinity so much as of our traditional concepts of God. We see a similar message expressed in more artistic form in the 1998 film *The Truman Show.* Truman Burbank has been held captive in an artificial world lorded over by a powerful God-like figure, who has the intriguing name of Christof. Toward the end of the film, Truman comes to grips with his need to put aside this world and its creator and to forge his own life. But Christof implores him to stay, saying, "There's no more truth out there than there is in the world I created for you . . . the same lies, the same deceit. But in my world, you have nothing to fear. . . . You can't leave, Truman; you belong here . . . with me." But leave he does. In a manner similar to the climax of *The Wizard of Oz,* Truman's disengagement from this God-figure reflects the trend toward autonomy and independence that marks the coming Aquarian Age.

Another cinematic example of this idea is the 1989 science fiction film *Star Trek V: The Final Frontier.* From an art standpoint, this movie has sometimes been criticized as the worst of the *Star Trek* movie series; yet its undeniable mythic resonance makes it in some ways the most interesting one. Part of this interest may stem from its astrological timing, since this film found its way into theaters the same summer we obtained our first close-up of Neptune through *Voyager II,* and several months prior to Saturn's passage over Neptune in 1989. This powerful emphasis on Neptune (the ruler of Pisces) meant this could be a pivotal point in the passage from the Piscean to Aquarian Age, and the closing-off of those symbols and concerns from the past. That sense of closure is reflected in this film in a striking way.

The crew of the *Enterprise* is led to the far ends of the universe by a charismatic religious leader named Sai Bak. They arrive at a region in space believed to be Heaven and come face-to-face with a God-figure straight out of the Bible: he's wrathful and bullying, and has a flowing white beard. But as in *The Wizard of Oz,* the anticipated encounter is a disillusionment: this "God" is nothing of the sort; he's an impostor. Eventually, this pseudo-God is destroyed by weapons from a spaceship piloted by Mr. Spock.

All in all, the film illustrates the transition between Ages beautifully, in the way that we see a textbook personification of the old religious worldview (Sai Bak, a Jehovah-like figure) taken down by a textbook personification of the new scientific worldview (Mr. Spock). In other words, the Piscean Age makes way for the Aquarian Age. As the final icing on the cake, the film concludes with Spock engaged in a discussion with Dr. McCoy and Captain Kirk on the matter of whether God exists. Kirk chimes in: "Maybe God doesn't exist out there . . . maybe He exists in here"—as he points to his chest. It's the same Aquarian message we've been seeing, that divinity resides within.

The New Face of God

All this discussion is not to say that there will no longer be any need for a God-concept in our future or in a belief in a supreme creative intelligence who regulates our world. Rather, it may mean that the route toward realizing that divine reality is more direct and personal now. The one-size-fits-all approach toward God that characterized many traditional societies won't work any longer in Aquarian culture. Each of us will have to learn how to connect with that "presence" in a manner best suited to our needs. So instead of an aged man with a flowing white beard, "God" may now have to sport a different face for each and every person on the planet. God will have to assume six billion faces—one for each member of the human race.

But hasn't the idea of God assuming human form been an integral part of our Western religious tradition for thousands of years, as exemplified by Christianity and ancient Greek religion? In one sense, yes; but there is a key difference in what we see with the emerging Aquarian mythos, and it may be expressed like this: rather than take on human form, God is now beginning to appear *as oneself* (or as someone "in the family"). This is an important step in the evolution of our religious sensibilities. To illustrate what I am talking about here, let's look briefly to the symbols offered by three of the most acclaimed science fiction films of recent decades: Stanley Kubrick's *2001: A Space Odyssey,* Robert Zemeckis's *Contact,* and Andrei Tarkovsky's *Solaris.*

***2001: A Space Odyssey* (Director, Stanley Kubrick):** Kubrick's self-styled "space opera" tells of a secret mission to the moon and Jupiter as a group of scientists attempt to solve a mystery involving intelligent life beyond Earth. Signals have been received first from the moon and then Jupiter, and astronauts have been sent to investigate. Along the way, problems arise with HAL, the spacecraft's computer, and only one astronaut is left to complete the mission. After a near-fatal confrontation with HAL, this astronaut leaves the ship and is drawn into a hyper-dimensional passage toward an unspecified reality.

At the climax of this psychedelic sequence, the astronaut finds himself in a brightly lit room, reminiscent of eighteenth century France. But what does he encounter during this climactic moment? Not aliens, not some bearded God-figure, but *himself,* or himself at progressively advanced ages. The movie concludes with the astronaut seemingly reborn as a star child floating high over the Earth.

As Joseph Campbell noted, each age and culture adapts the basic structures of the classic "hero's journey" to its own time and values. Kubrick's space opera places this quest in a stellar context. From one standpoint, the treasure at the climax of any heroic quest symbolizes the highest values of a particular culture; in one society, the boon might be a golden fleece, while in another, immortality. But in Kubrick's vision, the hero encounters himself. What does this mean about our own shifting relationship to the ultimate? It expresses the idea that the divine is taking on a more familiar form, and now is to be found by turning back toward ourselves.

***Contact* (Director, Robert Zemeckis):** Based on Carl Sagan's novel of the same name, this 1997 film tells of a female scientist engaged in a search for intelligent life in the universe. On discovering signals from deep space, scientists analyze them only to discover they encode instructions for building a spacecraft, one that would allow humans to travel somewhere. After many delays, the spacecraft is constructed, and the scientist endures a harrowing journey through mysterious realms. The craft eventually stops, and she finds herself on an ethereally beautiful beach, similar to Earth in some respects, but oddly different in others. She notices a figure approaching her; it is an alien disguised as her deceased father.

As with *2001: A Space Odyssey,* we see essentially the same archetypal symbolism here. It is a classic heroic quest: the central character embarks on a great journey, at the climax of which she undergoes a transformation. But here, too, that final encounter is not with a God-like figure, or some alien other, but rather a highly personal form—her father. If we read such encounters with the "other" as symbolizing our shifting relationship to the divine, then the visage of a family member at this key moment in the story reinforces the fact that our spiritual path is taking on more personal form now.

Solaris **(Director, Andrei Tarkovsky):** Based on a story by Stanislaw Lem, Andrei Tarkovsky's 1972 film is widely regarded as the finest science fiction film to come out of Russia in recent decades. The story centers on a group of scientists who have been sent to a remote space station orbiting a mysterious planet named Solaris. This is a watery planet that is an intelligent being in its own right. Strangely, each scientist on board finds that in the presence of this planet he experiences a series of highly personal hallucinations, based on his own buried memories from the past. In particular, the psychologist is haunted by memories of his beautiful wife who committed suicide years before.

Over the years, there have been many interpretations of this subtle and enigmatic work, which served as the inspiration for several English-speaking films, including *Event Horizon*. Yet from our perspective, it can be seen as one more variation on the same Aquarian point. In that confrontation with the "other," the film shows each individual having an experience that is unique and personal. Symbolically speaking, the divine is increasingly presenting itself in a more individualized manner, through filters or masks that befit our temperaments and destinies.

Religion in the Key of Jazz

What of the future of organized religion? Does this Aquarian oriented trend signal the end of conventional churches and denominations as a new-found spiritual individualism leads toward an "every man for himself" climate with no further need of religious institutions?

There are several possibilities to consider. The most obvious is that society will continue to become more pluralistic, kaleidoscopically harboring different religious viewpoints. To a great extent, America has already provided the template for this, with its diversity of religious faiths.

This is the other message in *The Wizard of Oz:* in addition to suggesting the "answer lies within," it depicts a coordination of diverse visions and journeys. Notice, for instance, the story doesn't simply depict one person setting out to obtain a dream, but rather a group of totally different creatures, each harboring totally different dreams. Despite their differences, they are somehow able to harmonize their quests in a way that proves greater than the sum of the parts. It's the kaleidoscopic, or jazz model again, in which multiple beings join forces.

It is worth comparing this model to earlier versions of the "group quest" in Western mythology. In variations of the Arthurian legends (chiefly the Old French version, *La Queste del Saint Graal*), the knights search for the Holy Grail on their own—a feature which Joseph Campbell said epitomized the spirit of the Grail as a symbol. As the original text describes it, "They agreed that all would go on this quest, but they thought it would be a disgrace to go forth in a group, *so each entered the forest at a point that he, himself,* had chosen, where it was darkest and there was no path [emphasis added]." To Campbell, this description offers an important insight into the Western approach to spirituality which differs from that found in Oriental mythologies, where individuality is less valued (Campbell 1990).

The Arthurian knights embark on their journeys individually, yet they are all searching for the same thing: the Holy Grail. In the Oz story, each character is searching for something different: for one, it is courage; for another, home; for another, brains; while for yet another, heart. That is a fundamental shift in the nature of the spiritual quest. In other words, the goal itself has changed, having become more individualized to best suit the needs of each quester.

Note that the knights don't coordinate their efforts. In their individualism, they strike out on their own into the "dark wood," which is a rudimentary stage of individualism, one could argue. In *The Wizard of Oz,* they are not only individualized but have learned how to coordinate their journeys without sacrificing their own visions. This offers a vital clue for our survival in the Aquarian Age: it is not simply a matter of awakening to our own dreams, we must find a way of *harmonizing* them, building a kaleidoscopic network of diverse spiritual visions within a group.

As to *how* this might achieved, we have several examples. The first example is global in scope, and illustrates how various faiths from around the world can coexist harmoniously. I'm referring to the Parliament of World Religions, first convened in Chicago in 1893, and then reconvened in 1993. Faiths from around the world came together to discuss the pressing issues of the times. It was a "United Nations" of religious faiths, one might say.

(Astrologically, both of these historic meetings were notable for having occurred *precisely* in tandem with rare outer-planet configurations at the time: the first Parliament coincided with the Pluto conjunction to Neptune still in effect in 1893, while the second Parliament coincided with the Uranus conjunction to Neptune in 1993.)

But it's also possible that the same kaleidoscopic pluralism can even exist within the confines of a single organization or religion, which is my second example. The Theosophical Society was founded in 1875 by H. P. Blavatsky; this organization undertook an essentially kaleidoscopic or jazz-style approach toward religion by allowing individuals of different spiritual orientations to join, sharing little more than an allegiance to certain fundamental principles, called by Theosophists the "three objects." One can be a Buddhist, Christian, or Muslim, and still join this organization.[3] In their own way, spiritual groups like the Unitarians and the Baha'i also show a kaleidoscopic approach to religious belief, while the California-based Institute of Noetic Sciences provides a secular example of how spiritually-oriented people can join forces within an organization, while simultaneously respecting the higher aims of modern science.

The Changing Shape of Personal Spirituality

But what of *individual* spirituality in the times ahead? If indeed we are to become more attuned to the idea that "God lies within us," what does this mean for the changing shape of spiritual practice itself?

Such a trend may produce what Huston Smith termed a "cafeteria" approach to religion, where individuals pick and choose from various traditions to create their own personalized religion. For many in the New Age community, this mix-and-match style has already become the option *du jour*, and will probably continue to be so for many centuries to come.

But there is a fundamental problem with this approach: while it may work fine for world-class religious founders like the Buddha, in the case of the average person it tends to produce a watered-down form of spirituality. As a yogi once remarked to Huston Smith, it is better to drill for water using one sixty-foot well than six ten-foot wells!

Along a different track, the democratizing influence of Aquarius will probably manifest for most people in a greater freedom of choice in their spiritual direction. Many of the same religions we are now accustomed to will persist in the coming Age; but in contrast to traditional times, we won't be obliged to practice whatever faith we were born into. Instead, we will have the option of electing whatever religion or denomination we want. Of course, the United States was founded upon this principle, a fact which shows another way this nation is the spearhead of the emerging order. Organized religions will continue to play a key role in our future, but people will have more latitude than in earlier periods of history.

A third possibility involves a reconciliation of the first two directions into a more integral approach, one which balances out the potential extremes of "pastiche" spirituality on the one hand, and traditional "monolithic" dogmatism on the other. This integral approach would involve subscribing to a specific technique or religion as one's *core* practice, while familiarizing oneself with the philosophies and principles of many different spiritual systems or beliefs. To say it another way, one will be eclectic in understanding but specific in practice.

The famed yogi Paramahansa Yogananda once said, "Learn a little about everything, and everything about one thing" (Yogananda 1997), and that could apply to spirituality in the coming era as well. Expand your horizons, but ultimately put your drill down *somewhere*, and take it all the way. Get the advantage of grounding and depth offered by a single path, with the breadth of understanding of many paths, a combination necessary for life in an increasingly complex and pluralistic world.

There are two further points pertinent to the future direction of personal spirituality in the Aquarian Age. First, as science continues to replace (and to some extent, discount) the standard myths of traditional religion, people will be turning away from an adherence to stories and looking increasingly toward spiritual methodologies as a basis for their religious practice—in short, looking for techniques rather than beliefs.

By way of example, think of Buddhism, which is more a methodology than a set of beliefs. Unlike more fundamentalist religions, one doesn't need to "believe" stories about the Buddha's life to get to "Heaven." The essence of Buddhism is a set of ethical precepts and spiritual practices, and such a structure is likely to be the wave of the future. Other examples include the Science of Mind, which eschews conventional mythic belief. Even within Christianity itself, we find signs of this shift entering in, as with the Christian Science movement. This system may be thought of as a hybrid of Piscean and Aquarian-style sensibilities, in the sense of being based on a Christian framework (Pisces), while stressing the importance of mind control (Aquarius).

The second point concerns something we might call the new perennialism. As our world grows more complex, we are being *forced* to transcend parochial dogmas and myths, and to focus our attention on commonalties which link us. One expression of this has been the rise of comparative religion in recent centuries, especially as it concerns the study of "perennial" principles. These are the core, universal ideas which undergird spiritual philosophies the world over. Over the last century, this new perennialism has been spearheaded by individuals like Carl Jung, Joseph Campbell, Frithjof Schuon, and Mircea Eliade, to name a few. Note, too, this approach doesn't necessarily require a *denial* of those features which are unique to a particular religion (a criticism commonly thrown at Joseph Campbell for his "universalist" approach). Rather, an integrative option is to balance an emphasis on universals with the particularities of each religion. This may offer the soundest option toward meeting the needs of our complex society.

Unraveling the Riddle of the Sphinx

In chapter 8 we drew upon the image of scientists watching children on a playground to convey one aspect of the Leo/Aquarius polarity—the sense of detached rationality that can occur when the human mind (Aquarius) becomes too dissociated from the immediacy and vitality of life experience (Leo). In this chapter we've seen a very different way of looking at the symbolism of this polarity which focuses on a more harmonious merging of these polar opposites. Instead of a one-sided emphasis on our humanity that denies the reality of God (Aquarius over Leo), or an emphasis on divinity that denies our basic humanity (Leo over Aquarius), this dimension concerns the possibility for an *integration* of the divine and the human, of the spiritual and the everyday.

Here a more appropriate image for conveying the potentials of the Leo/Aquarius axis would be the Egyptian Sphinx. We may never know what the Egyptians themselves intended with the symbolism of the Sphinx; even Egyptologists don't agree on this point. But as a symbol for our own times, the power of the Sphinx likely stems from the deep archetypal chords it strikes in us as an emblem for our emerging spiritual potentials, and for what we may *become*. Like the technology of solar power, the merging of the human and lion forms symbolically describes the joining of our spiritual and human natures as one, and the possibility of creating a society of fully integrated god-men and god-women.

Nearly a century ago poet William Butler Yeats hinted at the enormous power of this symbol for humanity's future when he wrote these lines heralding (or was it bemoaning?) the impending world age in "The Second Coming":

> Surely some revelation is at hand;
> Surely the Second Coming is at hand.
> The Second Coming! Hardly are those words out
> When a vast image out of *Spiritus Mundi*
> Troubles my sight: somewhere in sands of the desert
> A shape with lion body and the head of a man. . . .

17

The Mystery of Free Will: Aquarius and the Awakening of Self-Consciousness

As a spiritual force in humanity's evolution, the Aquarian Age is important on several levels. In the last chapter, we saw one important possibility, with the idea that it could open us to a reconciliation of our divine and human natures, by ushering in a more practical approach that manifests our spirituality in everyday contexts. But another aspect of this era's spiritual importance centers on the mysterious principle of free will. What *is* free will, exactly, and what possible relation could it have with Aquarius? To help answer questions like these, let us consider an idea I first encountered during a lecture by a spiritual teacher with whom I had been studying.

Aquarius—An Opening to Possibility

It was nearly twenty-five years ago that I sat and listened as the yogi recalled an experience he once had of "astrally projecting" to a realm esotericists call the Akashic Records. As interpreted by the conscious mind, he said, these records can take the form of twelve large books, in which are contained the knowledge of all that has occurred through time, though it is written in hieroglyphic-like symbols. What intrigued me about his tale was his comment about how one obtained knowledge from these books, specifically about the future. For this, he said, one turned to the eleventh volume of this series—an intriguing correspondence with the forward-looking sign of Aquarius, the eleventh sign of the zodiac. Here were encoded the potentialities of all that lie ahead, for oneself and the world. The clincher was, he said, as one turned to the last page of that eleventh volume, one discovered that it was never finished. Right before your eyes, words and letters continually form. Upon finishing those last words, a new page will "magically" appear, so that the 11th book forever remains incomplete, always in a state of becoming.

I don't know whether this man's story was truth or fabrication, nor did it matter. I knew that either way it contained an important insight about Aquarius. Yes, this sign is intimately involved with all matters pertaining to the future, as symbolically it's the zodiacal principle most often associated with hopes, dreams, and wishes. But for me, the deeper insight centered on the quality of open-endedness associated with the 11th volume, and its implication of free will.

If the twelve signs of the zodiac represent archetypal principles of the soul, then Aquarius is that point of the psyche through which we open up to the unbounded possibilities of existence, and the inner workings of destiny itself. In David Lean's *Lawrence of Arabia,* T. E. Lawrence proclaims "*Nothing* is written!"—and in so doing, he was expressing an Aquarian truth. The future may be predetermined to some extent, but it isn't set in stone; things *can* be modified, things *can* be acted upon. Aquarius is the state which allows us to step outside the ordinary framework of fate and do just that.

If this says something about the zodiacal sign Aquarius, then it also tells us something important about the Aquarian Age. The coming era could be a time when we gain access to our free will on a collective level. And there are indications this has already begun to happen. Roughly since the time of Uranus's discovery in the late 1700s, humanity has experienced a major shift in its attitudes toward what could be achieved in the world.

After believing for millennia that we were constrained by nature, ordinary men and women began entertaining the thought that they might master nature, and perhaps even attain that most precious of commodities—*freedom.* Just two or three centuries earlier, the notion that we could engineer our own destinies was virtually unthinkable for most people. Not only was this new spirit mirrored in symbols like aviation and modern democracy, but it expressed itself within a new view of history itself. Almost overnight, we shifted our attention from a once-powerful past to a suddenly boundless future. In a letter to John Adams, written in 1816, Thomas Jefferson remarked, "I like the dreams of the future better than the history of the past," and in so doing he became a mouthpiece for the new evolutionary impulse. Cultural historian Robert Heilbroner has described this novel shift in a passage that takes on special resonance for students of the emerging Aquarian consciousness:

> . . . until a few centuries ago in the West, and until relatively recent times in the East, it was the past and not the future which was the dominant orientation to historic time. . . . Ancient Egypt, Greece, Rome, the vast Asiatic civilizations, even the Renaissance, did not look ahead for the ideas and inspirations of their existence, but sought them in their origins, in their ancient glories, their fabled heroes, their pristine virtues real or fancied. . . . (Beginning with the seventeenth century, the past began changing) from a source of inspiration to a collection of mistakes, and the future, hitherto so featureless, had risen up like a Promised Land. By the eighteenth century, an immense optimism had swept over Europe, and no one voiced it so enthusiastically as the philosopher-historian Condorcet: "There is no limit set to the perfecting of the powers of man," he wrote (Heilbroner 1960).

The Gift of Knowledge

The question remains: why Aquarius? What is it about this sign that makes it so critical to understanding concepts like free will and the inner workings of destiny? Surely, such factors would seem more logically associated with a zodiacal sign like Leo, the sign of royalty and the source of our spiritual vitality. The image I had come to link with Aquarius—scientists standing outside a playground rationally observing the frolicking children—hardly seemed appropriate for expressing such notions as free will or freedom!

Yet over time, it became clear that it was the detachment underlying this sign which holds the key. By contrast, fiery Leo at the other end of the zodiac may relate to the principle of consciousness, but this is consciousness in a more experiential and immediate sense, more like the child bursting with enthusiasm than the reflective self-awareness of an adult. If one were to equate Leo with the proclamation "I AM!" then Aquarius could be expressed by "I AM *AWARE* THAT I AM!"—the consciousness *of* consciousness.

If you have ever had a guest drop in unexpectedly, you may have found yourself aware of an untidiness in your home you hadn't noticed moments before. It's as if you had an extra set of eyes by which to see your environment objectively. This objective viewpoint illustrates the principle of air as described by astrologers. As a psychological influence, the element of air gives one the capacity to be objective about things, to conceptually stand off and perceive oneself or situations from a detached viewpoint. Its presence (or absence) in someone's horoscope indicates their ability for setting aside emotional concerns or biases and to see things from a bird's-eye standpoint, like a neutral reporter.

On the global scale, this is why the modern media is a perfect symbol for the emerging Aquarian consciousness, since it represents an extension of our collective consciousness that has detached from itself and is now turning back to examine its own experience. In a sense, media is the embodiment of the Aquarian air principle in our world, in terms of a new style of self-consciousness awakening in us.

What does all this have to do with such concepts as free will or destiny? Simply put, that ability to stand apart in a detached fashion creates an opening in consciousness through which a new degree of choice enters into experience. It is a degree of choice absent when one is completely immersed in experience. To use a hypothetical example, imagine a community in which everyone plays a role in an intricately devised drama, but doesn't know it. That is because each has been hypnotized in the past, given inductions to act out pre-assigned parts, and programmed to forget they had ever been hypnotized. As a result, every one sets about their business, acting their parts, without realizing they're puppets, mechanically reciting scripted lines. Then one day an actor wanders "off-set," and accidentally stumbles upon a copy of the script they are living out. Leafing through the pages, he finds his own role delineated, each action and bit of dialogue laid out. More shocking, he finds lines and actions he is to perform in the coming week. How would *you* respond to such a discovery?

Apart from the existential crisis of it all, it would be hard to feel spontaneous from that moment on, since you would be constantly second-guessing every word and movement, wondering what was truly yours and what was scripted by some unseen writer. One major benefit would result from this: you would now have a certain element of *choice* in your actions from this point on. Why? Having glimpsed the script, you could now decide whether to act out that part as it was scripted, or not. That isn't an option yet available to the other actors in the troupe, since they have no way of knowing which lines were theirs and which were not. Through the gift of knowledge, in other words, you now have a degree of freedom you haven't experienced before.

Rewriting the Script?

In the same way, the detachment and knowledge conferred by air rationality introduces choice into our lives. As long as one is immersed in direct experience, running on impulse (the fire element), one has no choice but to act the way one is going to act. But by drawing back from that field of action to view it in a rational way, one now has a wider range of reactions from which to choose, perhaps even the ability to tinker with the script itself. This has a direct analogy with the Aquarian science of astrology, for by allowing one to see life from a detached, rational standpoint, the horoscope gives a peek at the script driving one's actions and thoughts. The reaction of many people to their first horoscope reading is similar to our hypothetical actor who realized he had been a puppet, moved involuntarily, except here the controlling influences consist of planetary "programs." While initially startling, it throws the door open to new possibilities and choices because you cannot be free of your karma until you first know what it is.

Humanity is undergoing an analogous awakening in its evolution now. Through the influence of air, we are becoming more detached from life in certain ways, something which has brought problems. Yet the same rational detachment has begun providing us the opportunity to stand back and catch a glimpse of the "script" which has been driving us for many millennia. On emotional levels, we can do this now through modern psychology, which has made us more aware of the workings of the human psyche in everyday life, and thereby allowed us to act upon behavior. In terms of the world-at-large, modern science has provided a knowledge of the laws that run our world, and has given us leverage over our environment. Astrology could play a similar role in the world, granting us knowledge of the workings of destiny.

Here we see another way in which the film *The Matrix* symbolically reflects the archetypal dynamics of our time. As noted earlier, this film tells of a society where men and women have been hypnotically enslaved within a collectively shared cyber-illusion. A few individuals in that world have awakened from the illusion and broken free of their enslavement. Like the actor in our example above, *The Matrix*'s men and women uncover the "script" which has been controlling their lives and see the hidden machinations that have been controlling—and creating—their world. But as a result of that detachment, they gain a degree of freedom, which others in the cyber-illusion do not have.

Symbolically, this film illustrates the process we have been exploring: humanity's awakening into the air element. As we develop the capacity for thinking, we learn to conceptually stand back and extricate ourselves from the "programs" of our instinctual natures and our enslavement to nature. Like this film's cyber-rebels, we are gaining a degree of choice in the process in determining our future. Note, too, that as in *The Truman Show* and *The Abyss,* this transformation is cinematically depicted as involving a transition from a water-based state to an air-based one, as *The Matrix*'s hero emerges from his amniotic sac into the real world of air.

This movement into the air element explains why Aquarius may prove to be such an important stage in the evolution of humanity's consciousness. As astrologers have long known (and as the story of the yogi and the Akashic Records underscores), there is something inherently open-ended about Aquarius which makes it hard to predict what will unfold from it. This is because of the element of choice and free will. In various esoteric sources through history, one sometimes encounters the idea that humans have a capacity for free will and spiritual growth that even God does not. How could this be? In a sense, it's precisely because of our separation from that cosmic source, resulting from our rational detachment—we have a certain leeway and capacity for choice that doesn't exist at higher levels of consciousness.

Compare the sun in its mighty course with a human on Earth. Which of these two has more free will, in terms of a capacity for choice? Of course, it's the human, for while the sun may be the source of all life in our solar system, it cannot be other than what it is, nor can it willfully change its orbit. On the other hand, because of the degree to which she is removed from that position of cosmic centrality, the human is free to choose whatever direction she wants, be that a beggar, businessperson, or farmer. This applies to Aquarius as well. This sign may be 180 degrees removed from the point of luminous consciousness represented by Leo, yet for that reason it exemplifies a degree of rational choice and free will which other signs do not.

With that choice now comes the possibility for spiritual growth. In chapter 2, I mentioned Carl Jung's remark that there is no morality without freedom. Unless one is responsible for one's actions, one cannot be held accountable for either evil or spiritual actions, since one is acting from instinct. Free will brings the possibility for choosing wisely or unwisely. This is why the awakening of rationality brings responsibilities *and* dangers; with the emergence of the Aquarian air, the ante is upped in *both* directions, toward tremendous spirituality or unparalleled destructiveness. Either way, it reflects a momentous step in the evolution of humanity.

There are other ways that the development of rationality can contribute to our spiritual development as a species. Take the example of someone who has lived in rural America, never having traveled outside of their county, let alone outside the United States. Can we say this person grasps what the "American experience" means, for better or worse? The fact is, such a person would probably be the *least* equipped to offer an assessment of this nation and its character, simply because he has been so immersed in it that he has nothing to compare it to. He has no objectivity.

But suppose he were offered the chance to travel overseas for a few months, and see the American culture from a distant vantage point. Having done that, he would have a new understanding of what it means to be an American, and presumably a richer grasp of its character. This example illustrates how detachment can sometimes be a holistic, enriching force in our lives. By perceiving an experience from an objective, rational perspective, we gain a depth of field or quality of three-dimensionality absent when viewed from a single viewpoint.

This epitomizes the virtue of the air element within the Great Ages. From one perspective, the Age of Aquarius could be a time when we become estranged from the divine source. Yet within a larger evolutionary perspective, that same sense of separation may grant us a more complete perspective on the divine than would be possible otherwise, in the same way that the man who left home thereby came to understand it more fully. The Talmud has an apocryphal dialogue between God and Abraham, in which God says, "If it wasn't for Me, you wouldn't exist." After a moment of thoughtful reflection, Abraham respectfully replies, "Yes, Lord, and for that I am very appreciative and grateful. However, if it wasn't for me, *You wouldn't be known*" (Schlain 1998).

Abraham's condition as a creature apart from God provided him the capacity to understand and appreciate God's mystery in a way not available even to God. In a similar way, the rational detachment of the Aquarian Age could similarly allow us to "know" the divine in a way that adds an important element to our evolutionary growth, by giving us a new depth of field or three-dimensionality regarding our perspective on that divine.

In his public lectures, the American philosopher Manly Hall sometimes described the impending stage in human evolution as a movement from the "Old Atlantis" to the "New Atlantis" (in reference to Francis Bacon's book of the same title). What exactly is the "Old Atlantis"? Hall defined this as life lived instinctually, unconsciously, where creatures follow the divine law perfectly yet blindly, like ants and bees going about their business. It is spirituality at its most primal yet unreflective of life "in the Garden." The "New Atlantis" represents a social order where beings live consciously and rationally, aligned with the divine order not through blind necessity but choice. Here we see the highest aspect of Aquarius, with its potential for enlightened rationality. We are permitted to *re*-enter the Garden of our own volition, through an understanding of universal law.

Lifting Our Sights

So what can we expect the Aquarian Age to bring? As this book has suggested, the coming era will likely be every bit as complex and multifaceted as every other Great Age that preceded it, possibly even more so. Some foresee an era of peace, love, and brotherhood, while others speak of a bureaucratic nightmare; but the truth probably lies within a constantly shifting variation between these extremes. In these last two chapters, we've looked at the optimal spiritual possibilities the coming era might bring. How realistic is it to expect such lofty potentials to manifest? For me, the more useful question here is what we can do to *encourage* such possibilities.

On the global scale, this means creating a society that fosters the emergence of such values and ideas. As Manly Hall put it, "If we create the body of civilization, then the soul body of civilization—which is the 'New Atlantis'—will move in and vitalize it. And instead of being a mechanistic culture defended only by mortal laws, it will be the manifestation of a living being receiving light from the Eternal source of light" (Hall 1998).

To achieve this, we will have to learn how to "fight fire with fire"—that is, to adjust our goals and means to the times. For example, it is probable that the forces of big business and technology will pose serious challenges for us in the times ahead; yet solving the problems caused by these forces will not come about by simply bypassing them but rather through *using* them in constructive ways—"working with the system." (In recent years we have been blessed with an abundance of useful resource guides that can help direct us in this regard, including books like *Conscious Evolution* by Barbara Marx Hubbard and *A Call for Connection* by Gail Bernice Holland.)

The other side of this picture is necessarily a personal one, in terms of how each of us must transform our lives to facilitate this process of global change. This is where we must turn our attention in the remainder of the book.

18

Preparing for the Times Ahead: A Personal Guide to Global Shift

If you were traveling in a "foreign" country for the first time, it would be common sense to spend time beforehand learning about the customs and culture to ensure your trip will go smoothly. The same might be said about entering a new Age. If one hopes to take advantage of the opportunities it has to offer and avoid its pitfalls, it is wise to learn its basic features and influences.

This book has mapped out some of these patterns and their possible effects on our lives. To round off this discussion, here is a brief list of "pointers" to help you navigate through the Aquarian onset ahead.

Leave Room for Silence in Your Life: We have all probably heard that oft-quoted Chinese curse which says, "May you live in interesting times!" Well, welcome to interesting times! Life has become louder and more fast-paced by the minute, and the Aquarian Age will continue providing us with amazing enticements of the most ingenious sort, designed to draw us out of ourselves a bit further. Can we resist the lure of these sensory pyrotechnics and retain some connection to our inner worlds?

One way to address this problem is to take time to simplify your life; begin cutting back on the noise and chaos in your environment. Ask yourself: Do I really need the radio or TV on all the time? Instead of watching that sports game at night, try reading an inspiring or thought-provoking book. Leave time for getting ready for work in the morning, so you can take things slowly and mindfully. You hardly need to reject civilization and its conveniences to buffer the effects of our modern age; but if you are *only* surrounded by noise and speed, how can you get in touch with your inner world?

Create a Center in Your Life: In an increasingly decentralized world, it is important that we find some way of creating our own hubs or centers. On a spiritual level, this may involve getting grounded in a daily spiritual practice. As the Zen tradition informs us, it is by establishing our connection to the Absolute (what other religious traditions might call God) that we can navigate through the realm of "the 10,000 things," the everyday world of phenomena and all its concerns. Taking the time to master a skill, whether that be gardening, sculpting, or yoga, can also help harmonize and centralize your energies on a daily basis and over the course of a life.

Resist the Deadening of Your World: Look around you right now. Are you surrounded by living bodies like people, plants, and animals? Or does your environment consist primarily of lifeless or manufactured items? What are the primary symbols around which your life activity revolves: Is it a child? The customers who visit your store? Something inanimate like a book or a computer?

One of the potential problems associated with the Aquarian Age, resulting from its root chakra emphasis, is the deadening effect it could have in our lives. While the coming era could be dynamic in terms of its fast pace and electrified technologies, it is also one that could see life progressively draining from our world in organic ways. One need look no further than the average office building to find examples of this, with rooms often comprised of synthetic items from top to bottom, from the light fixtures to the carpeting. One way to begin offsetting this imbalance is to bring more life into your environment, such as plants, animals, and more interactions with people. Reexamine your diet; do you eat primarily processed foods? Do you get all your nourishment through cans and hermetically-sealed packages? If so, consider introducing more living foods into your diet. Whenever possible, spend more time in nature; the more we become insulated from the natural world, the more we become cut off from our instinctual natures. Remember to make time for *play* in your life—preferably nonelectronic forms, if possible.

Maintain a Compassionate Heart: We have made much throughout these discussions of the role that awakened consciousness plays in the spiritual life, as well as the importance of the higher mind. Yet all this is but one half of the equation. Equally important is the role the awakened heart must play in our development in the times ahead.

By way of example, there are many times when we see people who have attained great levels of personal empowerment or high states of consciousness yet who have lost touch with basic values of compassion and ordinary goodness. Practical ways of nurturing this sensitivity include charitable work, loving-kindness meditations, exposing yourself to great art or music, or becoming involved with humanitarian groups or causes. You need not embark on any exotic project to develop yourself in this area; do it by simply being the most compassionate person you can be in everyday interactions.

Use the Power of Social Activism: In a mass society, it is easy to feel we can't make a difference in society. But if there is one lesson in the community-minded sign of Aquarius, it's that enormous power lies in numbers. Banding together in networks of individuals in a grassroots manner, we can effect enormous changes in world affairs. Emerging technologies (Internet, local access cable, community meetings, desktop publishing) are making these efforts even easier now. Figures like Martin Luther King and Mahatma Gandhi have shown that a ripple sent out from an individual can, when united with the power of the collective, swell into a wave of change across the planet.

Become More Self-Reliant: One doesn't have to be a survivalist to see the value of becoming less dependent on the "the grid"—the global infrastructure of energy, products, and information we feed off each day. Imagine that there were a cataclysm: How well would *you* cope? If you had to suddenly pull up stakes and move out of town in twenty-four hours, what would you bring with you? Thought-experiments like this can help you to prepare for this eventuality, and can help clarify what is valuable in your life. As an experiment, try giving up a different convenience for one week at a time—TV one week, the newspaper the next, coffee or sugar the next. Exercises like this can show you how dependent we have become on the many "things" in our life.

Avoid Being Hypnotized by the "Group Trance": More important than material self-reliance is the need to become free from society's *mental* "grid," the social-cultural matrix of beliefs and attitudes. Can you stand apart from the crowd and think for yourself? This is the lesson reiterated by many of our mythologies these days, such as films like *Dark City, The Matrix,* and *The Truman Show.* Have you ever noticed your mental state as you rushed to get in line for something in limited supply—a product or concert ticket? Remember the mental chaos that overcame you, how your breathing tightened up? Our minds are tugged and pushed all the time by our culture. Media advertisements are part of the picture, but what about the assumptions and biases that shape our perceptions and values every day? Such things comprise our "invisible environment" through which we move and breathe each day. To the extent we remain unaware of this environment, we remain susceptible to being *controlled* by it.

How does one break free of this influence? In addition to meditation during the day, cultivate a vigilant attitude of mindfulness throughout your life to become more aware of the effects of the world on your psyche. When a major political development occurs or new fad suddenly sweeps the nation, what reactions do you feel stirred in you? Be as informed as possible about current events—from several sources. Never assume the major TV networks and news outlets offer an objective or complete view of what is happening. Read alternative news sources like *Utne Reader* or surf the Web to see what foreign news services are saying. This can be helpful in providing a well-rounded understanding of things. Studying history or traveling to other countries are useful ways to step outside your provincial mindset and see your hidden cultural biases. Likewise, reading the classics of literature and philosophy can allow you to see the bigger picture underlying our current dramas of history. As Thoreau once remarked, "Read not the times. Read the eternities!" (Thoreau 1972).

Take Control of Your Everyday Attitudes: Abraham Lincoln once said that a person is as happy as he makes up his mind to be. That piece of wisdom applies to dealing with our changing times, too. If you can learn how to control your attitudes, then it doesn't *matter* how the Aquarian Age turns out, not in the sense of becoming apathetic, but in terms of not letting your environment control your states of mind.

The Ages may come and go, some more pleasantly than others; yet mystics have repeatedly underscored the importance of not letting our personal happiness be dependent on outer circumstances. As Paramahansa Yogananda once remarked, "You do not have to wait for the end of the world in order to be free. There is another way: rise above the age in which you are born" (Yogananda 1986).

Whether the Age of Aquarius turns out to be a utopia or an Orwellian nightmare, ultimately we have a responsibility for our own awareness and attitudes, and, in some ways, that is probably the most Aquarian lesson of all.

Appendix 1

The Dual Zodiac Problem: Just Who Is—or Isn't—an "Aquarius"?

About every ten years or so, a researcher comes forth with the startling claim that astrology has been "disproven" once and for all. How? By pointing out that astrologers have failed to take into account the "sliding zodiac" problem. This has to do with *precession*, an astronomical phenomenon that causes the visible constellations to slowly move out of sync with the zodiacal "signs" we normally associate with astrology.

For example, when we say someone is a Cancer or a Gemini, this generally has nothing to do with the stars, surprisingly enough, but is based on a twelvefold division of the sky arising out of the four seasonal points. According to this system (referred to as the tropical zodiac), the first degree of Aries is established by the first day of Spring; the first degree of Cancer is determined from the first day of Summer; the first degree of Libra from the first day of Fall; and the first degree of Capricorn from the first day of Winter.

Roughly two thousand years ago, this tropical zodiac was precisely aligned with the zodiacal band of the twelve constellations that are visible in the night sky. This latter grouping is conventionally referred to as the sidereal zodiac. But because of the slow drift of the Earth's axis, these two have drifted apart at the rate of one degree every seventy-two years, and are now out of sync with each other by roughly twenty-three degrees. This means someone born on the first day of Summer may be a sun-sign Cancer by tropical standards, yet, according to the sidereal (star based) zodiac, they would be classified a Gemini. As a rule, only those people born during the last seven or so degrees of a sign will tend have their sun in the same sign as described by *both* systems.

The fact of the matter is, most serious astrologers are aware of this predicament. For many, it is taken to mean there are two frameworks, each with its value and meaning. An analogous situation is found in modern physics, which also features different models of the cosmos, such as Einstein's and Newton's, which somehow manage to coexist, each valid in its own context. Another example is in health and healing. Western medicine operates along radically different theoretical lines from Oriental medicine, with the latter's concern for "meridians," "elements," and energy imbalances. Yet experience indicates that both systems can *work*, using different philosophies to address the same ailments. For example, a migraine headache might be soothed using acupuncture or aspirin. How can this be?

Archetypally speaking, we could say that there are many different ways to slice the same cake. That is, when dealing with the profundities of our world, the same phenomenon might lend itself to multiple interpretations, which in the end prove to be complementary rather than contradictory. The same applies to our understanding of the skies; one can draw different kinds of knowledge from the varied patterns of the stars without ever exhausting all the possible meanings encoded there. Hence, an astrological chart drawn up by a Vedic astrologer from India might extract one kind of information from a person's horoscope while a chart drawn up by a Western, tropical astrologer might extract another.

Yet that doesn't mean there aren't some knotty problems raised by this situation for astrologers. Indeed, one of these bears on the discussions in this book. I have cited certain figures from history as exemplars of Aquarian-Age themes or trends because of the way their horoscopes contain key planets in the (tropical) sign Aquarius. For example, Jules Verne was a sun-sign Aquarius (using the tropical system), and represents a "prophet" of certain Aquarian trends. However, according to the sidereal (star-based) zodiac, Verne was a sun-sign Capricorn. Why is this a problem? Because it is upon this sidereal method of interpreting the sky that we base our theory of the Great Ages! So how can we speak of someone who is an Aquarius within the one zodiacal system as being relevant to Aquarian themes or meanings as determined by the *other* zodiacal system (according to which Verne isn't an Aquarian)?

I have also referred to major planetary lineups in the sign of Aquarius, such as the great configuration of early February 1962, suggesting that these point the way to certain Aquarian-Age trends. Yet when converted to the sidereal zodiac, many of these same planets are found to be in Capricorn. Isn't this mixing apples and oranges in a way that is archetypally and practically unsound? Can we point to people *or* events positioned in tropical Aquarius as being in any way omens of trends related to the essentially sidereal Aquarian Age?

To highlight just how ludicrous a proposition this seems to some, it is sometimes noted that many thousands of years from now, these two versions of Aquarius (tropical and sidereal) will eventually be at opposite ends of the sky. So how can we say things taking place in one version of that sign will have relevance for the precessional phenomenon related to the other?

Based on my studies, I believe that, despite the seeming discrepancy between these two signs, there is *always* a symbolic link between the tropical and sidereal forms of any sign, however far apart they may be. I say this for several reasons.

On an empirical level, I have witnessed countless examples where planetary configurations taking place in tropical Aquarius give rise to Aquarian events or trends in society, rather than being Capricornian in nature as the sidereal system would suggest. A good example of this was that other significant Aquarian lineup during February of 1997. Beforehand, many of us in the astrology community predicted there might be important developments in science and technology during that period and with a "futuristic" flavor. As it turned out, this was when news of the cloning breakthrough involving Dolly the sheep in Scotland was released. I have often been astonished at how many of the historical figures involved in spearheading Aquarian trends have been sun-sign Aquarians or possessed key planets in this sign as determined by tropical standards (e.g., James Joyce, Thomas Edison, Jules Verne, Oprah Winfrey, Charles Lindbergh). Such findings have consistently reinforced my sense that there is indeed a significant link between the tropical and sidereal forms of Aquarius.

On a theoretical level, this possibility is also suggested by traditional astrology, where seemingly indirect correspondences of this sort are accepted as a matter of daily practice. For example, nearly all astrologers accept that the planet Mars is the symbolic "ruler" of the zodiacal sign Aries. As such, Mars is said to be in its "home" position when found in this sign. Yet as every astrologer knows, Mars can be positioned anywhere within the horoscope, in any of the twelve zodiacal signs, including the sign directly opposite it, Libra.

Yet, however far away it may be from that "home" point in Aries, there is always a certain correspondence or resonance between these factors, such that the condition of the Mars in someone's horoscope (by aspect, sign, or House placement) will always "feed back" to whatever house Aries is positioned on, and influence the fortunes of that House.

How can this be, skeptics ask, when Mars isn't anywhere *near* Aries? We can point to no "concrete" force linking these two areas; yet for astrologers, the link exists nonetheless, due to the power of correspondence and analogy whereby diverse objects or phenomena are attuned to the same archetypal vibration. In the same way, I argue that the tropical and sidereal forms of a sign are always harmonically linked, however far apart they may be in the sky.

This doesn't mean we should ignore the complex layers of meaning that result from such displacements. As the tropical sign Aquarius continues its slow glide through the background constellations, one can imagine that it assumes new "sub-tones" of meaning as befit those juxtaposed signs (just as Mars positioned in Libra will confer radically different qualities on that Mars than when found in its "natural" state).

For example, when the tropical and sidereal zodiacs were aligned two thousand years ago, Aquarius possessed a quality of pure Aquarius, without added layers of meaning. But now this sign is becoming transposed over the constellation of Capricorn, suggesting a hybrid symbolism that might be called Aquarius/Capricorn. When precession moves this sign all the way into the constellation of Leo, we can similarly expect a juxtaposition of those archetypal principles.

Appendix 2

The Varieties of Aquarian "Holism"

"Whatever befalls the earth, befalls the children of the earth. We did not weave the web of life, we are merely a strand in it. Whatever we do to the web, we do to ourselves."

This famed statement, widely (and probably mistakenly) attributed to the nineteenth-century Suquamish Indian Chief Seattle,[1] sums up an essential concern of the sign Aquarius: an awareness of interconnections. As we've seen, Aquarius is intimately associated with the principle of decentralization, and is thus involved with the complex relationships among parts in any system, be that a society, organism, or telecommunications network. We are indeed all elements within life's great web, with everything connected to everything else; and more than any other sign, Aquarius helps to make this realization possible.

Yet it is important to realize that there are many different kinds of systems in our world, not just one; each variation reflects a different facet of the Aquarian principle. For example, on a political level, a totalitarian state represents a type of system quite different from a society overrun by anarchy; both these are very different from the system found in a democracy.

So where do we begin to grasp the varieties of Aquarian systems for the coming Age? One simple approach is to reduce this discussion to the most fundamental components involved in any system: the relationship of the part to the whole. Every system, no matter how complex or simple, consists of a relationship between its component parts and the larger system which contains them. With this as a starting point, we can construct a spectrum of systems that characterize the styles of Aquarian holism. What follows is a fivefold arc of possibilities, ranging from those in which the system is dominant over its parts, to those where the parts are dominant over the system. Though this model doesn't exhaust all the possible dynamics and systemic nuances that can arise, it complements the ideas in this book.

Stage I: We find a system-dominant model where the larger network overrides the individual parts to an extreme degree; I call this the "totalitarian" model. In political terms, this is comparable to a society where the state holds complete sway over its citizenry, as in Nazi Germany, or *Star Trek*'s depiction of the Borg, a hive-mind race of aliens who operate as a collective. This stage is equivalent to a culture with only one government-run TV station, with no options or choices available to viewers aside from that channel.

Stage II: We have moved slightly beyond the anonymity of Stage I and see the first awakenings of individualism in the parts, but without any true differentiation. Symbolically, this stage could be illustrated by a media environment in which viewers have several channels to choose from, but still only a small amount of creative input, since the options for choice are limited.

Stage III: We find the individual elements now beginning to differentiate into autonomous, self-contained entities; there is a semblance of balance between the parts and the system in what I call the jazz model. In political terms, this is equivalent to a normal democracy: the citizens vote and are considered equals in essential rights.

At the same time, *true* individualism hasn't yet arisen; here, each unit is essentially similar in nature. In technological terms, this is comparable to a media environment where many choices are available to viewers (more channels or videocassettes) independent of what everyone else is watching. Yet the system is still not interactive since there is little creativity involved and the choices are predetermined by business interests. This is the weak jazz model.

Stage IV: Here the component parts have awakened into differentiated, autonomous entities, yet remain harmoniously coordinated among themselves. Unlike Stage III, those parts are not simply equal in status, but are now creative and participatory, free to pursue their own visions. In political terms, this is exemplified by a democracy in which citizens not only vote, but participate in the process through grassroots activism and/or creative involvement with their community.

Again using the symbolism of media technology, this stage could be illustrated by a culture where viewers not only watch whatever they want, but are involved in *creating* their own programming, or filming their own videos and films. In fact, the Internet offers a useful illustration of this stage, because of its striking element of interactivity through e-mail and the creation of personal websites.

I call this the strong jazz model, and it is related to kaleidoscopic holism. This stage includes any system where we see diverse elements joined together into a framework of meaning without compromising the integrity of the larger system. Examples include Disney's *Fantasia,* the Beatles' "white" album, the political melting pot of American society, the integral theoretical attempts to synthesize ideas by Jean Gebser, Roberto Assagioli, and Ken Wilber.

Stage V: The individual parts have become so differentiated that the system cannot withstand it; there is little (or no) coordination among the elements. This is not jazzlike autonomy but anarchy. Each entity in the system has awakened to its innate powers, but the system is unregulated and unbalanced. Politically, this is expressed by a society of anarchists or petty dictators. In technological terms, we might relate it to a system overrun by computer hackers.

This stage relates to what I call disintegrative kaleidoscopism, and can be associated with the cultural phenomenon of postmodernism in its negative form. This is the principle of the "fractured spectrum," aptly symbolized by the Frankenstein monster, a creature comprised of widely diverse parts with little sense of unity.

It is important to note that none of these five stages is inherently better or worse than any other, since all of them have value in one context or another. On the surface, it is tempting to think of the middle, balanced stage (Stage III) as the most spiritual; it's true, in some situations balancing between the parts and the larger system is the ideal condition. Yet any of these stages can be applied in constructive or destructive ways.

It is tempting to think of a Stage I system as inherently constrictive, an oppressive government crushing the life out of individuals (e.g., Orwell's *1984* or Terry Gilliam's film *Brazil*). Yet there are times when it might be *healthy* for the social web to assert its dominance over individuals, as in the case of a society clamping down on a child molester, or when the cells of your immune system rally against an invading virus. This intriguing point was portrayed in that otherwise lackluster film *The Postman* (1997). This movie tells of a time in our future when the United States has become *dis*-united and overrun by gun-toting militias, each defending its own turf. The federal system has broken down, and all its regions vie for control.

What was somewhat daring about this script (in the post-Waco mood of antifederalism) was how it featured a protagonist struggling not *against* the system, as has been the case in most films these days, but to *restore* it, to bring back the security and peace offered by a federal "grid." The message here is paradoxical but important for the Aquarian Age: namely, for freedom, there must be a strong system in place.

On the other side of things, the type of system represented by Stage V holism can indeed result in anarchy or overblown individualism, with no coordinating structure at all. Yet there are times when this kind of energy can be a restorative force in the world, as when a system *needs* to break down to make way for a new one. Consider schoolchildren subjected to nothing but rules and regulations for months on end, with no chance for spontaneity and fun. For such individuals, being allowed to run free on the playground with few rules might be a therapeutic situation. Take a political system which has grown rigid and corrupt; such a system might *benefit* from revolution and chaos every now and then. We think of computer hackers as a negative phenomenon because they disrupt service for millions through a misapplication of their computer skills. Yet in *Crypto: How the Code Rebels Beat the Government—Saving Privacy in the Digital Age,* Steven Levy tells how a group of individualistic computer geeks combated federal efforts to compromise the personal privacy of computer users—and won. Here the seemingly disruptive influence of lone individuals can be the very thing which counterbalances an overly rigid system.

We can also examine the balance point signified by Stages III and IV especially. While there are many situations where this can be a harmonious option, it may prove dangerous if applied in the wrong situations. Take a maximum security prison where democracy would signal disaster. Or take a large family of unruly kids, where a strong and constrictive system may be the only thing which keeps the family from breaking apart. Even on the political level, it may be naïve to think that democracy is always the preferable system for every nation. For example, Bhutan is a theocracy and seems to thrive in that kind of climate. There seems to be no pressing desire in its population to change that condition anytime soon.

So we need to be careful not to judge these various systems in simplistic, black-and-white ways; we must try to understand the applications of each, both constructive and destructive. Now let us turn our attention to further implications of this fivefold arc in terms of understanding history, past, present, and future.

One way to approach these stages is to see them as symbols for styles of Aquarian rationality. This fivefold framework can help us understand the evolution of the Western mind over the last few centuries. For example, during the era of the "Age of Reason" or "Enlightenment" (the 1700s), an era which I have proposed signifies the first noticeable wave of Aquarian consciousness, we see a form of rationality arising that expresses the qualities of Stage I holism, with its emphasis on universal truths and uniform meanings that ignore all particulars and differences. Ken Wilber writes about this era:

> There thus arose a positive mania for the universal and "common truths" of humankind, truths that could speak to everybody, and thus truths that must be "truly true," deeply true, for all peoples. All merely individual preferences and tastes, all peculiarities, all local differences, were dismissed as not being part of a common and universal humanity. . . . This search for a universal and unvarying set of codes and "natural law" (meaning universal law) swept through every branch of learning, science, political and social theory—and reached right down into the arts, into poetry, into painting, into architecture (Wilber 1995).

Yet it would not be long before this trend generated its opposite, in the counterbalancing trend of Romanticism. This form of rationality *cherished* differences and diversity, focusing on particulars rather than universal frameworks of meaning (Stages IV and V). This too, was a result of the emerging Aquarian rational movement, in that it extended far beyond any one cultural viewpoint to embrace a universal perspective, but it approached it from the other end of the spectrum. As Wilber points out, the romantic (he calls it "Eco-Romantic") rebellion was not so much *anti-rational* in spirit as it was *anti-uniformitarian.* It arose out of the same decentralizing spirit of the times, but emphasized the individualized "branches" of this tree rather than its centralizing trunks.

This was an equally momentous development in the evolution of modern thought, in terms of an ability to step outside one's provincial framework and honor the uniquenesses and differences of the world. Yet when taken to extremes, this approach had its problems as well, since it tended to glorify differences at the expense of acknowledging unifying frameworks or universal values of any sort. This is a problem that still affects us today in the postmodern crisis, wherein *all* meanings and frames of reference are rejected as repressive or useless.

Indeed, the evolution of the Western mind in recent centuries can be viewed as the playing out of these types of Aquarian rationality. Take the field of comparative religion and mythology. In studying world myths, the Stage I model has been expressed through the more "universalist" approach to mythology as articulated by figures like Joseph Campbell and Mircea Eliade. This approach focuses on the commonalties and universal meanings that unite religions, and has less concern for variations and differences among the systems. By this standpoint, the Christ story is significant more for the way it mirrors the hero archetype through history.

At the other end of the spectrum, the Stage V model is shown in the "particularist" approach to world mythologies through figures like Wendy Doniger; this school of thought tends to focus its attention more on the unique differences among the different world myths rather than their commonalties. Christ shares similarities with other hero figures through history (Osiris or Dionysus), but ultimately it's the unique touches which Christianity brings to that archetypal motif that makes it important. After all, we don't appreciate DaVinci's *Mona Lisa* simply because of how it *resembles* all other depictions of women or the divine feminine through history, but for its nuances.

Taken to an extreme, this "particularist" approach can overlook the insights offered by the universalist viewpoint. In between these two extremes therefore lies the more "integrative" approach toward world mythology which blends these opposing styles of scholarship and respects both the similarities and the differences that characterize all mythologies. The point is that *all* approaches have their respective values, depending on the context or the subject.

This fivefold model has implications for other areas of modern life, including business. For example, on the international scale, Stage I equates to a globalized business environment in which regional interests and distinctions are overpowered by multinationals. On the other hand, the part-dominant model represented by Stage V is comparable to an isolationist environment in which every country has its own business interests, but little contact with outside markets. The parts are all "doing their own thing," but there is little or no coordination or interaction among the various regional economies. The integrative or jazz-style approach represented by Stage III and IV is equivalent to a global environment where healthy trade exists between countries, but without sacrificing regional distinctions and creativity.

In terms of politics, the French Revolution illustrates Stage I holism. In reaction to the excesses of monarchy, the revolution went to the other extreme of emphasizing "the masses" so much that it eliminated personal rights. By contrast, the founders of the American Revolution realized the dangers of emphasizing "the system" over individuals, and took pains to make sure individuals (and states) retained certain rights; this revolution thereby expressed the balanced qualities of Stages III and IV. The recent history of democratic governments generally provides us illustrations of the tidal surges that can naturally occur between these extremes, as societies struggle to find the proper balance between the "parts" and the "wholes."

Throughout the Aquarian Age, we will see a complex interplay of these system types, in different fields and areas of experience. In some contexts, we can even expect to see forms expressing the juxtaposition of these extremes within the same situation. As an example, consider the image of the American cowboy. A seeming embodiment of rugged individualism, the truth of the matter is that most cowboys were company employees on a long leash, hired to get the cattle to market for their bosses back east. Behind the facade of the isolated individual was a corporate board! A better example of the contradictions in Aquarius is your average movie star, whose personality enchants the world, yet whose success is directly connected to the PR machinery of multinationals.

On a different front, this spectrum of possibilities can shed light on another problem of interest to astrologers. This is the question of which mythic figure is appropriate to symbolize the planet Uranus, ruler of Aquarius.

Most astrologers accept that the mythic names assigned to celestial bodies are somehow appropriate to their synchronistic character. From this perspective, the Greek god Ouranos would be the logical one to study to better understand the archetypal meaning of this planet. The aloof and tyrannical qualities of this primordial sky-god help us see the role this planet has in the lives of individuals and societies.

Yet writers like Richard Tarnas and Stephen Arroyo have proposed that Prometheus may be more appropriate to symbolize the qualities of Uranus.

Prometheus represented the forces of change and rebellion, and as Tarnas eloquently argues in *Prometheus the Awakener*, the tyrannical qualities of the old god Ouranos seem a poor match for the qualities often exhibited by this planet when it affects the lives of individuals or nations.

So which is it: Ouranos or Prometheus? Surely, these two mythic figures couldn't *both* express the qualities of Uranus—or could they?

My experience suggests that, as with Aquarius, Uranus features *several* faces. In this way, the seemingly contradictory qualities of Prometheus and Ouranos may be complementary aspects of the same astrological energy.

For example, consider the cases cited above of the cowboy or rock star, where something appears to be highly individualistic in nature (Stage V), yet is entwined with an anonymous collective (Stage I). Or consider historical manifestations which start out in one of these archetypal directions, yet eventually mutate into the opposite. Indeed, that is something that could be said about nearly any of the "Aquarian" developments explored in this book, including technology, science, capitalism, or America itself. Every one started out Promethean but mutated into Ouranean forms later.

Take modern technology, for instance. When the technological revolution began in earnest during the mid-eighteenth century, it was viewed as a "fire from the gods," in the way it conferred new powers and freedoms to individuals and businessmen (Stage IV or V manifestations). Yet over time, that same development became more constrictive, nearly overpowering its human creators (à la Mary Shelley's *Frankenstein*). Think of such things as the assembly line and industrialization. Like yin and yang, one extreme gave birth to the other, both expressing different faces of the same archetypal energy.

Much the same could be said about modern science. This began as a largely individualistic effort by amateur natural philosophers of the seventeenth and eighteenth centuries (Ben Franklin, Thomas Jefferson, Edward Bromfield), but over time gave rise to a corporate approach to scientific exploration in which large companies and universities tended to discourage individual ingenuity and initiative.

The United States offers a third example of this Aquarian mutation, in that it initially embodied a Promethean energy with its rebellious spirit of unlimited possibility and a break from the past; yet over time it drifted from that revolutionary impulse to become a heavy-handed military-industrial superpower.

The Promethean spirit of revolutionary change and the Ouranean spirit of tyrannical order may be necessary opposites in the same system. After all, one cannot be a rebel without an oppressive system to buck up against! This will hold true for the Aquarian Age, too. The Aquarian Age will probably continually witness an interplay between these extremes, on the creative, religious, scientific, and social fronts. It is a dynamic that has begun surfacing in most futuristically oriented stories and pop mythologies *(The Matrix, Terminator II, 2001: A Space Odyssey)*.

Appendix 3

Seeds of Revolution:
Assessing the Effects of the
May 2000 Planetary Lineup

Planetary lineups are among the most significant "cosmic triggers" in the unfolding of any Great Age. Like rolling the speedometer in one's car over at the 100,000-mile mark, major configurations are important milestones in our history. Themes of the old order are wrapped up and those of a new one begin in earnest. Both Kubrick's *2001: A Space Odyssey* and Jim Henson's *Dark Crystal* feature as prominent motifs the idea that major leaps in evolution are accompanied by multiplanet lineups.

The twentieth century saw a number of such lineups, including one in early February 1997, and the great Taurus lineup of early May, 1941. Yet by most accounts, the two most powerful configurations of this type from recent decades have been the seven-planet lineups of February 1962 and May 2000. Let's have a look at the effects of this most recent one.[1]

Shortly after the May lineup, I received a call from a friend wanting my opinion on the developments of that previous week. "So what happened?" he asked. "Everyone said the last two or three days would be a historic time, but I've been watching the news fairly closely these last few days and I haven't really seen anything spectacular taking place."

Big mistake, I thought—trying to gauge the full impact of a configuration like this by looking only to the events of two or three days. Like eclipses, major lineups exert their full effects only over the course of *many years*. The famed seven-planet lineup in Aquarius on February 4, 1962, was a classic example. Though the configuration lasted one day, its energies colored the 1960s. Looking just to those events around the actual point of closest approach doesn't give you a full sense of the scope of this lineup and its long-term impact on world culture.

But that hardly means the events around the configuration itself don't provide us with a number of useful clues to understand the larger trends to follow. It is during these early stages that the "entering wedge" of revolutionary change first emerges into view, making itself known through a variety of subtle omens and signs. For example, consider the case of singer-songwriter Bob Dylan, who was prominent, both artistically and politically, in the cultural revolutions of the 1960s. If we look back to the early part of that decade, we discover that his first album was released in February 1962, the same month as the great Aquarian lineup. In other words, though the full implications of this individual's influence unfolded over a longer period of time, they were subtly present from the start in "seed" form.

In that same spirit, it's worth pausing to take stock of the developments that have already transpired in the wake of the May 2000 lineup, to see what might lie ahead for us. As in the case of the 1962 conjunction, these sometimes take the form of events that may not appear especially momentous on their surface yet which symbolically point to broader trends. The following are my thoughts on the matter as an astrologer, compiled during the months following this event, and arranged in broad categories. Keep in mind that these developments are ongoing; so, by the time you read this, it's more than likely that other events along these general lines will have occurred.

Politics: To understand the "revolutionary" effects of major planetary lineups like this, it's helpful to recall the astronomical connotations of this word. A celestial body is said to make a full "revolution" each time it rotates completely on its axis or every time it comes back to its "home" point during a larger orbit. In other words, it's about something coming full circle, an old order is dying off and a new one starting up.

This certainly describes the events surrounding the period of the May lineup. For instance, on May 7, Russia's leadership saw the beginning of a new political era with the inauguration of Vladimir Putin as president.

Considering the proximity of this event to the lineup, it will be interesting to see what impact this former KGB spy eventually has on Russian and world politics. Closer to home, political pundits were heralding a possible shift in Cuban-American relations as a result of the Elian Gonzalez situation. In Europe, the days following the Taurus lineup saw a possible let-up in one of its long-standing conflicts: On May 6, the IRA announced it would disarm. Early June saw another possible breakthrough with the historic face-to-face meeting between leaders from North and South Korea.

There was a "changing of the guard" on other fronts, too. In New York politics, Rudolph Giuliani announced he would not be running for reelection in the wake of his battle with cancer and his impending divorce; a new candidate entered the race against Hillary Clinton and, as we know, lost. Also in New York, the Catholic Church appointed a new archbishop following the death of Archbishop O'Connor. Both Japan and Syria saw the deaths of old leaders and the arrivals of new ones, while England's young Tony Blair saw the birth of his child, Leo.

Economics: One of the more conspicuous effects of the Taurus lineup was the money mania that seemed to sweep across America during this period. This was reflected in a series of "get-rich-quick" TV shows *(Greed, Who Wants to Be a Millionaire?)* and in the near-maniacal fervor that erupted over a record Midwest lottery jackpot around the time of the actual lineup. There was also a frenzied spirit on Wall Street as stock prices fluctuated wildly.

But suppose you were to look back on this period a century from now with an eye toward the *larger* changes taking place in society that year. What would you see? No doubt you would notice the broader revolutions reshaping our world economy in 2000. For one, Internet "e-commerce" has made major changes in how global business is conducted. Then there is the influence of ever-larger corporate mergers, a disturbing development that is consolidating economic power into fewer hands around the world. Perhaps most significant of all is the profound restructuring of our world economy due to globalization. This is a trend that expands the power of multinational corporations and economic institutions like the World Trade Organization and the International Monetary Fund. These agencies affect the way business is run around the world and have considerable impact on the environmental and political policies of governments.

Here we see the flip side of this broader development. In response to these trends, we have begun to witness the rise of grass-roots attempts around the world to stem the influence of these agencies and the potential for injustice they can bring. No doubt, this is a reflection of the powerful Saturn-square-Uranus that was amplified by the Taurus lineup, and which suggested a clash between the forces of authority and those of rebellion. Starting with the so-called "Battle in Seattle," where protesters took to the streets in late 1999, we've seen ordinary people increasingly have an impact on the economic policies of these institutions; this dialectic will no doubt continue to transform the economic landscape for many years to come.

Along a similar line, this period saw the controversy over Napster, an Internet music-downloading service that has been threatening the power and profits of corporations and recording artists. Here, too, is another possible sign of the times that could foreshadow continuing tension between big business and the people in the years ahead. Still another "entering wedge" has been the China Trade Bill, which passed a major legislative hurdle during late May. This development is projected to have far-reaching effects on the American economy and the Chinese political landscape, due to the resulting stimulation of capitalism and Internet communication in that country.

Media and the Arts: The telecommunications industry experienced the shifts of "out with the old and in with the new." For example, a figure many regarded as the spirit of alternative media throughout the 1990s, talk show host Art Bell, retired on May 5 to tend to personal business; he was replaced by Seattle native Mike Siegel. (Art Bell returned to the airwaves a year later, on February 5, 2001.) Actor Michael J. Fox left his position on the popular TV show *Spin City* due to encroaching Parkinson's disease. *Beverly Hills 90210*, a TV show that for many embodied the youth culture of the 1990s, finally ended, and media personality extraordinaire, Oprah Winfrey, initiated a new magazine called *O*. In mid-May, the international news organization UPI was purchased by the Unification Church, prompting long-time journalist (and Washington icon) Helen Thomas to retire.

The Internet was a hot item during the first few days of May, primarily with news about a devastating computer virus attack called "Love Bug"—a fitting expression of the Venus-ruled energy of the period. Another possible sign of the times was news about the growing impact of the Internet on the entertainment industry, as reflected in made-for-Internet movies like *Quantum Project* or *Dead Broke*.

In some ways, the effects of this configuration might be compared to those of a lineup which occurred in Taurus during May 1941. Among other things, that was a period notable for the premiere of Orson Welles' *Citizen Kane*. Precedents like these portended a similar burst of artistic creativity during the spring of 2000.

One possible expression of that creative surge was the visually opulent film *Gladiator*, released nationwide on May 5. (Coincidentally, director Ridley Scott happens to be one of Orson Welles' biggest fans on the Hollywood scene; Scott and his brother produced 1999's HBO film on the making of *Citizen Kane*, titled *RKO 281*.) Beyond its stunning visual beauty, there are several ways *Gladiator* mirrored the energies of the Taurus lineup.

One of them was the unexpectedly devotional and heart-oriented thrust of the film, reflected both in the lead character's religious piety and his love for family (at the screening I attended that opening weekend, there wasn't a dry eye in the house at movie's end). We also see the Taurean emphasis in the film's recurring motif of the gladiator fingering ripened grain or handfuls of dirt at key moments, as a way to stay connected with his memories of home and his farm, in short, to savor the earth principle.

But the motif with the longest-term ramifications may prove to be *Gladiator*'s social message, its story of the struggle by "the little guy" to overcome the forces of tyranny (dramatized by the gladiator's efforts to establish republican rule in Rome, as requested by the dying Marcus Aurelius). One finds striking echoes of this theme in the news of spring 2000, not only in the antiglobalization protesters attempting to defy the forces of globalization, but in the presidential campaign of Washington gadfly Ralph Nader and the burgeoning controversy over Napster. You see a similar theme in the storylines of several other big-budget films from that month, including *Titan A.E.* and *Battlefield Earth*, both of which centered on rebels fighting an evil empire. As omens, what might all this mean? One possibility is that we may continue to see the rise of grass-roots efforts to combat an increasingly imbalanced monetary and political situation around our world.

The Environment: On another level, that poignant, earthy image of actor Russell Crowe (in *Gladiator*) fingering dirt and grain serves as an apt metaphor for the growing concern that has been developing over our environment, as a direct result of these economic and political trends. Of course, the ecological agenda was a major factor in those protests against the World Trade Organization during late 1999 and early May of 2000. On June 12, a disturbing report titled "Climate Change Impacts on the United States" was released, and it predicted that global warming over the next century could cause the Earth's temperature to rise anywhere from five to ten degrees, in turn bringing about drastic changes in the climate of this country. Among these effects would be severe droughts, mass migrations of species, increased risk of flood, and widespread erosion of coastal zones.

This period also saw several striking coincidences in the news that may reflect the broader dangers we are posing to ourselves through our ecological carelessness. On May 4, a fire set in New Mexico by the U.S. National Park Service as part of a "controlled burn" raged out of control and eventually destroyed 48,000 acres of land and more than 200 homes and apartment buildings. Several days later, an analogous situation took place in Europe, as fireworks set off in a residential district in the Netherlands grew out of control, destroyed a neighborhood, and caused numerous deaths. Early May also saw a bizarre string of structural collapses in the news involving bridges, piers, and buildings around the world.

There were several other notable stories involving the environment during this period, with possible long-term ramifications. During the first few days of May, scientists announced they had discovered huge cracks in the ocean floor off the east coast of America, which they claimed could eventually trigger killer waves or tsunamis that would affect the Mid-Atlantic states. And in late May, researchers noted an exceptional amount of geological activity around the world, ranging from earthquakes to volcanic activity.

Science: This was a period of major scientific breakthroughs in several areas. In biology, the biggest news centered on the announcement that scientists had completed a rough draft of the entire human genome, thereby bringing us one step closer to mapping our genetic code in a detailed fashion. In a particularly bizarre footnote to this story, scientists also proclaimed they had successfully combined genes from spiders with those of goats, giving us a new kind of goat's milk that possessed unique properties with various practical applications. During early May, cosmologists announced they had indirectly imaged the Big Bang for the first time by graphing the complex patterns of radiation emanating from the ends of the universe. Around this same period, it was also revealed that astronomers had finally solved a long-standing cosmological problem by detecting a large portion of the universe's missing hydrogen—a discovery that will help scientists map the large-scale structure of the universe.

Another surprising (and still contested) discovery from late May involved news that researchers in New Jersey succeeded in causing light to accelerate to 300 times its normal speed, a finding that could (if confirmed) open the door to further important discoveries in science and technology. One particularly odd aspect of the experiment was that the light pulse under study supposedly exited the test chamber before it entered it! This has led to speculation on the experiment's implications for the development of time-travel technologies, or even communication through time (an idea coincidentally featured in *Frequency,* a film playing in theaters around that same period). The speed of light is one of the cornerstones of modern science, and this breakthrough surely heralds some corresponding shift in the collective awareness—but what, exactly? Perhaps the answer will become clearer in the years ahead.

Archaeology: As humanity changes, so does its understanding of its own past. Time after time, we find evidence of major archeological discoveries arising in tandem, as if synchronistically, with important astrological patterns and broader intellectual revolutions throughout the culture. With that in mind, it is interesting to note the range of stories involving archeological themes that surfaced throughout May and June, some of which may hold major implications.

In the days surrounding the actual lineup, a story that made headlines involved new evidence that America's earliest inhabitants probably came not across the Bering Strait but from Europe—and thousands of years earlier than had been thought possible. Although theories about Pre-Columbian voyages to America have been proposed for years, these have generally been relegated to a fringe status; this announcement signaled a substantial shift in mainstream views toward this possibility.

Another story that sent shock waves through the archaeological community was the announcement in May of the discovery of a major civilization complex, dating back at least six thousand years, in the region of modern-day Syria. Historians had believed they had a reasonable understanding of how and where civilization first arose in the Middle East; but with this discovery of a previously unknown civilization, archaeologists realized that there may be major elements missing from their model, and that there could be other civilizations besides this out there awaiting discovery.

More controversially, May also saw the most public airing yet (via radio talk shows and Internet) of a story that's been making the rounds for years and which could have far-reaching implications for North American history. This is the controversial "Burrows Cave" site in southern Illinois, an underground chamber, discovered during the early 1980s, which supposedly houses thousands of handmade artifacts displaying ancient Egyptian and early Christian motifs. Though the authenticity of these items is far from certain at this point, there are several tenable theories being proposed as to how such artifacts might have wound up in the Midwest. For example, one scenario suggests that first century Christians from North Africa, fleeing Roman rule, sailed to America and traveled up the Mississippi, eventually settling in the Illinois region. (Curiously, the nearest big town in the Burrows Cave region is named Cairo.) What was significant about early May in this respect was the announcement that a yet-unidentified major university has finally agreed to examine the site and its contents in detail (another story worth following in the months or years ahead).

Some other stories of note in the news from this period:

• On May 12, the journal *Science* published the first scientific description of two 1.7-million-year-old skulls unearthed in the Republic of Georgia, a finding that researchers claim sheds new light on the early history of humanity's ancestor, *Homo erectus.*

• On June 3, marine archeologists announced they had found the 2,500-year-old ruins of submerged Pharaonic cities previously known only through Greek tragedies, travelogues, and legends.

• In mid June, it was reported that scientists found evidence from sites in the Czech Republic that clothing was woven on looms as far back as 27,000 years ago, roughly 20,000 years earlier than previously thought.

Miscellaneous: As we've seen, the Aquarian Age will likely involve humanity's discovery of/contact with nonhuman intelligence in the universe. One development from this period may hold far-reaching implications in this vein. During late May, NASA released 27,000 photos of the planet Mars taken by the Mars Surveyor spacecraft during the last two years. From a purely astronomical standpoint, this was significant; though for some, it held even greater potential by allowing us to finally verify—or dismiss—speculations about signs of life on this distant planet. Though most of the photos which have surfaced thus far have been too vague to establish anything conclusive, some of these images are provocative and merit closer study. Should any of them eventually turn out to harbor major discoveries along this line, it could well be the most significant legacy of the May 2000 lineup.

A possible connection to the lineup has been the growing epidemic of Mad Cow Disease throughout Europe and other countries, along with an unexpected resurgence of Hoof and Mouth Disease among livestock in these regions. Considering Taurus's ancient association with cattle, it is not hard to perceive a connection between these developments.

On occasion, major planetary lineups like this through history have coincided with the onset of major wars or conflicts, be these political or cultural in nature. For instance, the American Civil War occurred in close proximity with a major planetary lineup in 1861, when six planets were located within just 6 degrees of one another in Virgo. Early December of 1899 saw a six-planet lineup in Sagittarius, an event that coincided with the Spanish-American War. January 1914 saw a close multiple conjunction of six planets in Aquarius, all within 6 degrees, coinciding with the start of World War I. America's entry into World War II followed on the heels of the major lineup in 1941; and the multiple planetary lineup of 1962 preceded a major escalation in the Cold War, and the Cuban Missile Crisis in particular.

Does all this suggest the May 2000 lineup will bring about another major conflict in our world? Not necessarily; after all, though most major conflicts have been accompanied by planetary lineups, not all planetary lineups have been accompanied by major conflicts. But as of this writing (Spring, 2001), there are disturbing signs of unrest taking shape around the world, particularly in the Middle East, along with growing concerns over terrorist activity directed against the United States by militant factions from that region.

Perhaps this uneasiness shows another level of significance in *Gladiator*, released during the May 2000 lineup. In that film's first major sequence, imperial troops battle "barbarian" forces at the Empire's borders, using their superior technology. Set during the reign of emperor Marcus Aurelius, it is a turning point in the Empire's history; Roman power has reached its zenith, yet it will increasingly find itself threatened by those very barbarians—that era's equivalent to our modern-day third-world countries. One might see a parallel here with the state of affairs now facing superpowers like America in its dealings with Iraq or terrorists, like Osama bin Laden, though whether we will see a similar turning of the tide like that experienced by ancient Rome remains to be seen.

Finally, many believe that the full effects of a major planetary configuration like this don't manifest themselves fully until the children born under its influence reach their maturity, and in turn begin having an impact on the world. For instance, our example of Bob Dylan shows someone born near the end of the Taurus lineup of 1941 (though several of his personal planets overlap onto Gemini). Yet Dylan didn't hit his creative stride for another 25 years or so, at which point the energies at that lineup flowered into the collective consciousness. If we apply that view to our current Taurus lineup, we can likewise expect the effects of this period to manifest fully when the children born during *this* time attain their maturity, probably beginning around the 2020s and 2030s. Stay tuned!

Christmas 2.jpg @ 98%

Appendix 4

The World Trade Center Tragedy

While this book was completed and submitted for publication several months prior to the September 11th disaster, the following article¹ was written shortly afterwards, and offers an astrological perspective on the underlying dynamics of this pivotal event.

If there is any astrological lesson to be drawn from the tragedy of September 11, 2001, it might be that major historical events can reflect the convergence of several planetary factors simultaneously. In addition to the current tension between Pluto in Sagittarius and Saturn in Gemini that extends through both 2001 and 2002, and the volatile square between Mars and Uranus in Bush's inaugural horoscope, we should also consider the potential role of the extraordinary planetary lineup that occurred in Taurus during early May of 2000.

Traditionally, multiple planetary lineups have been regarded as among the most important "engines of change" in the astrological understanding of history, in their capacity to usher in cultural revolutions of various types. The major lineup of early 1962, for example, coincided precisely with the musical and artistic changes that were set into motion that same year, just as the lineup of 1941 before it opened the door to new experimentations in jazz, abstract art, and cinema for years to come.

On a more disturbing note, however, such lineups have also been associated with the onset of major wars through history. For instance, in 1861 a powerful lineup in Virgo coincided with the American Civil War; in 1899, an important lineup occurred in Sagittarius near the start of the Spanish-American War; in 1914, a lineup in Aquarius coincided with World War I, while the six-planet lineup in Taurus in 1941 was aligned with the onset of World War II. The seven-planet lineup in Aquarius of 1962 brought us to the brink of world war with the Cuban Missile Crisis. What made the May 2000 configuration unusually powerful was the fact that it followed closely on the heels of *two other* major configurations—the famous "Grand Cross" eclipse of August 1999, and the solar eclipse of February 2000 (featuring a tight conjunction with the planet Uranus in Aquarius). For astrologers, any one of these three configurations would have commanded attention as a significator of change; to find all three occurring so close to one another suggested that something truly extraordinary was in the air.

So what long-term changes would the seven-planet lineup of 2000 bring into the world? There are several ways to tell early on what to expect with such configurations; one of which is to study the zodiacal sign involved. In this case, that was Taurus—the sign of wealth, commerce, art, and environmental concerns. But an equally important key toward understanding such lineups lies within the primary planetary aspect involved— in this case, a square between rebellious Uranus and conservative Saturn. Indeed, not only was this aspect amplified by the May 2000 lineup, it was the single recurring aspect in *all three* of the astrological configurations mentioned above during 1999 and 2000. As the dominant theme sounding through all these patterns, it's safe to say that this planetary energy impresssed itself onto the collective psyche with a depth and duration far beyond its normal shelf life.

And some important clues were there right from the very start. In an article published in the October/November 2000 issue of the *Mountain Astrologer*, titled "The Seeds of Revolution" (see Appendix 3), I suggested that we could glimpse the long-term effects of any major planetary lineup by carefully examining the events around the first few days or weeks of the lineup, with these serving as "sneak previews" of a sort. For example, it's intriguing just how many aviation disasters occurred during the period leading up to the lineup, including the crash of JFK Junior's plane just one day before the first exact firing of the Uranus/Saturn aspect in mid-July of 1999, the crash of an Alaska Air jet off the coast of California, the freak crash of golfer Payne Stewart's Learjet, and the crash of EgyptAir flight 900, killing all aboard.

From an omenological standpoint, it is also worth remembering that in early February of 2000, close to the Solar eclipse conjunct Uranus, Afghan terrorists in London held passengers hostage for several days on an airport runway.

In addition, the influence of the Uranus/Saturn square was visible in the series of grassroots protests that took place around the world during 1999 and 2000, in defiance of the World Trade Organization and its economic policies. This unfolded with the "Battle in Seattle" during November of 1999, and reasserted itself during the week of the Taurus lineup, in early May of 2000. There was also the brewing controversy taking shape over Napster, the popular Internet service that provided free music to people and, in so doing, undercut corporate profits and control.

The Uranus/Saturn energy could also be clearly seen in the major attacks by computer hackers against corporate networks during both February and May of 2000 (including attacks on Yahoo! and eBay in February, and the unleashing of the famed "Love Bug" virus in early May). In the world of cinema, we saw a similar motif surfacing in the variety of films released from mid-1999 up through mid-2000, many of which featured a "David versus Goliath" theme—in movies like *The Matrix, Fight Club, Battlefield Earth, Titan A.E., The Insider, Hurricane,* and *Gladiator* (the last one being released precisely during the Taurus lineup), we find stories of rebellious or subversive elements doing battle against the "System."

In virtually all of these cases, the same astrological symbolism was at work—the clashing of Uranus in Aquarius with Saturn in Taurus. As such, these early events were tragic harbingers of the developments that would explode onto the world stage during September of 2001. For example, just as protesters had earlier fought the World Trade Organization and its financial policies, so the airborne terrorists in September targeted the World Trade Center as a leading symbol of Western materialism.

For this and other reasons, I've come to believe that the tragedy of September 11th is as much a lingering expression of the Uranus/Saturn aspect of 1999/2000 (amplified in particular by the Taurus planetary lineup) as it is of the Pluto/Saturn aspect of 2001, with the latter perhaps serving as a trigger for the former. This earlier connection is evident in the essential symbolism involved in the event: planes = Uranus, buildings = Saturn. An interesting side note here is how investigators discovered that a number of the hijackers involved in the September 11th incident settled in the U.S. in June of 2000 to begin flight school training in Florida—just weeks after the planetary lineup reached its peak intensity.

There is one other "omen" from the 1999/2000 period that is worth mentioning here—a cinematic image from David Fincher's violent master-piece *Fight Club*. In an article written for the April/May 2000 *Mountain Astrologer*, titled "Astrology Goes to the Movies," I discussed the surprising number of thematic parallels between this work and another acclaimed film of the period, *American Beauty* (released just weeks apart from one another during late 1999). In that article I noted how both of these films expressed the Uranus/Saturn energy in dramatic ways, such as in their stories of individuals rising up against the establishment and its values.

In *Fight Club*, this theme ultimately converges on a group of underground subversives (Uranus in Aquarius) whose primary goal is to destroy the major financial structures of society (Saturn/Taurus). Without giving away the film's ending, the closing shot now holds an eerie familiarity in light of recent events: the lead characters look out from a window high up in a skyscraper, as a series of corporate buildings around them—the last two of which bear a vague resemblance to the WTC towers—collapse to the ground in a heap of rubble, destroyed by explosives. As they say, truth is stranger than fiction; but sometimes, the two are almost indistinguishable.

Some Final Thoughts

"But what does it all *mean*?" a client asked me several days ago. In other words, is there some broader message contained in the New York City disaster that might relate to the broader changes shaping our world now? While it's too early to fathom all the levels at work in this tragedy, there are two possibilities I would mention as points for further reflection.

Occurring in the wake of the Taurus lineup, this event may partly represent the birth pangs of a new global economy, stemming from the influence of globalization and e-commerce. That it was so tragically Uranian in nature (i.e., jets plowing into corporate buildings) may underscore the profound challenge facing us as we attempt to reconcile individual or regional interests (Uranus/Aquarius) with the ever-expanding influence of corporate interests (Saturn/Taurus).

On a broader level, the recent crisis may take on special significance when seen in the context of the shifting Ages, as we move from Pisces to

Aquarius. Note that the attack was perpetrated by religious fundamentalists, specifically related to a Piscean Age religion (Islam). The image of religious extremists bent on destroying capitalist society may reflect the values of the previous Age clashing with those of the advancing one. From one perspective, the burgeoning conflict might therefore be characterized as a battle between tradition and progress, religion and industry, Piscean obedience and Aquarian freedom. How well we will succeed in reconciling these opposites will be a central question of the coming era.

Endnotes

Chapter 1

1. Depending on one's method of calculation, the duration of an age can differ by centuries. For example, if one divides the band of constellations into twelve evenly spaced segments, then each age lasts about 2140 years. But if one dates the beginning and end of each age by the actual size of the constellation the vernal point passes through, then its duration can be far shorter or longer than this figure. For example, the constellation of Cancer is small, giving rise to an Age of less than one thousand years in all. By contrast, the constellation of Pisces extends over a greater range of sky, and produces a Great Age over twenty-five hundred years in length. To complicate matters further, there is sometimes considerable overlap between the stars of adjoining constellations—making the question of where an Age ends and another begins problematic. Technically speaking, the vernal point is plotted to reach the first star in the constellation of Aquarius around 2700 A.D.; yet the stars in the constellation of Pisces extend *beyond* this celestial point. This means that, according to this method of calculation, the Piscean Age will formally continue beyond the beginning of the Aquarian Age by at least 100 years.

Another point should be noted here. The vernal point is only one of *four* astronomical points astrologers need to consider when trying to understand the influence of the shifting Great Ages. Positioned at 90 degree increments from one another, the other three are: the point of the summer solstice; autumnal equinox; winter solstice. When the vernal (spring) equinox moves into the constellation of Aquarius, the winter solstice is concurrently shifting into the constellation of Scorpio, while the summer solstice moves into Taurus and the autumnal equinox into Leo. Though these are important in their own ways, it is the vernal point (spring equinox) that, by all accounts, merits the greatest attention, being comparable in significance to the ascendant (or "rising sign") within a personal horoscope. (The latter half of this book deals extensively with the meaning and influence of the other zodiacal axis associated with Leo/Aquarius.)

2. Some critics, even a few astrologers, have questioned the Great Ages as an influence on world history because of how the doctrine often seems to involve a selective reading of historical events; the cultural manifestations often cited to illustrate various Ages are not always worldwide in their scope, e.g., during the Age of Taurus we saw an emergence of bull symbols in some cultures but not in others. But the same point could be made about virtually *any* astrological configuration, whether that be short or long-term.

Take the powerful planetary configurations that occurred during 1989; the effects that year were most dramatic in countries like Germany, China, and the Soviet Union, but less obvious in countries like Sweden or Egypt. That doesn't mean the effects of such astrological configurations are not real, simply that they are not homogeneous in their expression. The same applies to the Great Ages; the influence of the symbolism associated with any one Age may be more concentrated or obvious in certain cultures, but will be felt by people across the entire planet in different ways.

3. I have borrowed this analogy between Roman imperialism and the development of the human ego from James Hillman's *Re-visioning Psychology* (Hillman 1975).

4. As an archetypal expression of our times, modern psychology represents another "transitional" phenomenon in the way it partakes of the qualities of Piscean and Aquarian Ages. For instance, to the degree that it concerns the interior lives of individuals, as with the depth psychology of Freud and Jung, it has roots within the Piscean Age and its legacy of emotionality and interiority. But to the extent that psychology represents a nuts-and-bolts science of human personality (e.g., B. F. Skinner's "Behaviorism"), it expresses the spirit of the emerging Aquarian ethos. To say it another way, the Piscean Age contributed enormously to the rise of modern psychological thought, yet the notion that the study of human nature could serve *as an end in itself,* divorced of metaphysical or religious considerations, is primarily an Aquarian innovation.

5. The "breaking out of prison" theme dramatized by the storming of the Bastille has recent echoes in pop culture. During the powerful Uranus/Neptune conjunction of the early 1990s, several of the most notable films from this period featured this theme, presented in literal or metaphorical ways. These included *The Shawshank Redemption* (1994), in which a wrongfully accused prisoner struggles to break out of jail, and Jane Campion's fascinating *The Piano* (1993), about a woman who feels *emotionally* imprisoned (a bad marriage and the old-world—*Piscean*—values of her time) but who breaks free.

6. Another "transitional symbol" involving whale symbolism can be found in Disney's *Fantasia 2000,* the sequel to the 1941 original. The timing of this film's release, on the first day of 2000, along with the fact that it followed in the footsteps of one of history's landmark films, made this a film worth watching for symbols. In the sequence widely considered the best (set to Resphigi's richly orchestrated *Pines of Rome*), we are treated to images of whales who go from a water-bound state to airborne, working their way into the upper reaches of the sky. In other words, here is the transformation of the Piscean consciousness (whales, the ocean) into the Aquarian consciousness (flying, clouds, the stars).

Chapter 2

1. The fact that America may be the vanguard of the Aquarian era does not mean it will necessarily remain the leading world power for the next two millennia.

(Indeed, some might read the publication of Gibbon's *Decline and Fall of the Roman Empire* in 1776 as synchronistically underscoring that fact.) A possible analogy here is ancient Jerusalem, which was in some respects the womb of the Piscean Age, yet this city did not remain a key political force for much of that Age.

Another point to bear in mind is that as the various characters in a play further the unfolding of that play's storyline, so there are *many* nations feeding into the emerging Aquarian mythos in different ways. A basic list of candidates includes:

Germany—in music (Ludwig van Beethoven, Wolfgang Mozart, Richard Wagner); science and technology (Albert Einstein, Werner Heisenberg, Max Planck, Werhner von Braun); philosophy (Friedrich Nietzsche, Goethe); cinema (Fritz Lang, F.W. Murnau); psychology (Sigmund Freud).

England—in science (Sir Isaac Newton, Charles Darwin, Stephen Hawking, William Herschel, Michael Faraday); technology (the industrial revolution, the development of computers); popular music (the Beatles); politics (the Magna Carta, John Locke); philosophy (Francis Bacon, Alfred North Whitehead, Arthur Koestler); literature (Aldous Huxley, Lord Byron, Percy and Mary Shelley, H.G. Wells, Arthur C. Clarke, William Blake, W.B. Yeats); economics (Adam Smith); astrology (Charles Carter, Alan Leo, Charles Harvey).

France—in literature (Jules Verne, Paul Verlaine, Charles Baudelaire); art (Claude Monet, Cézanne); music (Claude Debussy, Maurice Ravel); politics (public education, domestic abolition of slavery, women's rights, Napoleonic legal codes); aviation (the Montgolfier brothers); cinema (the Lumiere brothers, George Melies, François Truffaut, Jean Cocteau); warfare (universal conscription, modern military tactics).

Russia/the former USSR offers an intriguing case study in the ways this culture combines the qualities of both adjoining ages. In some ways, this culture seems more oriented toward Piscean Age values, as reflected in its emotional temperament, long history of suffering, and embrace of a distinctly Piscean economic system, communism. (Also, note that the last leader to preside over a communist regime in that country, Mikhail Gorbachev, was a Pisces, while the first major leader to preside over a democratic regime, Boris Yeltsin, was an Aquarius.) Yet in other ways, Russia/USSR has been on a par with the United States in advancing Aquarian trends.

In science and technology, for instance, it was the first to send both a satellite and a human being into space; it was instrumental in the development of both TV and cinema, especially through pioneers like Sergei Einsenstein. In music, it gave us Igor Stravinsky; and in religion, there was H.P. Blavatsky, whose writings on Theosophy influenced W.B. Yeats, Wassily Kandinsky, L. Frank Baum, and Thomas Edison, to name a few.

To be sure, there are other nations besides these contributing to the birth of the Aquarian Age, but in particular, I would call attention to China, Japan, and Australia as potential players in this unfolding drama—though exactly when and how remains to be seen.

2. Writing during the nineteenth century, historian and social analyst Alexis de Tocqueville described the leaders of the French Revolution as having formed a new "turbulent and destructive race . . . that stipulates that there are no individual rights, indeed that there are no individuals, but only a mass which may stop at nothing to attain its ends" (Dunn 1999).

3. In a slightly different way, this imbalance between the "higher" and "lower" aspects of the American psyche is one of the defining themes of Orson Welles' *Citizen Kane*. A young man rises to great power only to experience a fall from grace.

But in the end we learn that his tragic flaw was his stunted emotional growth, symbolized by his childhood sled Rosebud, an emblem of his lost youth. The character of Charles Foster Kane never truly had a childhood; he lost his mother at a young age and was sent off to guardians in the city, and thus he had no emotional foundations to build his character upon. He was thrust onto the stage of adulthood at an early age (not unlike Welles himself), and thereafter sought to fill the gaping void within himself by acquiring women or possessions.

In an analogous way, America really didn't have a "childhood" either; that is, America didn't have a rooted tradition of its own, having essentially imported European culture and planted it in its own soil. This lack of tradition has been both America's greatest strength and weakness ever since. On the one hand, having so few roots is precisely what has allowed it to become the great innovator and pioneer in so many areas, since it wasn't hindered by tradition in the way most European cultures had been. Yet it also meant America sprung onto the scene as a full-blown adolescent, a prodigy with enormous power and a bright mind, but without the benefit of a normal psychological growth process, such as we find with most other cultures around the world.

Without that emotional grounding, America has been paying a heavy price ever since, in terms of an ongoing battle between "North" and "South"—its highly developed mental nature and less developed emotional nature. That's why Charles Foster Kane's story is reflective of America's. It's intriguing that the original title of Welles' film had simply been *American*. At some level, Welles and cowriter Herman Mankiewicz sensed the deep relevance of their story to the American experience in general. But in giving us this story, they also provided us a valuable glimpse of the workings of the emerging Aquarian psyche.

Chapter 3

1. A more recent example of how wars can act out the archetypal dynamics of the Great Ages would be the war over Kosovo in 1998. On one side, there were the airborne soldiers armed with cutting-edge technology, ostensibly representing the Aquarian forces of religious tolerance and humanitarianism; on the other side, there were the ground-based Serbian forces involved in the ethnic cleansing of Muslim inhabitants in the region, mirroring Piscean religious intolerance and persecution. (See chapter 12 for another example of warfare symbolism as played itself in the 1991 Gulf War.) The nature of war itself changes fundamentally with each Great Age. Hence, while the Age of Aries played host to wars of conquest, the Piscean Age gave us wars of ideology and religion, and the age of Aquarius will presumably see wars of information and technology or corporate interests.

2. For a fascinating depiction of both Bram Stoker's story and the unique qualities of *fin de siècle* Europe in the 1890s, see Francis Coppola's 1992 film *Dracula*, particularly its London-based sequences involving Gary Oldman and Winona Ryder. With its art nouveau motifs, absinthe bars, and ornate costumes, these sequences provide an intriguing look into the combination of ethereality and sensuality that characterized the period of the Pluto/Neptune conjunction. Also of interest is the intriguing way Stoker's story itself reflected the qualities of the Pluto/Neptune configuration in effect when he wrote it. Pluto symbolically governs factors like power, violence, and underworldly activities, while Neptune rules (in its negative aspect) parasitical influences. Combine these two and what do you get? A powerful underworldly figure who literally drains the life out of others!

3. The blending of past and future Ages in musicians like Debussy is also visible in many other artists of that period. Another example is the painter Paul Gauguin; he brought to a colorful head many of the qualities associated with the Piscean Age, as in his exotic and oceanic subject matter, not to mention the profoundly escapist qualities of his life (penniless, he abandoned his family for Tahiti in 1891). Yet like Debussy, his work prepared audiences for futuristic trends with his gift for abstraction and nonnaturalistic colors, elements that were crucial to the development of twentieth century art.

4. Among the more notable spiritually oriented magazines of the 1990s were *Gnosis* and *The Quest*. What is worth noting here is how closely the fortunes of both these publications waxed and waned in tandem with the Uranus/Neptune conjunction of the time (a period extending roughly five years on either side of 1993). Both journals began publication during the late 1980s, came into relative prominence during the early 1990s, and eventually faded from sight during the later part of the decade—*The Quest* being converted and scaled down to a members-only publication of the Theosophical Society in 1998, and *Gnosis* ceasing publication entirely that same year.

Chapter 4

1. Though the Lumiere brothers are credited with the first public screening of a motion picture, the actual invention of film technology is generally credited to Laurie Dickson, who worked in Thomas Edison's workshop. During the early 1890s, Dickson perfected the first fully functioning movie camera and viewing devices, beginning with the Kineotograph and followed by the Kinetoscope.

2. To the synchronistically minded, there is something provocative about the fact that just as the Lumieres were perfecting their cinematic "dream machine" in 1895, another epochal development was taking place that called attention to human dreams and fantasies: Sigmund Freud's intellectual breakthrough concerning dream symbolism. Writing in a letter to his associate Wilhelm Fliess, Freud speculated that some day a monument might be erected which read, "Here, on July 24, 1895, the secret of dreams was revealed to Dr. Sigm. Freud" (Tarnas 1995).

3. My thanks to Keith Cunningham for this insight concerning the nature of modern film as a corporate product.

4. In addition to *The Abyss*, the summer of 1989 saw many other films with possible synchronistic links to the *Voyager II* Neptune mission. For example, one finds a thoroughly Neptunian mood in such films as *Dead Poets Society* (a reawakening of nineteenth century Romanticism at its best and worst); *Indiana Jones and the Last Crusade* (which centered on the quest for the Holy Grail—the great symbol of esoteric Christendom); *Field of Dreams* (the power of fantasy and lost dreams); *Star Trek V* (a tale of charismatic religious leaders and religious self-deception—see chapter 17); *Wired* (the life of John Belushi and his long-standing battle with drugs—released the day after *Voyager II*'s closest approach); the French film *Camille Claudel* (an outstanding biopic on the self-destructive life of Rodin's alcoholic mistress); and *Ghostbusters II* (a tale of encounters with the paranormal).

Other, real-world, events from this period expressed a strong resonance with the energies of the Neptune fly-by: a series of news stories centering on the ocean (including the discovery of the underwater wreck of the *Edmund Fitzgerald* and a major conference on the condition of the world's oceans); on the actual day of the fly-by, researchers announced a possible cure for crack addiction; on August 16, an agent for the DEA (the U.S. Drug Enforcement Agency) was seized for smuggling drugs; and religious battles reached a fever pitch in Lebanon and India, highlighting the dangers of religious intolerance. In the months leading up to the fly-by, an account from Pittsburgh said hundreds of people claimed they saw a statue of Christ in a local church *close its eyes*. Even if dismissed as nothing more than a mass hallucination, such an experience echoes the subliminal realization of a passing era, in that the Piscean Age consciousness, too, was "closing its eyes" to modern humanity.

5. In their own way, the Wachowski brothers may reflect another side of Uranus in Gemini as found in both the United States' horoscope and this planet's discovery chart. As any astrology text will show, Gemini is the zodiacal sign most associated in symbolism with siblings. When Uranus is positioned in this sign, that symbolism can refer to siblings of a more innovative or even futuristic sort. For example, consider these notable siblings from the last two centuries who were involved with cutting-edge developments in distinctly Aquarian areas: in aviation, the Montgolfier and Wright brothers; in astronomy, William Hershel and his sister Caroline (jointly responsible for many of his key discoveries); in politics and space travel, John and Robert Kennedy; in modern literature and philosophy, Henry and William James; in astrology, the Sibley brothers of late eighteenth century England; and in cinema, the Lumiere brothers, Joel and Ethan Coen, and, as we noted, the Wachowskis.

6. It's often said that *Citizen Kane* encapsulated the evolution of film up to that point, while heralding those trends yet to follow. In light of that observation, it seems like a synchronistic "passing of the torch" that the man often described as the father of modern film editing, Edwin Porter *(The Great Train Robbery)*, died on April 30, 1941, the day before *Citizen Kane*'s world premiere.

7. The key astrological configurations in effect at the time of *Citizen Kane*'s premiere (May 1st, 1941) were: Jupiter and Uranus in precise conjunction (0-degrees alignment); Uranus and Neptune in precise trine (120-degrees alignment); Jupiter and Neptune in precise trine (120-degrees relationship); and a six-planet lineup in Taurus that also included Uranus. That so many outer-planet relationships were culminating at once is unusual enough; the fact that Uranus factored so prominently in virtually all of these further suggests the importance of this window for Aquarian trends. And if one extends out the range of influence here (what astrologers refer to as "orb"), one could also include other major alignments from this period, such as the alignment between Jupiter and Saturn and another between Saturn and Uranus. Synchronistically, it is also worth mentioning that this general period (May of 1941) witnessed significant artistic developments on other fronts, including the first public exhibition at the newly opened National Gallery of Art in Washington, D.C., and the birth of Bob Dylan on May 25th, 1941.

Chapter 5

1. The idea of "news" is normally associated by astrologers with the sign Gemini, yet this more appropriately relates to traditional forms of news gathering or dissemination, such as regional newspapers and ordinary letter-writing. The rise of the global electronic media is more properly associated with the sign Aquarius, while its news gathering function reflects the coupling of Aquarius with information-oriented Gemini.

Chapter 6

1. Though I have personally drawn this system of astrology/chakra correspondences from teachers in the Kriya Yoga tradition (as taught by Goswami Kriyananda and Shelly Trimmer), it's important to note this system of correspondences isn't exclusive to any one spiritual tradition, and has been supported by many other writers through the years with affiliations to different traditions, including Jeff Green, David Frawley, and Marc Edmund Jones.

2. For a more in-depth discussion of my own thoughts on the implications of the chakra/astrology model, see my 1996 book *The Waking Dream*, chapter 10; see also my chapter in the 1997 anthology *Eastern Systems for Western Astrologers*.

3. While sometimes classified as being "expressionist" in its style, Orson Welles brought remarkable touches of realism to *Citizen Kane*. In addition to featuring a decidedly secular subject (the rise and fall of a materialistic tycoon), we see the influence of realism in its naturalistic dialogue and the mock-newsreel footage which opens the film (complete with scratches and editing errors). Another exquisite example is the deathbed scene involving Kane's second wife, Susan Alexander (played by Dorothy Comingore).

In most films of the 1930s and '40s, leading actresses were shown in an idealized light, even when in dire or traumatic circumstances. As a comparison, the film *Wuthering Heights* was released just two years prior to *Citizen Kane*, and shows its leading lady on her deathbed, photographed through gauze filters and a beatific glow bathing her head. But in *Citizen Kane*, the heroine is shown at her crucial moment with disheveled hair and sweat pouring down her face—a startling sight for movie goers of the time who were unaccustomed to such forthright depictions of emotional tragedy.

Chapter 7

1. Though Galileo may have been the first in modern times to engage in a "scientific" study of phenomena, he was by no means the first to do so in history. There are several prominent instances of traditional cultures engaging in a rational, experimental investigation of natural phenomena. For instance, the Babylonians used a scientific approach when tabulating their famed "omen series," a process that involved observing phenomena over time, developing theories, then cross-checking these against subsequent observations. In Egypt, the "Edwin Smith surgical papyrus" likewise testifies to the way this culture was perfectly capable of empirical-rational studies of phenomena, untainted by superstition or religious preconceptions. (See *The Temple of Man* by Schwaller de Lubicz for an in-depth discussion of this remarkable document.)

The chief difference between these traditional examples and modern forms seems to lie primarily in the underlying intent with which they have been applied. In ancient cultures like Babylonia and Egypt, these instances of scientific thinking were subsets of a larger, spiritually oriented culture; in our time, the scientific approach has become a dominant mode of thinking unto itself.

2. As the final two signs of the zodiac, *both* Aquarius and Pisces are associated with the awareness of systems. The difference is that with Pisces, individual distinctions are largely erased relative to the greater system, whereas in the case of Aquarius, individual distinctions tend to be *preserved* within the system—as shown in my example of the jazz band (Aquarius) versus the traditional Gregorian choir (Pisces).

3. The question of whether or not systems thinking represents a more "spiritual" approach toward our world is a subtle one, for the reason that there are many different *kinds* of systems we must take into account. For instance, in this chapter I am primarily critiquing "horizontal" forms of systems thought, those which address phenomena occurring on a single plane of experience. An example of this is standard ecological theory, which examines all the interrelated forces and creatures inhabiting an ecosystem, without taking into account the spiritual or subtle energies that underlie this system. While more "holistic" in spirit, it is nevertheless a more "Flatland" approach to systems thinking, since it focuses only on physical, measurable entities.

There are more *vertical* kinds of systems which involve multiple levels of reality beyond the physical, and which could be called "spiritual" in nature. An example of this is the integral philosophy of Jean Gebser, who pioneered a model of human evolution which drew upon many ideas and levels of consciousness, and in so doing created a "systems" approach to human knowledge that was not "Flatland" or "horizontal."

Chapter 8

1. In addition to symbolic pairings like Jesus and the Virgin Mary, the combined influence of Pisces and Virgo can also be seen in the widespread trend toward doctrinal and theological hair-splitting that characterized Western thought for much of the last two thousand years. Turning to the previous Great Age, Jungian astrologer Alice O. Howell offers observations on how the zodiacal polarity of Aries and Libra manifested in human culture. Not only was this an era of great empires and military leaders like Alexander the Great and Ramses II, but it was a time which saw the rise of great laws and lawgivers (e.g., Moses with his Ten Commandments, Hammurabi and his Code, Solon and his Edicts, and the codification of the Twelve Tablets of Roman Law), reflecting the influence of Libra.

Howell points out how this influence is especially obvious in the Oresteia trilogy, where the people of Athens are told that the best way to deal with injustice is by means of a jury and the wisdom of rational consensus. (See Howell's *Jungian Synchronicity in Astrological Signs and Ages* [1990].) This counterbalancing influence of Libra might also be seen in the extraordinary works of sculpture and art found in cultures like Greece at its height, whose works displayed an elegance and grace different from the timeless and monumental qualities of much Taurean Age art and sculpture.

2. Astrologer Liz Greene associates the mythic figure of Prometheus with the zodiacal sign Aquarius (Greene 1984). My own experience has led me to associate this mythic figure more broadly with the entire Aquarius-Leo axis. In this way, the "drawing down of fire" motif takes on added resonance in relation to Aquarius's interplay with its opposing sign, fiery Leo. (See appendix 2 for further thoughts on how the Promethean myth relates to both Aquarius and Uranus.)

Chapter 9

1. Michael Wilmington, *The Chicago Tribune*, Sept. 26, 1999 (7, 1). Also, 1962 was a turning point for cinema in certain non-English-speaking countries as well; for example, that was the year that twenty-six young filmmakers in Germany issued their manifesto declaring, "The old film is dead. We believe in the new film."

2. Beyond pioneering the theme of "mind control," John Frankenheimer's *The Manchurian Candidate* may have been prophetic in other respects. It was the first

Hollywood film to feature a martial arts fighting sequence (between Frank Sinatra and Henry Silva). Its theme of political assassination proved ominous in light of JFK's assassination the following year, an event which led in part to the film being withdrawn from public circulation for several decades. This raises the possibility of a further synchronicity: in the real-life assassination of JFK, the alleged killer was named Lee Harvey Oswald, while in *The Manchurian Candidate*, the trained assassin in the film was played by an actor named L. Harvey (Lawrence Harvey).

3. Though primarily emphasizing the polarity between Leo and Aquarius, the great planetary lineup of 1962 formed a powerful relationship with Neptune in Scorpio (what astrologers call a "T-square"). Since Neptune governs mysticism and delusion, this caused the "heroic" energies of the Leo/Aquarius opposition to be tainted by a certain messianic quality. This was reflected in the way the cinematic version of T. E. Lawrence becomes more deluded about his powers and importance as the story progresses (he even refers half-jokingly at one point to his ability to walk on water). In turn, that same involvement of Neptune in Scorpio seems to underlie Lawrence's fall from grace as depicted in the film, when his inflated ego is suddenly deflated by an unsavory sexual encounter in a Turkish jail.

The influence of Neptune in Scorpio is also visible in many other films from 1962, such as *Dr. No*, with its themes of covert spies and their sexual escapades; and in *Days of Wine and Roses*, a story of alcoholism and renewal. As seen in the context of the 1960s, the lingering influence of this Neptunian pattern may be responsible for the powerful Dionysian trends which ran through this period, as reflected in the expanding popularity of sex, drugs, and rock and roll.

4. *Schindler's List* was released in 1993, the same year as the powerful conjunction between Neptune (altruism, compassion) and Uranus (the entrepreneurial spirit), planetary rulers of the adjoining Piscean and Aquarian Ages. The release of this film at that time provided another illustration of how the values of these two ages might be combined toward a harmonious end in our future, with the application of business to spiritual and humanitarian ideals.

5. The symbol of the empowered child has existed in world mythologies through history. The difference now is that this archetypal theme, rather than being exclusively associated with one or two key figures in society (like Krishna in Hindu mythology), is becoming democratized through the emergence of *many* gifted children in society (especially in terms of intellectual and technological aptitude).

Chapter 10

1. The news of Dolly the sheep burst into prominence during late February of 1997 at a time when there was a major planetary lineup in the sign Aquarius. The news of Dr. Seed's controversial announcement one year later, in early January of 1998, was likewise accompanied by a multiple lineup in Aquarius, though this time involving only four planets.

2. For a more extended discussion of genetics and the theory of "morphic fields," see Sheldrake 1995.

Chapter 11

1. On the day news of the Monica Lewinsky scandal first broke, a four-planet lineup in Aquarius was being triggered by an exact alignment between Mars and Jupiter within that configuration. Symbolically interpreted, the Aquarian emphasis

here relates to the involvement of global media in the scandal, while the role of these two planets relates to the sexual (Mars) and judicial (Jupiter) nature of the ensuing controversy that would unfold in its wake.

2. There are other possible synchronicities to be mined from the films and TV shows released at the height of the Clinton/Lewinsky saga, which could shed light on the dynamics underlying this scandal. As 1998 unfolded, I began to notice echoes of this story appearing in apparently unrelated places, and which pointed to other forces at work behind the scenes. This centered on a series of prominent films and TV shows of the time which featured images of public figures being systematically taken down by hidden killers, specifically under the supervision of covert interests. In view of growing charges from many quarters that corporate interests and well-heeled enemies of Clinton may have been involved in encouraging these political attacks, I decided to pay attention to this.

To begin with, there was Warren Beatty's film *Bulworth* (released during early 1998) in which the lead political figure is picked off at film's end by an assassin hiding in the shadows. Though we don't actually see the killer pulling the trigger, the implied villain is corporate America—specifically, the insurance industry.

Then, in May of that year, we had the much-touted season finale of *The X-Files*, pivoting around a chess match being played out in the center of a large auditorium. A hidden assassin attempts to kill one of the players (a psychic child).

Around this same time, Brian DiPalma's film *Snake Eyes* was released; it featured a stunningly similar scene centering on an assassination plot at a boxing match, with the triggerman lurking in the shadows, acting on behalf of corporate interests.

A month later, John Frankenheimer's *Ronin* came out; it had a pivotal scene involving an assassination in a public arena (an ice skating rink) by a killer hiding in the rafters. A curious detail linking all of these cases was the assassination scenes were shown being videotaped and/or televised—another clue in this drama.

If we take this as a synchronistic trend of the time, how do we interpret it? On a literal level, it points to the possibility that the attacks on Clinton were partly bankrolled or in some way spurred on by hidden interests. Whether or not this involved some "vast right-wing conspiracy" as some Clinton defenders claimed, I don't know; however, it is well-known that Clinton developed powerful enemies while in office, including special interest groups like the gun, medical, and tobacco lobbies. It was interesting to learn over the course of the scandal that the independent counsel appointed to run the investigation had been previously employed by the tobacco industry, and that the congressmen and senators most involved with attacking Clinton had previously received the most campaign and lobbying dollars from tobacco companies. None of this diminishes Clinton's mistakes in the matter, but highlights the extent to which moneyed interests might influence the political process.

Viewed symbolically, this scandal may underscore the profound tension that exists between corporate interests (Aquarius) and individuals who threaten them (Leo). As such, it highlights the serious challenge we may *all* face in the coming Age, not only in our efforts to separate special interests from the political process, but in trying to remain free-thinking individuals in a mass society. The close involvement of the media in these cinematic examples and the real-life scandal points up the intimate role that telecommunications technology could continue to play in all these sociological dramas.

Chapter 12

1. The aviation experiments by the Montgolfier brothers occurred in several stages. In November of 1782, the first of their balloons was a simple construction of fine silk over fire. Then in 1783, Joseph and Etienne used a sheep, rooster, and duck as the first living creatures to partake in a balloon experiment. It was only in October of that year that a living human became part of a tethered balloon flight, for an ascent of only four and a-half minutes. Finally, in November (though some sources cite a December date), two associates of the Montgolfiers became the first human beings to pilot a free-flight of an untethered hot-air balloon.

2. Breakthroughs in aviation consistently appear to be associated with astrological configurations involving either Aquarius or Uranus. To cite three examples: the Wright brothers made their first controlled flight on December 17, 1903, when Uranus was aligned with the sun and opposite its discovery position in 1781, suggesting this was a noteworthy Aquarian "window." When Robert Goddard made his first successful launch of a liquid fuel rocket on March 16, 1926, the sun was again aligned with Uranus. Lindbergh made his famed landing in Paris in 1927, when the discovery point of Uranus from 1781 was also emphasized prominently, and Uranus was in relationship with Mercury, Jupiter, the sun, and the moon—all indicating a significant resonance with the emerging paradigm.

3. In early 1998, astrophysicists announced the discovery that the universe was expanding faster than it "should," at least as dictated by gravity. This was taken to mean there might be an unusual new "repulsive" force operating in our cosmos, perhaps related to Einstein's early notion of the "cosmological constant." Though seemingly similar to Fischbach's idea proposed in the 1980s, the repulsive force announced in 1998 operates on a grander cosmic scale; Fischbach's "hyper-charge" was described as functioning over short distances of perhaps no more than 600 feet. Another notable development during the twelve months leading up to the *Voyager II* fly-by past Uranus was the surprising upsurge of globally televised humanitarian events involving rock stars in different cities around the world linked by satellite hook-ups. Among these were the famed "Live Aid" and "We Are the World" benefits—a truly Aquarian blending of humanitarian concerns with telecommunications technology.

4. This individual, Richard Andresen, has since signed a statement confirming that this conversation took place prior to the disaster.

5. Even before the *Challenger* disaster, the image of an exploding rocket ship was already viewed by some as a symbol for the problematic side of industrial civilization. Several years earlier, the independent film *Koyaanisqatsi* received widespread distribution. This quasi-experimental feature displayed a succession of images illustrating humanity's destructive impact on nature; the opening and closing shots centered on a rocket taking off and exploding in pieces over the Earth—a heavy-handed metaphor for the failure of modern technology. First released in the early 1980s, the film was still widely screened in the art house circuit at the time the shuttle exploded.

6. At another level, the movie *Pleasantville* can be viewed as a brilliant illustration of dynamical systems theory. Among other things, this theory demonstrates how the transition from a less complex system to a more complex one can (superficially at least) appear to be a movement toward greater chaos and destruction, when what is actually occurring is a movement toward greater order. The transition from life as an embryo to an independent adult might be viewed from the standpoint of the

embryo as a "fall" into greater chaos and suffering, considering all the problems and headaches that attend normal adulthood. Yet from a long-range perspective, this is a step forward in evolutionary complexity to be accompanied by greater pains, sure, but greater joys and rewards as well.

Chapter 13

1. Having studied arguments on both sides of the ET question for many years, I've often found proponents of the pro-contact viewpoint to be more rigorous and "scientific" in their approach to this field than their skeptical counterparts in groups like CSICOP. As one example, when UFO researcher Stanton Friedman set out to investigate reports of the famed Roswell, New Mexico, case, he interviewed more than a hundred witnesses before formulating any conclusions. When the leading skeptic in this field approached this same case, he reached his conclusions as an "armchair theorist," without interviewing a single witness. (Only after much criticism did he relent by conducting a handful of interviews.)

Further, when one reads any of the respectable UFO publications, one almost always finds heated debate among writers on the merits of major cases (such as the Roswell incident or the notorious "Alien Autopsy" footage). By contrast, look through either of the two leading skeptical journals on newsstands (e.g., *Skeptical Inquirer* and *Skeptic*); one rarely finds writers breaking ranks with the "debunk-at-all-costs" party line—strongly suggesting these researchers have come to the table with predetermined agendas rather than the critical open-mindedness of the actual skeptic.

Chapter 14

1. For a discussion of this and other possible evidence for lost civilizations, see Cremo and Thompson's *Forbidden Archeology* (1993).

2. Of the critical studies put forward on the Piri Reis map over the years, to my mind the most credible is that of geologist Robert Schoch, in *Voices of the Rocks: A Scientist Looks at Catastrophes and Ancient Civilizations* (New York: Harmony Books, 1999). For a more sympathetic (and to my tastes more compelling) viewpoint, see Rand Flem-Ath's and Colin Wilson's *The Atlantis Blueprint* (London: Little, Brown and Company, 2000).

3. One objection to the argument that the Sphinx was carved during the Age of Leo centers on the fact that the early Egyptians probably didn't *understand* the concept of the Great Ages (or for that matter the constellations) as we now do. If they didn't, however, that raises an equally vexing set of problems, such as how to explain the dramatic shifts in Egyptian religious symbolism that occurred in tandem with the shifting Great Ages, such as the shift from bull imagery to ram symbolism during the transition from Taurus to Aries around 2100 B.C.

Yet another possibility to consider is that humans have *always* acted out the dynamics of the Great Ages, whether they consciously knew it or not. The dynamics of the Great Ages are based on principles of universal symbolism; as such, it's probable that they shape our lives with or without our consent or understanding. So it's possible the construction of the Sphinx could have been undertaken in a way that mirrored the archetypal energies of the Age of Leo without there being any conscious awareness of this correlation. Sadly, until there is some way of conclusively dating this monument one way or another, all speculations on this subject are destined to remain little more than that.

4. For example, in *The Orion Mystery*, Robert Bauval and Adrian Gilbert proposed that the layout of the Giza pyramids reflects stellar patterns as they existed over Egypt 12,000 years ago—a theory that has sparked enormous controversy in both archeological and astronomical circles. Until further evidence surfaces settling the matter one way or the other, the question of Egypt's true antiquity or historical understanding will remain an open one.

5. The castration motif underlying the Ouranos story may shed light on certain other trends which have taken place in recent years related to configurations involving Aquarius or Uranus. For example, early 1997 hosted a significant planetary lineup in the sign Aquarius, including a powerful alignment between Jupiter and Uranus (an expansive and futuristic combination). The weeks following this lineup saw an uncanny number of news stories involving astronomical, spiritual, or New-Age themes of one sort or another. Among these: the March 24 cover story of *Time* centered on humanity's changing perceptions of heaven; the March 24 *Newsweek* focused on the Hale-Bopp comet; on March 31, the *U.S. News and World Report* cover story dealt with "life after death"; *TV Guide*'s cover on March 29 featured the title "God and Television," while the March 31 *Newsweek* featured as a cover story "The Mystery of Prayer." Also, March 13 was the date of the now-famous "Phoenix lights" incident, when thousands of Arizona citizens observed unusual lights moving through their skies.

In the wake of all these, late March of that year revealed grisly details of a mass suicide by the Heaven's Gate cult in California, an event spurred by unfounded rumors concerning the Hale-Bopp comet. In some ways, this group embodied an approach to religion that was Aquarian at its most dissociated and spaced-out, with their belief in an ideal utopia located literally among the stars, far from the grime and crude vibrations of Earth. Their ritualistic rite of passage in embarking on this final journey? Physical castration!

6. There are many examples illustrating the way archeological discoveries seem to coincide with powerful periods of social transformation. A prime example was the powerful Uranus/Neptune alignment of 1993. That year saw the network premiere of the show *Mystery of the Sphinx* (as well as the return to print of John Anthony West's book *Serpent in the Sky*, on which the show was based); the publication of Cremo and Thompson's enormously controversial *Forbidden Archeology;* and the discovery of the mysterious (and still unexplored) "Gattenbrink shaft" within the Great Pyramid. The years immediately adjoining that conjunction proved fertile for books and research in both mainstream and alternative branches of archeology, with the popularity of authors like Graham Hancock *(Fingerprints of the Gods)*, Robert Bauval and Adrian Gilbert *(The Orion Mystery)*, David Frawley *(Gods, Sages, and Kings)*, and Rand and Rose Flem-Ath *(When the Sky Fell)*.

Considering that Uranus rules astronomy and Neptune governs spirituality, it seems appropriate that this combination included an explosion of popular interest in archeoastronomy, the study of how traditional myth and religion connect with ancient star beliefs. In addition to the above-mentioned authors, this interest was evident in the work of writers like Jane Sellers, David Freidal, Joy Parker, David Fideler, Linda Schele, Anthony Aveni, and Edwin Krupp. Also noteworthy is the way many of these breakthroughs had their roots in seminal works published during previous "future windows." For example, many of these writers were in debt to 1960s writers like Charles Hapgood (*Maps of the Ancient Sea Kings* 1966), Giorgio de Santillana and Hertha von Dechend (*Hamlets Mill: An Essay Investigating the Origins of Human Knowledge and its Transmission through Myth* 1969) and Virginia Trimble

("Astronomical Investigations Concerning the so-called Airshafts of Cheops Pyramid," a seminal paper published in 1964).

Virtually *all* these developments in the 1960s and 1990s owe their genesis to the work of Norman Locklear, who proposed his controversial views on the astronomical dimension of ancient monuments in 1894 (close to the Pluto/Neptune conjunction of 1892). Arguably the single greatest breakthrough in Egyptology occurred exactly in tandem with the conjunction of Uranus and Neptune in 1821: Champollion's deciphering of hieroglyphics using the Rosetta Stone.

Chapter 15

1. Over the years some have questioned whether Welles was directly responsible for the multiple-viewpoint approach of *Citizen Kane.* Though we may never know for sure, what we *can* say is that this stylistic convention meshes perfectly with Welles' own creative impulses both before and after the film. For example, arriving in Hollywood, Welles' first planned movie was to be a daring cinematic adaptation of Joseph Conrad's *Heart of Darkness,* which would play on the question of perspectives by centering principally on a first-person viewpoint of the protagonist. (The project was ultimately scrapped due to budgetary constraints.) Following *Citizen Kane,* Welles returned to the notion of splintered perspectives in a more symbolic way, with the climactic fun-house sequence in *The Lady from Shanghai* in which the lead characters are shown as shattered reflections in broken mirrors.

2. When speaking about "integral" creativity in contemporary society, it's useful to make a basic distinction between "flat" and "deep" forms of this process. By "flat," I refer to those forms which integrate various elements in a single form, but on a single plane of experience. For instance, modern science's effort to synthesize the four basic forces of the universe might be called "integral," yet it does not extend any higher than the physical world in scope. Likewise, brilliant as *Citizen Kane* may be in drawing together multiple perspectives and stylistic conventions, it is a largely secular work, with few if any spiritual implications or elements. On the other hand, Roberto Assagioli's system of psychosynthesis offers an example of integral, kaleidoscopic creativity that draws together multiple systems and levels of consciousness across a more vertical spectrum of experience, from lower forms of emotionality to the spiritual states of consciousness.

3. Whether or not one agrees with Ken Wilber's ideas, it can't be denied that he articulates many of the pressing themes of the coming era in a way that makes his work essential reading for anyone interested in this area. This is especially apparent in the areas under discussion here—the emerging "integral" approaches toward psychology, spirituality, business, and society itself. (For a good overview of integrative trends in modern thought, see Ken's introductions to his *Collected Works* series, volumes 7 and 8.)

Though Wilber himself doesn't seem inclined toward an astrological view of such things, a propensity for cutting-edge trends is clearly indicated by the patterns in his own horoscope. Born January 31, 1949, Wilber has the sun, Mercury, and Mars in futuristic Aquarius, while his Uranus is positioned at twenty-six degrees of Gemini—close to the point where it was when first discovered in 1781. All of these factors suggest a possible attunement to the intellectual themes of the emerging paradigm.

Chapter 16

1. Both the Aquarian and Piscean approaches to spirituality, when taken to extremes, can lead to problems. On the one hand, Piscean-style spirituality tends to be overly dependent on external God-symbols or savior figures, while Aquarian mysticism can stress personal autonomy and the belief in "the God within" to a narcissistic, even solipsistic degree, and thus overlooks the valuable tools offered by Piscean devotionality and ego-surrender. To that extent, the oft-heard criticism from Christian fundamentalists about New Age (i.e., superficially Aquarian) spirituality, that it is dangerously "me-oriented," is somewhat valid. Too often, it *does* fixate on the ego and the surface personality to the exclusion of a communion with one's higher nature.

2. Even within overtly mystical cultures like India it can be argued that the majority of worshippers have traditionally adhered to their faiths in a relatively exoteric manner, in approaching their deities and gurus as essentially superior and exterior to themselves—just as most conventional Western worshippers have done over the last two thousand years.

3. In some ways, the "three objects" that comprise the mission statement of the Theosophical Society can be viewed as foreshadowing the guiding ideals of the Aquarian Age itself. These are: 1) To form a nucleus of the universal brotherhood of humanity, without distinction of race, creed, sex, caste, or color. 2) To encourage the comparative study of religion, philosophy, and science. 3) To investigate unexplained laws of nature and the powers latent in humanity.

Appendix 2

1. It's now widely believed that most versions of Chief Seattle's speech consist largely of words attributed to him by later writers, in particular screenwriter Ted Perry for a 1972 TV documentary titled *Home* (Jones and Sawhill 1992).

Appendix 3

1. This piece appeared in slightly different form in *The Mountain Astrologer* magazine ("The Seeds of Revolution: Assessing the Effects of the May 2000 Lineup in Taurus"), Oct/Nov 2000, p. 51.

Appendix 4

1. This piece appeared in slightly different form in *The Mountain Astrologer* magazine ("The World Trade Center Tragedy and the May 2000 Planetary Lineup"), Dec 2001/Jan 2002, p. 4.

Bibliography

Allan, D. S., and J. B. Delair. *Cataclysm!: Compelling Evidence of a Cosmic Catastrophe in 9500 B.C.*, with a forward by Rand Flem-Ath. Santa Fe: Bear and Company, 1997.

Allt, Peter, and Russell K. Alspach, eds. *The Variorum Edition of the Poems of W. B. Yeats.* New York: MacMillan Company, 1966.

Algeo, John. "The Wizard of Oz on Theosophy" *The Quest* (Nov.–Dec. 2000).

Bauval, Robert. *Secret Chamber: The Quest for the Hall of Records.* London: Century, 1999.

Bauval, Robert, and Adrian Gilbert. *The Orion Mystery: Unlocking the Secrets of the Pyramids.* Toronto: Doubleday Canada, 1994.

Bellah, Robert N. *Beyond Belief: Essays on Religion in a Post-Traditional World.* New York: Harper and Row, 1970.

Bernstein, Carl. "The CIA and the Media." *Rolling Stone* (Oct. 20, 1977).

Bertalanffy, Ludwig von. *General Systems Theory.* New York: Braziller, 1968.

Blavatsky, H. P. *The Secret Doctrine.* Wheaton, Ill.: Theosophical Publishing House, Quest Books, 1933.

———. *Collected Works XIV.* Wheaton, Ill.: Theosophical Publishing House, 1985.

Bohm, David. *Wholeness and the Implicate Order.* Boston: Routledge, 1980.

Byrne, Dennis. "Man Declares Himself God—Then Cashes In." *Chicago Sun Times.* Quoting Richard Seed on National Public Radio. (Jan. 8, 1998).

Callow, Philip. *From Noon to Starry Night: A Life of Walt Whitman.* Chicago: Ivan R. Dee Publications, 1992.

Callow, Simon. *Orson Welles.* New York: Viking, 1996.

Campbell, Joseph. *The Masks of God.* 4 vols. New York: Viking, 1959–62.

———. *Transformations of Myth Through Time.* New York: Perennial Library, 1990.

———. *The Inner Reaches of Outer Space.* New York: Alfred Van Der Marck Editions, 1996.

Campion, Nicholas. "The Age of Aquarius: A Modern Myth," in *The Astrology of the Macrocosm.* Joan McEvers, ed. St. Paul, Minn.: Llewellyn, 1990.

———. *The Great Year: Astrology, Millenarianism and History in the Western Tradition.* London: Arkana, 1994.

Capra, Fritjof. *The Turning Point: Science, Society, and the Rising Culture.* New York: Simon and Shuster, 1982.

————. *The Web of Life: A New Scientific Understanding of Living Systems.* New York: Anchor Books, 1996.

Case, George. Letter to the editor. *Time* (April 2000).

Chambers, John. "Message From Space: An Interview with Edgar Mitchell." *Kindred Spirits* 6, no. 3 (Summer 1997).

Clark, Kenneth. *Civilisation, a Personal View.* New York: Harper and Row, 1969.

Clark, Rosemary. *The Sacred Tradition in Ancient Egypt.* St. Paul, Minn.: Llewellyn, 2000.

"Climate Change Impacts on the United States." http://prod.gcrio.org/NationalAssesment

Coleman, Loren. *Curious Encounters.* Boston: Faber and Faber, 1985.

Cremo, Michael, and Richard L. Thompson. *Forbidden Archaeology: The Hidden History of the Human Race.* San Diego: Bhaktivedanta Institute, 1993.

Cunningham, Keith. "Myths, Dreams, and Movies." *The Quest* (Spring 1992).

De Santillana, Giorgio, and Hertha von Dechend. *Hamlet's Mill: An Essay On Myth and the Frame of Time.* Boston: Nonpareil Books, 1969.

Dick, Steven, ed. *Many Worlds: The New Universe, Extraterrestrial Life and the Theological Implications.* Philadelphia: Templeton Foundation Press, 2000.

Dickinson, G. Lowes. *The Greek View of Life.* Ann Arbor, Mich.: Ann Arbor Paperbacks, University of Michigan Press, 1966.

Doniger, Wendy. *Other Peoples' Myths.* New York: Macmillan, 1988.

Dossey, Larry. *Prayer Is Good Medicine: How to Reap the Healing Benefits of Prayer.* San Francisco: HarperSanFrancisco, 1996.

————. *Meaning and Medicine: Lessons from a Doctor's Tales of Breakthroughs and Healing.* New York: Bantam, 1991.

Dunn, Susan. *Sister Revolutions: French Lightning, American Light.* New York: Faber and Faber, 1999.

Ebert, John David. *Twilight of the Clockwork God: Conversations on Science and Spirituality at the End of an Age.* Tulsa, Okla.: Council Oaks Books, 1999.

Edinger, Edward F. *Ego and Archetype: Individuation and the Religious Function of the Psyche.* Baltimore: Penguin, 1973.

————. *Transformation of the God-Image: An Elucidation of Jung's "Answer to Job."* Toronto: Inner City Books, 1992.

Eliade, Mircea. *The Sacred and the Profane: The Nature of Religion.* Translated by Willard R. Trask. New York: Harcourt Brace, 1959.

Feidelson, Charles N. *Symbolism and American Literature.* Chicago: University of Chicago Press, 1974.

Ferguson, Marilyn. *The Aquarian Conspiracy: Personal and Social Transformation in Our Time.* New York: J. P. Tarcher, 1987.

Feuerstein, Georg. *Structures of Consciousness: The Genius of Jean Gebser: An Introduction and Critique.* Lower Lake, Calif.: Integral Publishing, 1987.

————. *Wholeness or Transcendence: Ancient Lessons for the Emerging Global Civilization.* Burdett, New York: Larson, 1992.

Feuerstein, Georg, and Tricia Lamb Feuerstein. *Voices on the Threshold of Tomorrow.* Wheaton, Ill.: Quest Books, 1993.

Fideler, David. *Jesus Christ, Sun of God: Ancient Cosmology and Early Christian Symbolism.* Wheaton, Ill.: Quest Books, 1993.

Flem-Ath, Rand, and Rose Flem-Ath. *When the Sky Fell: In Search of Atlantis.* Toronto: Stoddart, 1995.

Flem-Ath, Rand, and Colin Wilson. *The Atlantis Blueprint.* London: Little, Brown and Company, 2000.

Frawley, David. *Gods, Sages and Kings: Vedic Secrets of Ancient Civilization.* Salt Lake City: Passage Press, 1991.

Freidel, David, Linda Schele, Joy Parker, Justin Kerr, and MacDuff Everton. *Maya Cosmos: Three Thousand Years on the Shaman's Path.* New York: William Morrow and Company, 1993.

Friedman, Thomas L. *The Lexus and the Olive Tree: Understanding Globalization.* New York: Farrar, Straus, and Giroux, 1999.

Gebser, Jean. *The Ever-Present Origin.* Athens: Ohio University Press, 1985.

Gerbner, George. Interview by Michael Toms. "Saving Our Cultural Environment: Putting the 'Vision' Back into Television. A Conversation with George Gerbner." http://www.newdimensions.org/article/gerbner.html (1998).

Geyer, Georgie Anne. "Spreading the American Developmental Gospel." *The Chicago Tribune* (Dec. 31, 1999).

Gibson, William. *Neuromancer.* New York: Ace Books, 1984.

Godwin, Joscelyn. *The Theosophical Enlightenment.* Albany: State University of New York, 1994.

Gottesman, Ronald, ed. *Focus on Citizen Kane.* Englewood Cliffs, New Jersey: Spectrum/Prentice-Hall, 1971.

———. *Focus on Orson Welles.* Englewood Cliffs, New Jersey: Prentice-Hall, 1976.

Grasse, Ray, "Myth in the Modern World: An Interview with Wendy Doniger." *The Quest* (Winter 1990).

———. "A Synchronistic Approach to Mundane Astrology, Part I." *Welcome to Planet Earth* 10, no. 6 (1990).

———. *The Waking Dream: Unlocking the Symbolic Language of Our Lives.* Wheaton, Ill.: Quest, 1996.

———. *Eastern Systems for Western Astrologers* (anthology). York Beach, Maine: Samuel Weiser Inc., 1997.

———. "Drawing Down the Fire of the Gods: Reflections on the Leo/Aquarius Axis." *The Mountain Astrologer* (February/March 2000).

Greene, Liz. *Relating: An Astrological Guide to Living with Others on a Small Planet.* York Beach, Maine: Samuel Weiser Inc., 1978.

———. *The Outer Planets and Their Cycles: The Astrology of the Collective.* Reno, Nev.: CRCS Publications, 1983.

———. *The Astrology of Fate.* York Beach, Maine: Samuel Weiser Inc., 1984.

Groothuis, Douglas. *The Soul in Cyberspace.* Grand Rapids, Mich.: Baker Books, 1997.

Grosso, Michael. *The Millennium Myth: Love and Death at the End of Time.* Wheaton, Ill.: Quest Books, 1995.

Guttman, Ariel, and Ken Johnson. *Mythic Astrology: Archetypal Powers in the Horoscope.* St. Paul, Minn.: Llewellyn, 1998.

Guttmann, Allen. *From Ritual to Record: The Nature of Modern Sports.* New York: Columbia University Press, 1978.

Hall, Manly Palmer. *The Foundation of the Great School in America* (unpublished), 1944.

———. *The Secret Teachings of All Ages.* Los Angeles: The Philosophical Research Society Inc., 1977.

———. *Landmarks of Esoteric Literature.* "Francis Bacon-*New Atlantis.*" no. 1, Philosophical Research Society, Inc. Audio, 1998.

———. *The New Atlantis* (unpublished).

Hancock, Graham. *Fingerprints of the Gods: The Evidence of Earth's Lost Civilization.* New York: Crown Publishers Inc., 1995.

Hand, Robert. *Essays on Astrology.* Gloucester, Mass.: Para Research, 1982.

Hapgood, Charles H. *The Earth's Shifting Crust: A Key to Some Basic Problems of Earth Science.* New York: Pantheon, 1958.

———. *Maps of the Ancient Sea Kings: Evidence of Advanced Civilization in the Ice Age.* Philadelphia: Chilton Books, 1966.

Harman, Willis. *Global Mind Change: The Promise of the Last Years of the Twentieth Century.* Indianapolis: Knowledge Systems, 1988.

Harvey, Andrew. *The Direct Path: Creating a Journey to the Divine Through the World's Mystical Traditions.* New York: Bantam Doubleday Dell Publishers, 2000.

Hawass, Zahi. "Solving the Puzzles of Giza." *Egypt Revealed* (March/April 2001).

Hawking, Stephen. Interview with Nigel Farndale. *Sunday Telegraph* (Jan. 2, 2000).

Heelas, Paul. *The New Age Movement: The Celebration of Self and the Sacralization of Modernity.* Oxford: Blackwell, 1996.

Heilbroner, Robert L. *The Future as History: The Historic Currents of Our Time and the Direction in Which They Are Taking America.* New York: Harper and Brothers, 1960.

Heller, Erich. *The Importance of Nietzsche: Ten Essays.* Chicago: University of Chicago Press, 1988.

Henderson, Hazel. *Building a Win-Win World: Life Beyond Global Economics.* San Francisco: Barrett-Koehler Publishers, 1966.

Hillman, James. *Re-visioning Psychology.* New York: Harper and Row, 1975.

Hoeller, Stephan A. *Freedom: Alchemy for a Voluntary Society.* Wheaton, Ill.: Quest, 1992.

Holland, Gail Bernice. *A Call For Connection: Solutions for Creating a Whole New Culture.* Novato, Calif.: New World Library, 1998.

Houston, Jean. *Jump Time: Shaping Your Future in a World of Radical Change.* New York: J. P. Tarcher/Putnam, 2001.

Howell, Alice O. *Jungian Synchronicity in Astrological Signs and Ages.* Wheaton, Ill.: Quest, 1990.

Hubbard, Barbara Marx. *Conscious Evolution: Awakening the Power of Our Social Potential.* Novato, Calif.: New World Library, 1998.

Huxley, Aldous. *The Perennial Philosophy.* New York: Harper and Row, 1944.

———. *Brave New World.* Leichester: Charnwood, 1983.

Hynek, J. Allen. *The UFO Experience: A Scientific Inquiry.* Chicago: Henry Regnery Company, 1972.

Iyer, Pico. *The Global Soul: Jet Lag, Shopping Malls, and the Search for Home.* New York: Knopf, 2000.

James, Henry. *The Notebooks of Henry James,* edited by F. O. Matthiessen and Kenneth B. Murdock. New York: Oxford University Press, 1947.

James, William. *A Pluralistic Universe.* Cambridge: Harvard University Press, 1977.

Jenkins, John Major. *Maya Cosmogenesis 2012.* Santa Fe: Bear and Company Publishing, 1998.

Jervis, Robert. *System Effects: Complexity in Political and Social Life.* Princeton: Princeton University Press, 1997.

Jones, Malcolm, Jr., and Ray Sawhill. "Just Too Good to Be True: Another Reason to Beware of False Eco-Prophets." *Newsweek* (May 4, 1992).

Joyce, James. *Ulysses.* New York: Random House, 1967.

Jung, C. G. *Collected Works of Carl Gustav Jung.* 20 vols. Translated by R. F. C. Hull, and edited by H. Read, M. Fordham, G. Adler, and W. McGuire. Princeton: Princeton University Press, 1953–79.

———. *Psychology and Alchemy.* Vol. 12 of *Collected Works of Carl Gustav Jung,* Translated by R. F. C. Hull. Princeton, NJ: Princeton University Press, 1968.

Kaku, Michio. *Hyperspace: A Scientific Odyssey through Parallel Universes, Time Warps, and the 10th Dimension.* New York: Oxford University Press, 1994.

Kael, Pauline. *For Keeps: 30 Years at the Movies.* Citing Jesse Zunser. New York: Dutton, 1994.

Kant, Immanuel. *Critique of Pure Reason.* Buffalo, New York: Prometheus Books, 1990.

Keel, John. *The Mothman Prophecies.* Citing Charles Fort. New York: Saturday Review Press, E. P. Dutton and Co., 1975.

Kriyananda, Goswami. *The Spiritual Science of Kriya Yoga.* Chicago: Temple of Kriya Yoga Press, 1988.

Kuhn, Thomas S. *The Structure of Scientific Revolutions.* Second Edition. Chicago: University of Chicago Press, 1970.

Kurzweil, Ray. *The Age of Spiritual Machines: When Computers Exceed Human Intelligence.* New York: Viking, 1999.

Lasch, Christopher. *The Culture of Narcissism.* New York: Norton, 1978.

LaViolette, Paul. *Earth under Fire: Humanity's Survival of the Apocalypse.* Schenectady, New York: Starburst Publications, 1977.

Lawton, Ian, and Chris Ogilvie-Herald. *Giza: The Truth.* London: Virgin, 1999.

Leary, David E., ed. *Metaphors in the History of Psychology.* New York: Cambridge University Press, 1990.

Lemkow, Anna F. *The Wholeness Principle: Dynamics of Unity Within Science, Religion and Society.* Wheaton, Ill.: Quest Books, 1990.

Levine, Stephen. *Planet Steward: Journal of a Wildlife Sanctuary.* Santa Cruz: Unity Press, 1974.

Leviton, Richard. *The Imagination of Pentecost: Rudolf Steiner and Contemporary Spirituality.* Hudson, New York: Anthroposophic Press, 1994.

Levy, Steven. *Crypto: How the Code Rebels Beat the Government—Saving Privacy in the Digital Age.* New York: Viking, 2001.

Lockyer, Sir Norman. *The Dawn of Astronomy.* Cambridge, Mass.: MIT Press, 1973.

Mander, Jerry. *Four Arguments for the Elimination of Television.* New York: Quill, 1978.

Maslow, Abraham H. *The Farther Reaches of Human Nature.* New York: Penguin/Arkana, 1993.

McKenna, Terrence. Radio interview with Art Bell. March 19, 1998.

McLaughlin, Corinne, and Gordon Davidson. *Spiritual Politics: Changing the World from the Inside Out.* New York: Ballantine Books, 1994.

McLuhan, Marshall. *Understanding Media: The Extensions of Man.* New York: McGraw-Hill, 1964.

———.*The Medium Is the Message.* New York: Random House, 1967.

Meece, E. Alan. *Horoscope for the New Millennium.* St. Paul, Minn.: Llewellyn, 1997.

Melville, Herman. *Moby Dick.* New York: Hendricks House, 1962.

Miller, Mark Crispin. *Boxed In: The Culture of TV.* Evanston, Ill.: Northwestern University Press, 1988.

Murphy, Michael. *The Future of the Body: Explorations into the Further Evolution of Human Nature.* Los Angeles: J. P. Tarcher, 1992.

The Mystery of the Sphinx. The Sphinx Project, Inc. Magical Eye/North Tower Films Production, 1993.

Narby, Jeremy. *The Cosmic Serpent: DNA and the Origins of Knowledge.* New York: Jeremy Tarcher/Putnam, 1998.

Nasr, Seyyed Hossein. *The Need for a Sacred Science.* Albany, New York: State University of New York Press, 1993.

Nietzsche, Friedrich. *Also Spake Zarathustra.* In *The Portable Nietzsche*, ed. Walter Kaufmann. New York: Viking, 1968.

Noonan, John T., Jr. *The Lustre of Our Country: The American Experience of Religious Freedom.* Berkeley: University of California Press, 1998.

Olds, Linda. *Metaphors of Interrelatedness.* Albany, New York: State University of New York Press, 1992.

Orwell, George. *1984.* Leichester, England: F. A. Thorpe, 1982.

Paglia, Camille. "The Human Imagination Unleashed in All Its Glory." in Salon.com (April 5, 2000). http://www.salon.com/people/col/pagl/2000/04/05/mcmedia/index.html

Pearce, Joseph Chilton. *Evolution's End: Claiming the Potential of Our Intelligence.* San Francisco: HarperSanFrancisco, 1992.

Radin, Dean. *The Conscious Universe: The Scientific Truth of Psychic Phenomena.* New York: HarperCollins, 1997.

Ridpath, Ian. *Star Tales.* New York: Universe Books, 1988.

Russell, Peter. *The Global Brain Awakens: Our Next Evolutionary Leap.* Palo Alto, Calif.: Global Brain, 1995.

Scarfone, Jay, and William Stillman. *The Wizardry of Oz: The Artistry and Magic of the 1939 MGM Classic.* New York: Random House, 1999.

Schlain, Leonard. *Art and Physics: Parallel Visions in Space, Time, and Light.* New York: Quill/William Morrow, 1991.

———. *The Alphabet Versus the Goddess: The Conflict between Word and Image.* New York: Viking/Penguin, 1998.

Schoch, Robert M. *Voices of the Rocks: A Scientist Looks at Catastrophes and Ancient Civilizations.* New York: Harmony Books, 1999.

Schuon, Frithjof. *The Transcendent Unity of Religions.* New York: Harper and Row, 1976.

Schwaller de Lubicz, Rene. *Esotericism and Symbol.* Translated by Andre and Goldian VandenBroeck. New York: Inner Traditions, 1982.

———. *The Temple of Man: Apet of the South at Luxor.* Translated by Robert and Deborah Lawlor. Rochester, VT: Inner Traditions, 1998.

Schwartz, Joseph. *Cassandra's Daughter: A History of Psychoanalysis.* New York: Viking, 1999.

Sellers, Jane B. *The Death of Gods in Ancient Egypt: An Essay on Egyptian Religion and the Frame of Time.* London: Penguin Books, 1992.

Sheldrake, Rupert. *A New Science of Life: The Hypothesis of Morphic Resonance.* Rochester, New York: Park Street Press, 1995.

———. *Seven Experiments That Could Change the World: A Do-It-Yourself Guide to Revolutionary Science.* New York: Riverhead, 1995.

Sitchin, Zecharia. *The Wars of Gods and Men.* New York: Avon, 1985.

Smith, Huston. *Forgotten Truth: The Primordial Tradition.* New York: Harper and Row, 1976.

———. *Beyond the Post-Modern Mind.* Revised Edition. Wheaton, Ill.: Theosophical Publishing House, 1989.

Solomon, Robert C., and Kathleen M. Higgins. *What Nietzsche Really Said.* New York: Schocken Books, 2000.

Stapp, Henry P. "S-Matrix Interpretation of Quantum Theory." *Physical Review* D3, 1303 (1971).

Sykes, Charles J. *The End of Privacy: Personal Rights in the Surveillance Society.* New York: St. Martin's Press, 1999.

Talbot, Michael. *The Holographic Universe.* New York: HarperCollins, 1991.

Tarnas, Richard. *The Passion of the Western Mind: Understanding the Ideas that Have Shaped Our World View.* New York: Harmony Books, 1991.

———. *Prometheus the Awakener: An Essay on the Archetypal Meaning of the Planet Uranus.* Woodstock, Conn.: Spring Publications, 1995.

Teich, Mikulas, and Roy Porter, eds. *Fin de Siécle and Its Legacy.* Cambridge: Cambridge University Press, 1990.

Teilhard de Chardin, Pierre. *The Phenomenon of Man.* New York: Harper, 1959.

Thompson, William Irwin. *Imaginary Landscape: Making Worlds of Myth and Science.* New York: St. Martin's Press, 1989.

Thoreau, Henry David. "Life Without Principle." In *Thoreau: The Major Essays.* Edited by Jeffrey L. Duncan. New York: E. P. Dutton, 1972.

Thornton, Bruce S. *Plagues of the Mind: The New Epidemic of False Knowledge.* Wilmington, Del.: ISI Books, 1999.

Thurman, Robert. *Inner Revolution: Life, Liberty, and the Pursuit of Real Happiness.* New York: Riverhead, 1998.

Toynbee, Arnold J. *America and the World Revolution.* New York: Oxford University Press, 1962.

Turkle, Sherry. *Life on the Screen.* New York: Simon and Shuster, 1995.

Wertheim, Margaret. *The Pearly Gates of Cyberspace: A History of Space from Dante to the Internet.* New York: Norton, 1999.

West, John Anthony. *Serpent in the Sky: The High Wisdom of Ancient Egypt.* Second Edition. Wheaton, Ill.: Quest, 1993.

Whitman, Walt. *Leaves of Grass: Poems of Walt Whitman.* Selected by Lawrence Clark Powell. New York: Thomas Y. Crowell Company, 1964.

———. "Give Me the Splendid Silent Sun." From *Leaves of Grass.* New York: New American Library, 2000.

Wiker, Judith. "A New Look at the Aquarian Age: An Interview with Ray Grasse." *The Monthly Aspectarian* (June 1989).

Wilber, Ken. *The Holographic Paradigm, and Other Paradoxes: Exploring the Leading Edge of Science.* Boulder, Colo.: New Science Library, Shambhala, 1982.

———. *Quantum Questions: The Mystical Writings of the World's Great Physicists.* Boulder, Colo.: Shambhala, 1984.

———. *Sex, Ecology, Spirituality: The Spirit of Evolution.* Boston: Shambhala, 1995.

Williamson, Marianne. *The Healing of America.* New York: Simon and Schuster, 1997.

Wilmington, Michael. "The Best Years of the Century." *Chicago Tribune* (Sept. 26, 1999).

Wilson, Colin. *From Atlantis to the Sphinx: Recovering the Lost Wisdom of the Ancient World.* New York: Fromm International, 1996.

Wright, Paul. *Astrology in Action.* Sebastopol, Calif.: CRCS, 1989.

Yates, Frances. *Giordano Bruno and the Hermetic Tradition.* Chicago: University of Chicago Press, 1991.

Yeats, William Butler. *The Collected Poems.* London: Macmillan, 1952.

———. *A Vision.* New York: Macmillan, 1956.

Yogananda, Paramahansa. *The Divine Romance.* Los Angeles: Self-Realization Fellowship, 1986.

———. *Journey to Self-Realization: Discovering the Gifts of the Soul.* Los Angeles: Self-Realization Fellowship, 1997.

Index

About the Author

Ray Grasse worked on the editorial staffs of Quest Books and *Quest* magazine for ten years. He currently works as an editor, writer, and teacher. In 1996, his book *The Waking Dream* was published by Quest, a study on synchronicity and symbolism, and received favorable reviews in the *Institute of Noetic Sciences Review, Gnosis*, and *Intuition*. It was called by Patricia Barlow "the best book on the esoteric issues underlying synchronicity."

Grasse has published articles in many magazines, including *Magical Blend, NCGR Journal, The Mountain Astrologer, Welcome to Planet Earth*, and *The Quest*. He also contributed to the anthology *Karma: Rhythmic Return To Equilibrium* (Quest, 1990), and wrote the opening chapter in the acclaimed anthology *Eastern Systems For Western Astrologers* (Weiser, 1997). Grasse received a degree in filmmaking from the Art Institute of Chicago in 1974 under experimental film pioneers Stan Brakhage and John Luther Schofill. From 1972 to 1986, he studied extensively with two teachers in the Kriya Yoga tradition, and in 1986 studied Zen meditation at Zen Mountain Monastery in New York. In recent years, he has been involved in a journalistic capacity with important archaeological investigations taking place in Egypt.

Hampton Roads Publishing Company

... for the evolving human spirit

Hampton Roads Publishing Company
publishes books on a variety of subjects,
including metaphysics, health, integrative medicine,
visionary fiction, and other related topics.

For a copy of our latest catalog, call toll-free
(800) 766-8009, or send your name and address to:

Hampton Roads Publishing Company, Inc.
1125 Stoney Ridge Road
Charlottesville, VA 22902

e-mail: hrpc@hrpub.com
www.hrpub.com